Out in the Union

Out in the Union

A Labor History of Queer America

MIRIAM FRANK

TEMPLE UNIVERSITY PRESS
PHILADELPHIA

TEMPLE UNIVERSITY PRESS
Philadelphia, Pennsylvania 19122
www.temple.edu/tempress

Library of Congress Cataloging-in-Publication Data

Frank, Miriam.
  Out in the union : a labor history of queer America / Miriam Frank.
    pages cm
  Includes bibliographical references and index.
  ISBN 978-1-4399-1139-6 (hardback : alk. paper)
  ISBN 978-1-4399-1141-9 (e-book)
  1. Gays—Employment—United States.   2. Labor unions—United
States.   3. Gay liberation movement—United States.   4. Gay labor union
members—United States.   5. Sexual orientation—United States.   I. Title.
  HD6285.5.U6F73 2014
  331.5'30973—dc23   2013042505

Printed in the United States of America

081214-P

For Desma Holcomb and Ruth Frank-Holcomb,
with love and gratitude

Contents

Acknowledgments   ix

A Brief Chronology of LGBT Labor History, 1965–2013   xiii

Prologue: *Love and Work and Queer Survival*   1

I Coming Out

1 From Construction to Couture: *Coming Out in Unionized Workplaces*   17

2 Outsiders as Insiders: *Sexual Diversity and Union Leadership*   48

II Coalition Politics

3 From Common Enemies to Common Causes: *The Labor Movement and the Gay Movement in Action and Coalition*   75

4 The Heart of the Matter: *Union Politics, Queer Issues, and the Life of the Local*   102

III Conflict and Transformation

5 Organizing the Gay Unorganized: *Talking Union, Talking Queer*   135

Epilogue: *When Connie Married Phyllis*   165

Notes   175

Bibliography   201

Index   211

Acknowledgments

Out in the Union began with a modest handbook that Desma Holcomb and I co-authored in 1990. *Pride at Work: Organizing for Lesbian and Gay Rights in Unions* documented new labor-gay alliances in collective bargaining and organizing and featured interviews with New York City unionists. Gay-labor activists around the country began using *Pride at Work* to guide their projects. I wanted to know more about that work and about their lives on the job and in their unions.

I discussed my questions with Debra Bernhardt, Colette Hyman, and Roberta Schine and devised a plan for oral history and archival research. Dorothy Sue Cobble, Steve Curry, Paula Ettelbrick, and Daniel Walkowitz endorsed my proposal, and in 1994 I was awarded New York University's Stephen Charney Vladeck Junior Faculty Fellowship. Interviews started in New York City that summer, and I traveled to six other cities the next year.

Friends and family housed me, helped me understand their cities, and reflected with me on the findings of the day. I thank my hosts: in Boston, Laurie Israel and Elaine Sidney, Enid Eckstein and Dick Monk; in San Francisco, Michael and Millianne Lehmann; in Oakland, Lois Rita Helmbold, Connie Cronin; in Detroit, Pam Weinstein and Jim, Robbie, and Charlie Dwight; in Washington, DC, Hector and Maria Figueroa, Barbara Feldman and Barry Whitebook; in Seattle, Rita Shaw and Joan Sandler; in Tacoma, Virginia LaGasa; in Portland, Joe, Haven, Dan, and Margaret Frank.

I am grateful to local activists who introduced me to so many outstanding narrators. Tom Barbera (in Boston), Howard Wallace (in San Francisco), Van Alan Sheets (in Washington, DC), Ron Woods and Elaine Crawford (in Detroit), Rita Shaw (in Seattle), Virginia LaGasa (in Tacoma), Anne Montague (in Salem), and Connie Ashbrook (in Portland) recommended wonderful sources.

My conversations with Allan Bérubé continue to guide my own "desire for history." From 1995 to 1996, I participated in his seminar on queer working-class history at the Center for Lesbian and Gay Studies at City University of New York Graduate Center, and I presented interview excerpts to his undergraduate students at the New School. Allan's analytic power and profound generosity have inspired all that is good about the writing that has followed.

My travels were followed by research on issues and organizations and more interviews, often by telephone. I received summer grants from New York University in 1999 and 2005 and a semester's leave in 2001. Colleagues in General Studies (later Liberal Studies)—Josiane Gregoire, Robert Jeske, Roberta Newman, and Fred Roden—commented on early drafts of the manuscript, as did my friends Jon Bloom, Joan Reutershan, Dagmar Schultz, and Pam Weinstein. During the summers of 2006 and 2007, I finally found a narrative shape that worked. I thank Denice Lombard and Nancy Wohlforth for their quiet place in the country, where I finally saw *Out in the Union* clearly enough to push it to conclusion. In 2011, a Liberal Studies Dean's Award for Research and Scholarship provided a semester's leave to prepare the manuscript for submission to Temple University Press. I thank Dean Fred Schwarzbach for that boost.

My colleagues Joyce Apsel, Robin Goldfin, Jacqueline Jaffe, Karen Karbiener, Heather Masri, Joe Portanova, Ron Rainey, Nancy Reale, Anthony Reynolds, Kyle Wanberg, and Heidi White supported me through the stops and the starts. Longtime friends listened and believed: Ron Alpern, Karen Brown, Bill Bryce, Connie Cronin, Jacqueline Friedrich, Atina Grossmann, Wendy Henry, Ika Hügel-Marshall, Karin Kirshner, Richard Millen, Gerald Orange, Louise Radanovich, and Jaye Spiro.

I thank Pennee Bender, Paula Finn, Tami Gold, Gerald Hunt, Kitty Krupat, Pat McCreery, Priscilla Murolo, and Jane Slaughter. They published my findings, used my material in their media projects, and invited me to speak in their classes and to collaborate on conferences. Thanks go to Tim Retzloff for sharing research and insights about LGBT lives in the Motor City; to Dana Frank and Colette Hyman for incisive reviews and excellent questions; to Lois Rita Helmbold and Jane LaTour for quick and practical edits on a late set of drafts; and to Michael Anderson, whose expert readings transformed my storytelling and my scholarship.

Central to this labor history of queer America are the experiences and insights of more than a hundred individuals. They let me record their memories of organizing and everyday work, their angers, loves, fears, and triumphs. *Out in the Union* is built on excerpts from those interviews, but it is only one book; much has been left behind. I have deposited the *Out in the Union* oral history collection at the Robert F. Wagner Labor Archives/Tamiment Library, New York University, and it is open to the public.

Debra Bernhardt supported the project, suggested people to interview, and took my trove into the Wagner Labor Archives with her collector's glee. I have resorted often to the resources of Wagner/Tamiment, and I thank Rachel Bernstein, Bob Eberwein, Peter Filardo, Erica Gottfried, Andrew Lee, and Gail Malmgreen for their collegial help whenever I came in to dig.

Staff at the New York Public Library's International Gay Information Center Collection aided my many expeditions over the years. Richard Wandel welcomed my searches in the National Archive of Lesbian, Gay, Bisexual, and Transgender History in Greenwich Village. I received efficient and generous help from Kayleigh Stalstrand at the Lesbian Herstory Archives in Brooklyn and from Caitlin Birch at the Northeastern University Archives and Special Collections in Boston. I thank the staff of the ONE National Gay and Lesbian Archives at the University of Southern California and the staff of the Walter P. Reuther Library of Labor and Urban Affairs at Wayne State University.

Several narrators whose vibrant memories form the backbone of this history are no longer living. Some were queer; some were allies—their work endures. Honor, then, goes to Walter Johnson, Harry (Kitty) Kevorkian, Jean Laberge, Ed Mayne, James Mitchell, Bill Olwell, Yolanda Retter, Bill Roberts, Michael Rubino, Van Alan Sheets, Sidney (Sylvia Sidney) Sushman, Peter Tenney, Howard Wallace, and Hank Wilson.

Other people who are part of the history died before I had the opportunity to meet them. It is our good fortune that they are remembered by surviving colleagues, friends, and lovers, whose testimonies I recorded. These friends (whose names follow in parentheses) devoted portions of their interviews to tributes: Steve D'Inzillo (Ruth Jacobsen, Jean Laberge), Carol Ernst (Susan Schurman), Barry Friedman and Tom Stabnicki (Bailey T. Walker, Jr.), Robin Lutsky (Sally Otos), George Mendenhall (Howard Wallace), Bob Ralphs (Becky Capoferri), Bill Taylor (Joe Izzo, Arthur Shostak), and John Ware (Ellis Boal). I also wish to honor Debra Bernhardt and Allan Bérubé, who supported *Out in the Union* from the start, as did Paula Ettelbrick; unfortunately, they did not live to see its completion. Regrettably, the same is true for Michael Nash, who headed Tamiment/Wagner from 2002 to 2012.

The talented people at Temple University Press stayed with this book, and I have benefited from their guidance. Michael Ames, now at Vanderbilt University Press, acquired *Out in the Union* in its earliest drafts. Micah Kleit took up the manuscript, and he and Sara Cohen readied it for Temple's Spring 2014 list. Thanks go to Joan Vidal, who has managed all editorial functions with crisp focus and pragmatic forbearance. Expert indexing by Nancy Newman and sharp copyedits by Susan Deeks have produced a book that I hope will be useful and fun to read. I thank Kate Nichols, the production director, and Mia Risberg, the cover designer/illustrator, for the fine cover design, and I am grateful in advance to the Marketing Department staff; their work has just begun. I thank the two anonymous reviewers, whose astute suggestions improved the final text. Any errors are, of course, my responsibility alone.

Out in the Union is dedicated to Desma Holcomb, my wife, and to Ruth Frank-Holcomb, our daughter. Desma has been my muse and first reader, a devoted co-parent, and an intrepid organizer, whose ambitious projects regularly amaze me. Ruth, who was in kindergarten at the start of this project, is now completing her master's degree in elementary education. I thank her for being simply herself: curious and impatient, silly and kind, always an inspiration.

New York City
March 2014

A Brief Chronology of LGBT
Labor History, 1965–2013

1965

Judy Mage, an emerging lesbian, leads eight thousand employees of New York City's Department of Welfare as they walk off their jobs in early January.[1] The strike, initiated by the independent Social Service Employees Union in coalition with American Federation of State, County, and Municipal Employees (AFSCME) Local 371, defies state law and continues for twenty-eight days. Mage and eighteen other leaders from both unions are arrested, jailed, and released. Union members return to their jobs, and negotiations resume. A settlement in June breaks new ground on wages, reductions in case loads, and defined union rights for all municipal workers.

1969

Bill Olwell, a closeted gay man, stands for reelection as president of Retail Clerks Local 1001 in Seattle. As president of the King County Labor Council, he wields influence beyond his home local; his public stands against the war in Vietnam and in favor of racial integration of the building trades have angered other union leaders on the council. They find an opponent to run against him and finance a campaign of queer-baiting smears. Olwell offers members his record of excellent service and is easily reelected. He never again hides his gayness.

1970

The Executive Council of the American Federation of Teachers (AFT) approves a resolution to "protest any personnel actions against any teacher solely because he or she practices homosexual behavior in private life."

1972

The National Organization for Women and the Mexican American Legal Defense Fund file suit against AT&T for sex- and race-based job discrimination. The consent order requires the company to integrate its best-paid jobs in installation, repair, and maintenance. Women apply, many of them lesbians who seek the high pay and the physical challenges of technically tough jobs.

1972–1974

Gary Kapanowski, a young shop steward at a bathtub factory in suburban Detroit and a member of United Auto Workers (UAW) Local 212, is out to a few of his co-workers but not to his father and other family members who work at the plant. Rumors of a shutdown prompt Kapanowski to run for shop chairman. He loses to the incumbent, who negotiates a new contract loaded with giveaways. The business is sold, and the new owners prepare to send the work to Tennessee. Kapanowski and his caucus discover serious depletions of the pension fund and evidence that UAW officials have participated in a very bad deal. During Kapanowski's second run for shop chairman, his opponents cover the shop with flyers that proclaim him "a faggot," but he and his slate win by a 2–1 margin. They participate in a wider insurgency in Local 212 at the huge Mack Stamping Plant in downtown Detroit and then reach an agreement with the bathtub company and the union that $1 million will be paid into the pension fund. When the plant finally closes, Kapanowski is the man handing out severance checks and the last to exit the building.

1973

The AFT approves a resolution at its national convention to support the "repeal of state laws and school district regulations which attempt to punish acts committed by teachers in the course of their private lives."

1974

Bar patrons in San Francisco's gay Castro neighborhood support a strike by beer truck drivers from Teamsters Local 888 and add their rowdy queer vigor to an ongoing boycott of Coors beer. The campaign spreads throughout the region and then nationally to address Coors's antigay, antilabor employment practices. Coors's offenses inspire continued protests for twenty more years.

Two AFSCME local unions negotiate collective bargaining agreements that include nondiscrimination clauses for sexual orientation: Local 693, a unit of bus drivers employed by the Ann Arbor Transit Authority, and Local 2083, the Seattle Public Library Workers.

The National Education Association adds sexual orientation to its constitutional nondiscrimination policy.

1975

Johnny Cisek, an assembly line worker at the General Motors (GM) plant in Lordstown, Ohio, and a member of UAW Local 2112, takes leave to undergo sex reassignment surgery. She returns to work as Joni Christian and deals with hostile co-workers. Supervisors, however, hound her with special aggression. Christian uses her union's legal services benefit to sue GM for invasion of privacy. She wins a satisfactory settlement, and her workmates learn to accept her presence. After thirty years at the plant, she retires with a pension in 1999.

1977–1978

Lesbians head an organizing committee to form the Boston school bus drivers' union, Local 8751 of the United Steelworkers of America. The union wins renown in Boston's labor scene for its openly queer leadership, its proactive grievance process, and, in the 1980s, its involvement in Boston's Gay and Lesbian Labor Activists' Network.

President Jimmy Carter issues Executive Order 11246, which gives women access to apprenticeships in the building trades. Many lesbians sign up for the programs. The training is rigorous; the harassment is harsh. But those who endure to achieve journey- and master-level standing in their trades earn top wages.

Right-wingers target gay male schoolteachers as predators of young boys and organize successful referendum campaigns that rescind standing gay rights ordinances in Miami-Dade County, Florida; Wichita, Kansas; St. Paul, Minnesota; and Eugene, Oregon. An alliance of Seattle's public employee and service sector unions, gay organizations, and religious and civil rights groups mounts an effective defensive campaign, and Proposition 13 is rejected at the polls. In the State of California, a broad coalition beats back the Briggs Initiative (Proposition 6), a referendum to dismiss queer school workers and their allies from their jobs.

1980

The gay and lesbian caucus of San Francisco's Hotel Employees and Restaurant Employees Local 2 supports an insurgent campaign for new union leadership and then publishes its first (and only) edition of *Dishrag*, "America's Leading Journal for Lesbian and Gay Hotel Restaurant and Bar Employees."

1982

Staff at the *Village Voice* in New York City negotiate extension of the paper's health plan to "spouse equivalents." The union, District 65–UAW, already insures unmarried cohabiting heterosexual couples at the *Voice*. Under the new contract, the arrangement is eventually formalized as "domestic partner benefits."

At AFSCME's national convention in Atlantic City, delegates approve by acclaim a gay rights resolution, "Civil Rights for Gay and Lesbian Citizens." Similar resolutions a few months later win unanimous approval at assemblies of the AFL-CIO's building trades and industrial union departments.

1984

The AIDS Committee of the Service Employees International Union (SEIU) Local 250, the union for hospital workers in San Francisco, publishes its influential brochure "AIDS and the Health Care Worker." The union develops AIDS training for hospital and health care workers throughout the San Francisco Bay Area, and SEIU distributes the booklet and its Spanish translations nationally through five editions.

1987

Workers at the new Ed D. Edelman Clinic for AIDS care at the Gay and Lesbian Center in Los Angeles join SEIU Local 399 by direct recognition and ratify their first contract.

A national gay rights march on Washington in October includes a contingent of gay-labor activists carrying the banner "Pride at Work." A day ahead of the march, the AFL-CIO sponsors an official reception to welcome LGBT union members to its headquarters.

1989

Workers at the Northwest AIDS Foundation, a social services agency in Seattle, petition for representation by SEIU Local 6. Management hires a consulting attorney and then promotes several workers to supervisory status, thus whittling down the bargaining unit. SEIU Local 6 is elected by a thin margin in November, and a first contract is ratified in July 1990.

1992

Right-wing voter initiatives are on the ballots of Oregon and Colorado. Oregon's Measure 9 proposes dismissal of all gay public employees and their sympathizers. SEIU Local 503, the Oregon Public Employees Union, collaborates with gay and civil rights activists and appeals to unions throughout the state. Voters reject the measure by 57 percent. Colorado's Article II proposes the abolition of standing gay rights ordinances and a ban on new attempts. The union membership rate in Colorado, a right-to-work state, hovers at 10 percent and below throughout the 1990s. Gay organizations and unions fail to coalesce. Voters approve Article II by 53.4 percent.

1993

Ed Mayne, president of the Utah AFL-CIO, and his wife, Karen, of the AFT, support an initiative by Cal Noyce, a telephone technician and a vice-president of CWA Local 7704, to organize a gay-labor group in Salt Lake City. The Utah Coalition of Gay, Lesbian, and Bi Union Activists and Supporters continues for another six years, supporting union efforts throughout the state and displaying "Union Yes" signs on Noyce's pickup truck at Salt Lake City's annual gay pride fair.

1993–1994

As president of Local 1002 of the International Union of Electrical Workers (IUE), Kim Ramsey is quietly out at work and devoted to her two hundred members, all employees of General Electric's jet engine plant in Seattle. Top union officials ignore her inquiries when the factory is scheduled to be shut down and remain detached as she seeks support. She learns that the closing will enable GE to supply machinery to a jet plane factory in Turkey; what is not exported abroad will be transferred to a nonunion facility in the U.S. Southeast. Ramsey rallies the community and attempts to arrange alternative job training and placements. The plant ceases operations in July 1994, just a few months after the national board of the IUE approves a prohibition of discrimination within the union based on sexual orientation.

Workers at the Gay Men's Health Crisis in New York City are initially enthusiastic about a union drive sponsored by District 1199 in 1993, but the board consults with aggressive antiunion attorneys, and the campaign loses its way. A vote is scheduled for February 1994, with two electoral groups. The larger unit of clerical and back-office workers rejects the union. The smaller unit of direct-service professionals is certified, but negotiations never occur. Organizing committees at the San Francisco AIDS Foundation (SFAF) and at Whitman-Walker Clinic in Washington, DC, initiate their campaigns with affiliates of SEIU in 1994, and both unions certify that year. The union at SFAF negotiates with weak security and does not survive past its second contract cycle. Whitman-Walker's union starts out strong and twenty years later continues to represent the clinic's employees.

1997

The AFL-CIO welcomes Pride at Work, the national organization of lesbian, gay, bisexual, and transgender unionists, into the federation as an official constituency organization.

1999

The Chrysler Corporation (DaimlerChrysler) agrees to the UAW's proposal for a feasibility study on domestic partner benefits, and Ford and General Motors join the deal. The coverage is absorbed into the overall package of wages and benefits of the current agreement, to be instituted mid-contract. The "Big Three" join 3,400 corporations, nonprofit organizations, and state and local governments—18 percent of U.S. workplaces—that offer benefit equity to gay and lesbian employees.

2004–2013

A ruling by the Massachusetts Supreme Court to legalize same-sex marriages goes into effect in May 2004, but opponents propose a constitutional amendment at the state's legislature to block further progress. Building on many years of statewide labor-gay collaborations, SEIU's Massachusetts State Council, which represents 85,000 members, the state Teachers and Nurses' Associations (memberships of 96,000 and 22,000), and local affiliates of the UAW and International Brotherhood of Electrical Workers join other unions to endorse the court's ruling, lobby legislators, and rally in Boston at the State House. The hostile amendment fails to pass.

Labor support for marriage equality plays an increasingly crucial role in states where unions are strong: Connecticut (2008), where a ruling at the State Supreme Court is backed by a bill that passes both houses of the legislature and is signed into law in 2009; New York, where the legislature passes its Marriage Equality Act in 2011; and Maine, Maryland, Minnesota, and Washington, where marriage equality is affirmed by statewide referenda in 2012. Maine and Washington begin issuing marriage licenses in December 2012, Maryland in January 2013. The referendum in Minnesota rejects a standing ban on same-sex marriage, and in May 2013 a new marriage equality bill passes both houses of the state legislature. Weddings commence in August 2013.

Prologue

Love and Work and Queer Survival

This labor history of queer America begins with a tale of survival. In 1900, a thirteen-year-old girl was rescued from a hurricane that destroyed her hometown of Galveston, Texas, and wiped out her family. Dressed as a boy, the orphan took the name Bill and journeyed north, working at menial jobs along the way. By 1902, Bill was in St. Louis, employed at the American Rattan Works, making baskets and chairs. As told by the British sexologist Havelock Ellis, Bill associated "with fellow-workmen on a footing of masculine equality. . . . [S]he drank, she swore, she courted girls, she worked as hard as her fellows . . . and she did not flinch when the talk grew strong."[1]

Bill joined the International Brotherhood of Boilermakers as an apprentice, "wielding a hammer and driving in hot rivets."[2] St. Louis was a major railroad hub; Bill was most likely initiated into Boilermakers Lodge 27, which represented the trade of locomotive engine repair. He was popular enough among his fellow workers to be elected secretary of the lodge and well-disguised enough to pass a doctor's exam when he applied for insurance. Ellis brings Bill's story to an abrupt end. In 1909, "in a moment of weakness, she admitted her sex and returned to the garments of womanhood."[3]

Records of Lodge 27 (later Lodge 35) are scant and make no mention of Bill's sojourn, but the story is believable.[4] Before and after Bill, American women passed as men. Some did so to survive economically, or to study, or to participate in the military world; others wanted to live openly as husbands in lesbian relationships or to present the masculinity they felt in themselves.[5] But the anecdote of Bill's gamble is special: our first hint of any gender or sexual variance in the life of any American union member, let alone an elected official in the heavy metal workshops of the Boilermakers' trade.

A century later, transgender people are in the mix of sexual minorities at unionized workplaces. And some of them, along with gay men, lesbians, and bisexuals, have come out in the union to make their place in labor's campaigns for economic justice. Lesbian, gay, bisexual, and transgender (LGBT) caucuses have formed coalitions to integrate civil rights into the constitutions of their national unions; LGBT activists have articulated winnable demands for local unions' collective bargaining agendas; and LGBT employees have led successful campaigns at their workplaces for collective bargaining rights.

Bill and his union brothers would be astonished to see any of this. In their day, unions were struggling for fair pay and an eight-hour limit to the workday. The eight-hour day and other standards for wages, hours, and working conditions endure as law. The hard fights today are the enforcement of those standards and the continuity of contractual gains that advance members' basic priorities.

The rights of transgender workers were first affirmed in labor agreements during the 1980s, in contracts negotiated by the Amalgamated Clothing and Textile Workers Union with industrial laundries in New Jersey. The topic came up because a shop steward was harassed after returning to work from male-to-female surgery. She raised the issue with her union representative, Clayola Brown, who resolved the issue at the shop. The laundry contract cited sexual orientation in its antidiscrimination articles, but for Brown and the steward, that was not enough. They wanted explicit protections for transgender workers. In the next round of contract talks, labor and management agreed to add "change of sex" to the list of protected classes, a specific acknowledgment of transgender rights.[6]

The issue advanced in 1997 when employees of the Whitman-Walker clinic in Washington, DC, negotiated their second contract. The clinic specialized in AIDS-related services, and the staff union was affiliated with District 1199-E DC Service Employees International Union (SEIU). Some workers who were making the transition from male to female "wanted to wear skirts without supervisors threatening them," said Joe Izzo, a member of the negotiating committee. The five-year agreement was ratified with protection for "gender expression" in its equal rights articles.

In 2005, two unions went beyond discrimination and equal rights when they negotiated for transgender rights as economic topics. One of the unions was the Graduate Employees Organization (GEO) of the University of Michigan, founded in 1970 and affiliated with the American Federation of Teachers (AFT) as Local 3550; the other was the union at Whitman-Walker. Both unions expanded health care coverage to all transition-related treatments and procedures, including sex-reassignment surgery. Whitman-Walker's unit of fewer than two hundred workers ratified transition-related coverage as an extension of rights that had been won in the previous contract of 1997. AFT Local 3550/GEO, a larger unit of 1,600, achieved antidiscrimination protections as well as transgender health coverage in one round.

Three years earlier, GEO negotiators had focused on inequities in benefits and had demanded subsidies for child care to raise overall incomes of parents in low-wage jobs. The university affirmed the subsidies after a one-day walkout that drew robust participation from the entire unit. In preparation for contract talks that would start up in 2004, the negotiating committee researched inequities in compensation across the university and found a wide range of unequal hours and rates of pay. Disproportionately clustered in the lowest-paid job classes were parents, international students, racial minorities, and sexual minorities.

Early in 2004, André Wilson, a former steward and a graduate student in architecture, traveled to San Francisco for sex-reassignment surgery. The health plan of his domestic partner had been covering hormonal treatments, but money for the operation had to come directly from his family. The release he experienced when the surgery was complete startled him to action. "It was suddenly clear to me that these procedures should be accessible to everyone who needs them," he said. He returned to Ann Arbor with a new name, a new look, and a mission: to make comprehensive transgender health benefits a priority for GEO's next contract.

"I went on strike in 2002 for members who needed child care," said Wilson. "Now I wanted the union to stand for members who are transgender." He discussed his ideas with the Negotiating Committee. "I wanted to bargain on gender identity and nondiscrimination as a matter of equal rights and equal access. Benefits are a mandatory subject in contract talks. I said we should propose a health plan with treatments and procedures necessary for the health and survival of people in transition." The committee discussed how to develop a set of demands that would deflect contention among the unit's diverse minorities. Wilson pointed out that transgender health benefits were likely to be cost-effective. "At the time, I was the only out trans- person in the union." The committee decided to link transgender rights and benefits to the needs of GEO's other constituencies and appointed Wilson to lead negotiations.[7]

Talks that began in November continued until March 25, when GEO walked out for one day and announced plans for a longer strike. Just short of the deadline, the university and the committee reached a settlement that was ratified early in April. The agreement included cost-of-living raises, improvements in dental benefits, equal protection for gender identity and gender expression, and coverage for sex-reassignment surgery.[8]

Bill the Boilermaker and André Wilson the college instructor: their identities as workers and as trade unionists are as different as how they lived their queerness. In the first decade of the twentieth century, Bill learned his craft and served his union, even as he attempted and accomplished, briefly, his own survival as a man. A century later, Wilson made his transition and then led negotiations for a contract that pledged protection for gender identity and expression and access to transgender-inclusive health benefits: explicit safeguards and supports for the lives of union members in transition.

Since Bill's time, the labor movement has found its place in the economic and political life of the United States; the movement for LGBT rights is younger and less well established. But the two movements share an ethic. Throughout its history, the labor movement has accompanied its economic programs with the principles of solidarity, often expressed in the century-old motto "An injury to one is an injury to all." That call to political unity and human dignity is similarly essential to the modern movement for gay pride.

The Labor Movement and Gay Rights

Labor's interventions—organizing drives, strikes, political campaigns—have benefited the material welfare of an American working class that has always included lesbian, gay, bisexual, and transgender people. Landmark union battles during the first half of the twentieth century were sustained with the talent and support of queer workers in the ranks and queer volunteers in allied organizations.[9] What they accomplished as trade unionists is part of labor's legacy, but the queer spheres of their lives exist only as fragments and guesses. Long years of truths untold have left little more to glean than anecdotes, episodes, and broken connections.

Some of those gaps have been examined by a new generation of scholars who have researched queer lives in working-class communities. They have documented the decades "before Stonewall" in terms of sexual behavior; romances; vice-related arrests; social connections in cafés, bars, parks, and other public meeting places; political groupings; and legal restrictions.[10] But these histories make neither union participation nor life on the job their central subjects.

Allan Bérubé's historical studies have been the significant exception. His *Coming Out under Fire: The History of Gay Men and Women in World War II* describes military workplaces and assignments of queer-seeming GIs and WACs to cross-gender jobs: men to clerical, medical, and chaplain's services; women to the motor vehicle corps.[11] Bérubé's next project, a history of the Marine Cooks and Stewards Union (MCS) of the Congress of Industrial Organizations (CIO), develops his insights about "queer work."[12] The MCS organized on the waterfronts of the West Coast among workers who served in dining rooms, galleys, and private living quarters of luxury cruise ships. The union welcomed black, white, Asian, and gay workers and encouraged their leadership. The MCS flourished from the late 1930s through the late 1940s. Refusals by officers to sign noncommunist affidavits required by the Taft-Hartley Act of 1947 led to the union's expulsion from the CIO in 1949. The MCS held on for another five years and then disbanded.[13]

Red-baiting persisted as a common political practice during the 1950s, but the period was not uniformly repressive. Section 14(b) of Taft-Hartley weakened attempts by unions to recruit by permitting state legislatures to enact restrictions on organizing; however, in regions where "right-to-work" legislation did not prevail, peacetime industrial growth actually improved the climate for organizing. In 1953, the economy was booming, and unions represented 32.5 percent of the U.S. workforce, a peak that gradually fell off to 28.5 percent during the next twenty years.[14]

Lesbians, gay men, and bisexuals sustained prejudice and persecution, too, but the dominant culture of sexual conformity could not inhibit all freedoms at all times. Queer subcultures survived and evolved, especially in large cities. Alfred Kinsey's best-selling *Sexual Behavior in the Human Male* (1948) and *Sexual Behavior in the Human Female* (1953) enlightened a curious public about homosexuality and bisexuality, topics typically forbidden in conventional society.

Gay men in Los Angeles founded the Mattachine Society in 1951 and lesbians in San Francisco founded the Daughters of Bilitis (DOB) in 1955. Both groups conducted business with stealth and pseudonyms, as was the custom of the time.[15] Ambitions were big, beginnings modest; the Mattachine Society started as a discussion forum, and the Daughters of Bilitis as a social club. Working-class people participated in both groups, but little is known about their union affiliations. One of Mattachine's first branches in Southern California included a cluster of factory workers. As for DOB, programs and purposes shifted during its early period, though a core of blue-collar women remained loyal.[16] Chapters of DOB and Mattachine formed in other cities, and monthly newsletters—the *Mattachine Review*, DOB's *Ladder*, and *One*, an independent magazine—reached subscribers beyond the urban enclaves. But actual numbers for readership and membership were very low. On the basis of Kinsey's data, activists estimated that 15 million or more Americans were homosexual; the vast majority were still quite isolated.[17]

A cultural thaw in the early 1960s awakened public interest in sexual freedom and encouraged a new wave of alliances and protests. The Society for Individual Rights, founded in San Francisco in 1964, offered community activities for migrants new to the city, including political forums, cultural evenings, service projects, and a bowling league.[18] In the East, Mattachine and DOB joined with civil libertarians to demand an end to harassment by the police. Homophile activists picketed the White House, the United Nations, and Philadelphia's Independence Hall in 1965; they returned to Philadelphia for the next four years, always on July 4. Although they walked in silence, their demands were clear: "Equality for Homosexual Citizens" read one sign; "HOMO-SEXUALS should be judged as individuals" read another.[19]

A younger generation of organizers arose in the 1960s. Lesbians and gay men among them were less brave about their queer identities than the homophile activists but more militant in their politics. Some came from working-class backgrounds; others, from privilege. They were at the March on Washington for Jobs and Freedom in August 1963, and they volunteered for voter registration drives during "Freedom Summer" in Mississippi in 1964. A few years later, they protested at local draft boards and boarded union-sponsored buses to mobilize against the war in Vietnam. Few were open about their gayness in the context of these movements, but many who went to the big rallies brought lovers or gay friends and found tacit tolerance. Through these great movements, many gay men and lesbians discovered their own courage, political ideals, and capacities for leadership. They were already activists when they came out in the late 1960s to organize the fresh new work that became the gay liberation movement.[20]

Political ethics—freedom, equality, justice, peace—did not always work out as personal values. Women's liberation of the late 1960s proposed a different paradigm: personal experience at the center of political dialogue. Feminists identified male chauvinist behavior as a corruption of movement ethics and focused on power as the primary element in gender relations. The basic organizing model for women's liberation was the process of consciousness-raising. Groups met regularly for intimate and confidential discussions that would affirm women's solidarity while locating sources of oppression. Feminist theory and practice developed from those insights, and sex itself became a central political issue.[21]

Lesbians participated in feminist consciousness-raising. Some found the discussions about men annoying; others benefited from the support; and still others came out while they were in the groups. Gay men developed their own models for raising consciousness. They read feminist pamphlets and newspapers and discussed gender, power, and personal dynamics.[22] But gay liberation's flash point was not a discussion group.

Riots in June 1969 following a police raid at the Stonewall Inn, a gay bar in New York City, ignited a decisive turn toward public, militant action. The flying bottles and rocks, the spontaneous rage, the meetings and rallies during the weeks and months that followed released what first seemed impossible and then inevitable: a political transformation. Stonewall's influence was lasting because the foundations for change—two decades of homophile resistance and the contemporary thrust of radical liberation—were so firmly in place.[23]

Racial equality, peace, women's liberation, gay liberation: the new mass movements challenged a labor movement that was no more united than the rest of the country. While the United Auto Workers (UAW) committed huge resources to the March on Washington, unions in the building trades restricted access to apprenticeships for racial minorities. Top leaders of the AFL-CIO endorsed continued military escalation in Vietnam even as the peace movement was persuading more and more union families, local officers, prominent leaders, and their entire organizations that the war must come to an end.

The rights of gay citizens became a national political issue in July 1972, at the Democratic Party's convention in Miami. A gay rights plank for the party platform was proposed, rebutted, and then voted down. Two months later, George Meany, president of the AFL-CIO, mocked the initiative during his keynote speech to the United Steelworkers at their convention in Las Vegas.[24] Those delegates applauded, but the issue was not to be dismissed.

In other sectors of the labor movement, fair treatment for gay workers was no joke. The AFT in 1970 and 1973 and the National Education Association in

1974 discussed the issue at executive meetings and at national conventions and then adopted resolutions and policies to affirm homosexual colleagues' rights to practice their professions without discrimination.[25]

Lesbian- and gay-labor activists took note of the teachers' resolutions and explored feasible goals within their unions' structures. Some union leaders rejected gay proposals out of hand, but others acknowledged the sexual diversity of their membership and sponsored appropriate policies and programs. Labor's formal methods of negotiated alliances and patient pragmatism diverged sharply from what gay liberationists were projecting for their brave new movement. But without the radical breakthrough in public awareness that was Stonewall, proposals to adopt policies of tolerance never would have carried.

Historically and structurally, the labor movement and the movement for LGBT rights developed along distinctly different trajectories. Labor's primary program was always an economic one: to organize workers in all industries and thus better the material lives of all Americans. Included in labor's economic intentions are LGBT workers who do benefit materially from collective bargaining.[26] By contrast, LGBT movements for liberation and justice made their primary goal the affirmation of civil rights already assumed by the predominant straight majority: freedom from discrimination based on sexual orientation or gender expression.

Although the gay movement always encouraged LGBT people to come out, most of the estimated 2 to 10 percent members of the U.S. population that are thought to be queer have kept their sexual identities private.[27] LGBT people could count neither on the law nor on the goodwill of neighbors, co-workers, or families to support their interests. Even in seemingly enlightened environments, gay people could still be intimidated by blackmail or violence. Masking or denying queer identity often seemed like a reasonable strategy for basic survival.

Clandestine activity and threats of violence lie deep in labor's heritage, too. Until the 1930s, workers who organized unions and negotiated contracts did so without legal protection. Some workers had to sign "yellow dog contracts" promising not to join a "combination" before they were hired. Organizers would hold union meetings at night in unlit rooms to keep company spies from recognizing their workmates; known union supporters risked being blackballed or beaten. Nor is antiunion intimidation a remnant of the distant past, as organizers who recruited in southern textile towns during the 1960s could testify. Those campaigns were waged in states with right-to-work statutes that hamper organizing and collective bargaining.

Gay communities and the labor movement have common foes and common friends. Until the 1960s, sodomy was a felony in every state, with gay men the likeliest targets for arrest and prosecution. Between 1961 and 2002, antisodomy laws were repealed or struck down in thirty-six states. Then, in 2003, the U.S. Supreme Court's decision in *Lawrence v. Texas* (539 U.S. 558 [2003]) struck down antisodomy laws in the fourteen remaining states. Of those states, twelve were among the twenty-four that maintain right-to-work statutes: Alabama, Florida, Idaho, Kansas, Louisiana, Mississippi, North Carolina, Oklahoma, South Carolina, Texas, Utah, and Virginia. Michigan, an antisodomy state at the time of *Lawrence*, adopted right-to-work sanctions in 2013. As for common friends, in 2013, seventeen states included sexual orientation and gender identity as protected classes in their employment discrimination statutes; four other states protected sexual orientation only. None of these twenty-one states had ever been a right-to-work jurisdiction; nor did any of them wait until 2003 to abolish their antisodomy laws.

Teachers' resolutions of the early 1970s influenced reforms in other national unions and in local organizations. In 1974, municipal bus drivers in Ann Arbor and librarians in Seattle negotiated the addition of sexual orientation to their contracts' nondiscrimination articles. In 1978, a gay male couple at Boston City Hospital, a security guard and a laundry worker, represented an insurgent slate in a local union election. They were baited and then elected—the security guard to the presidency, and the laundry worker to the Executive Board. And in 1982, staff at the *Village Voice* in New York City ratified a contract that included full health benefits for domestic partners, straight or gay (the term in use was "spousal equivalent benefits," and the plan was the first in the nation).

By the mid-1980s, unions in the public sector were developing policies and proposing contractual innovations to reflect the everyday realities of sexual minorities within labor's mainstream. Every reform suggested new directions. A turning point had come toward a new and continuous political relationship. No longer would the labor history of queer America be a disconnected series of occasional events. Some in leadership continued to wonder what labor's stake could be in supporting gay rights, but others quickly appreciated the possibilities. LGBT people would be coming out at work and would be looking to their unions to back them up.

Out in the Union

Out in the Union tells the continuous labor history of queer America from the mid-1960s through the turn of the twenty-first century in three major parts: "Coming Out," "Coalition Politics," and "Conflict and Transformation."

Part I: Coming Out

Chapter 1, "From Construction to Couture: Coming Out in Unionized Workplaces," and Chapter 2, "Outsiders as Insiders: Sexual Diversity and Union Leadership," explore coming-out experiences of LGBT workers at unionized workplaces and of union officers and staff. Part I also follows queer and straight advocates for gay rights who stood against harassment at their workplaces and in their union halls.

Chapter 1 concentrates on workplace cultures and friendships and hostilities among workmates. Although coming out on the job, for some unionized workers, was a statement of the obvious in a tolerant environment, many more held to the closet, knowing not to rely on the union to defend them as they tried to earn a living. The chapter surveys a range of employment sectors to demonstrate a breadth of experience, including that of office workers who navigated boundaries of social prejudice and tolerance; lesbians who were baited and harassed as they broke into the telephone crafts and construction trades; autoworkers who faced down bigotry on the line and in the union; drivers who affirmed queer solidarity in the bus yards of Ann Arbor and Boston; and high-fashion sales clerks who rallied community support during their battle for a contract by putting on a runway show—in drag.

Chapter 2 focuses on the political consequences of personal revelations—that is, of coming out in the union. I describe the experiences of unionists who stood as candidates for local office, competed for seats on regional executive boards, served as staff at headquarters, and organized in the field. They were union insiders with very public careers who lived their queer (and sometimes hidden) lives outside the social mainstream. Some were open and risked being shunned; others feared disgrace and held back.

Many unions of the late twentieth century endured rough internal politics. Chapter 2 highlights LGBT leaders of dissident caucuses. Their reform campaigns targeted corruption and other problems in the administration of their unions. Gay issues were not the point. The insurgents held to their strategies—elections, lawsuits, public protests—even when their opponents attacked with queer smears.

Part II: Coalition Politics

Chapter 3, "From Common Enemies to Common Causes: The Labor Movement and the Gay Movement in Action and Coalition," and Chapter 4, "The Heart of the Matter: Union Politics, Queer Issues, and the Life of the Local," describe how organizers in queer communities built comprehensive alliances with labor activists to prioritize gay-labor issues at national union conventions and in community-wide and regional campaigns. At local union levels, these gay-labor collaborations initiated important innovations, including contractual protections against discrimination, domestic partner benefits, and AIDS education in the workplace.

Chapter 3 highlights broad coalitions of national consequence: the twenty-year labor-gay boycott of Coors beer; the adoption of gay rights resolutions by the American Federation of State, County, and Municipal Employees in 1982 and by the entire AFL-CIO in 1983; the growth of regional and union-wide gay-labor networks in the 1980s and 1990s; the founding of Pride at Work in 1995 and its recognition as an official constituency group of the AFL-CIO in 1997. The chapter also describes the wave of national countermovements in the late

1970s that threatened queer communities and union principles. Right-wing ballot initiatives successfully overturned standing municipal gay rights ordinances in four cities where unions and LGBT groups failed to collaborate; in Seattle, a solid coalition of labor, gay, and civil rights advocates beat back a similar attempt. A statewide initiative in California intended to amend the state's constitution to have all openly gay teachers and their allies fired (Proposition 6). But unions, gay organizations, religious groups, civil libertarians, and grassroots activists collaborated on a vigorous "No on 6" campaign that defeated the amendment.

Chapter 4 studies local unions as the basic organizing units of the labor movement and examines how gay issues have been integrated into collective bargaining, grievances, and other everyday union functions. Adding sexual orientation as a protected class to the contract's equal rights articles has been the foundation for grievances on AIDS discrimination and managerial and worker-to-worker harassment.[28]

During the 1990s, LGBT caucuses in local unions connected with similar groups in their national unions and in their regional labor movements. In 1992, the gay and lesbian caucus of SEIU Local 503, the Oregon Public Employees Union, made the defeat of Ballot Measure 9 union business. The referendum proposed the abolition of standing civil rights protections for sexual minorities and dismissals of openly gay state-employed workers and their public sympathizers. Local 503 joined a broad coalition of religious and civil rights groups and garnered support from the statewide labor movement. Ballot Measure 9 was defeated.

Part III: Conflict and Transformation

Part III examines gay-labor campaigns that broke new ground. Chapter 5, "Organizing the Gay Unorganized: Talking Union, Talking Queer," describes recruitment drives to win collective bargaining rights at queer community-based businesses and service agencies. The Epilogue, "When Connie Married Phyllis," covers the ambitious campaign to win popular and legislative support for the marriage equality bill that became law in the State of New York in June 2011.

Chapter 5 begins with the growth of queer communities and their economies during the 1970s in California. Gay entrepreneurs flourished but resisted fair labor codes. Organizing was haphazard at first; unions did not understand the cultures of queer communities, and workers walked out without planning their strategies. During the early 1980s, two important local unions in San Francisco began targeted organizing among small businesses in gay neighborhoods. Employers put up hard resistance, and some campaigns failed, but a few drives were strong enough to achieve certification and solid contracts.

By the mid-1990s, AIDS service centers had become the best-funded and leading employers of gay people in the nonprofit sector, and the second half of Chapter 5 studies union drives at those agencies. Unions were certified at five important centers during the heaviest years of the epidemic, some after bitter campaigns. The governing boards of two agencies were dominated by wealthy business leaders who took strategic advice from antiunion consultants; at both clinics, management successfully undermined bargaining, and the unions could not maintain their position. The three other service centers have changed in their missions and organizational structures, but workers still have union representation, and collective bargaining continues.

The early years of the twenty-first century have been harsh for working-class Americans and for a diminished labor movement. Union participation in the private sector has continued its decline, and unions in the previously well-fortified public sector took huge and heavy hits, especially following the recession of 2008. By 2012, unions represented only 12 percent of the workforce. LGBT union members shared in these losses, even as they took heart from the surging movement for LGBT rights and its development as a distinct and respected force in U.S. politics.

The Epilogue brings the labor history of queer America up to date with the story of a sweet and signal victory: the passage of the Marriage Equality Act in the State of New York in June 2011. Same-sex marriage emerged as a popular and achievable goal in the early years of the twenty-first century, and by 2010 it had become a matter of law in five states and the District of Columbia. The AFL-CIO of the State of New York first endorsed marriage equality in 2008 and maintained support as the campaign gathered force. Unions in 2011 represented 24.1 percent of the state's workforce, more than double the national average of 11.9 percent.[29] Some of the state's largest unions were especially generous with resources and trained volunteers. New York's intense labor mobilization set a pattern that campaigners adapted for the next four states. Maine, Maryland, Minnesota, and Washington won marriage equality in 2012.

Making Out in the Union

Connie Kopelov and Phyllis Siegel were the first of 484 couples in New York City to be pronounced married the first day that the Marriage Equality law took effect. I first met Connie in the late 1970s, and in the 1980s we both served on the board of the New York Labor History Association. I interviewed her during the summer of 1994, just after New York University awarded me the Stephen Charney Vladeck fellowship that allowed me a semester's leave to launch my research. Neither Connie nor I had any notion that gay marriage would ever be a reality, but Connie was hopeful that a new generation would overcome the prejudice that she and other lesbians had experienced doing union work.

Connie shared her memories, opinions, and contacts. She led me to several other older lesbians with union backgrounds, and they introduced me to their friends. Connie's interview became the first of more than 100 recorded conversations that have formed the groundwork of this book. Along with that central series, I used notes and transcripts from earlier interviews conducted in the late 1980s for *Pride at Work: Organizing for Lesbian and Gay Rights in Unions*, a staple-bound organizing handbook that Desma Holcomb and I co-wrote and published with New York City's Lesbian and Gay Labor Network (LGLN) in 1990.

There were few other sources. I researched lesbian and gay union issues in published books and archives, journals, and other print media and found some leads but was often disappointed that writings on "working-class" gay lives rarely mentioned life on the job, union participation, or collective bargaining. When I searched for "unions" and "lesbian and gay rights," the one publication that always came up was *Pride at Work*. Early in the project, I knew that the center of my research would have to be the interviews themselves, and luckily, the booklet's popularity led me to the very people I would need to meet.

LGLN distributed *Pride at Work* and used as its contact number the home phone number I shared with Desma. For the next two years, we fielded calls from all over the country, most of them not about book orders. People were excited about LGLN's vision of gay rights in unions and interested in the strategies that *Pride at Work* suggested. Regional labor networks were finding their work confirmed in our reports; union-wide caucuses in AFSCME and SEIU were tucking the pamphlet into conference packets; labor studies centers put it on their reading lists.

By the spring of 1995, I was in touch with key activists in communities where labor-gay organizing was especially lively, including Boston; the San Francisco Bay Area; Washington, DC; Seattle/Tacoma; and Portland, Oregon. Detroit in 1995 did not have a lively gay-labor organizing culture. Most of the male auto-workers I interviewed there were not activists. But I had lived in Detroit during the 1970s. That is where I came out and where I worked as a union educator for the Amalgamated Clothing and Textile Workers Union. I left in 1981 but have kept up with the city and its political communities.

For each of these major cities, I interviewed main contacts and the people they suggested. In greater Detroit, I sought gay male autoworkers, including one Chrysler worker with a job and home in Windsor, Ontario, who "lived gay" when he crossed the Detroit River and the international border. Usually, however, I looked for a variety of experiences in unions, workplaces, and local queer communities. At the Labor Notes conference in Detroit in April 1995, I found activists from Salt Lake City and Toronto, and at the Pride at Work conference in Oakland in June 1996, I interviewed California activists and one more autoworker, from Kenosha, Wisconsin.[30] Until I wrote my first draft in 2000, I recorded all interviews on tape; thereafter, while I researched, wrote, and revised, I interviewed sporadically and made verbatim transcripts.

Out in the Union is not comprehensive. Important working-class communities and whole sectors of the unionized workforce are missing. Southeastern Michigan was the only midwestern region that I visited; after Bill the Boilermaker in St. Louis, there are no more reports about queer union members in the steel, oil, mining, or manufacturing centers of the heartland. And while there is some material from the Southwest, I skimped on Texas, a hub for airline labor, as well as Las Vegas, which before the 2008 recession was the fastest-growing city in the country and supported by an economy based in the highly unionized hospitality, entertainment, and gaming industries.[31]

This labor history of queer America is rooted in the events and controversies that have shaped unions of the late twentieth century: the country's last industrial organizing drives in textile towns of the South; the decades-long sweep of plant closings that devastated hundreds of communities that had long been union strongholds; the union megamergers that initiated new, aggressive organizing in the service and industrial sectors.

Conventional labor history has not told it this way, but LGBT union people were involved in those events and in many other powerful issues that have shaped unions and work in America. In the 1960s, LGBT social workers, teachers, and hospital workers organized successfully in public and service sector workplaces, where union participation grew steadily for the next forty years.[32] Beginning in the 1970s, lesbians and bisexual women were among the brave female pioneers who broke through gender barriers to enter transportation services, the building trades, telephone, printing and film crafts, and other "nontraditional" trades. Their paths followed earlier efforts by black workers who broke the color bars of their trades during the 1960s and 1970s. During the 1970s and 1980s, LGBT union activists participated in rank-and-file movements that challenged leadership at local union halls and at national headquarters of the UAW, SEIU, the Hotel Employees and Restaurant Employees Union, the Office and Professional Employees International Union, the International Brotherhood of Teamsters, and the International Union of Electrical Workers. Many of the dissidents were radicals committed to community causes, from women's and immigrant rights to the fights against plant closings and for community-based AIDS education.

This labor history of queer America is about the survival of unions and the survival of queer communities. Sophisticated LGBT labor activists have long understood that the labor movement and the movement for LGBT rights need each other as essential allies. The two movements first found their way to cooperation through issues of mutual concern, such as the adoption of antidiscrimination resolutions by national unions. But they also responded to each other's crises, and they persevered on reforms that emphasized lasting results. From organizing unions at AIDS clinics to battling the right at the ballot box and negotiating transgender health benefits, they collaborated on common causes and worked out connections of mutual respect. *Out in the Union* tells the stories of people who stood for their unions and for their communities. With love, anger, humor, and insight they survived, and they thrived. Their enduring coalitions continue to shape the politics and culture of contemporary America.

I

Coming Out

1

From Construction to Couture

Coming Out in Unionized Workplaces

"I never told anyone that I was gay": Jackie Harris, an African American lesbian, reflected on her twenty-seven years (1964–1991) as a caseworker and supervisor in New York City's welfare system. She always controlled her personal information, switching the genders of her pronouns, staying detached while mixing collegially. "The only people who knew were the few that I knew to be gay. I socialized with a gay guy on the job. If he needed a straight date, he would take me."[1] Harris belonged to Social Service Employees Union (SSEU) Local 371, a municipal union with a reputation for political liberalism. She participated regularly in all of the union-endorsed work actions and union-sponsored rallies for civil rights, welfare rights, and opposition to the Vietnam War. As eager as she was to contribute to the union's fight for social justice, she did not fight for her own rights as a lesbian; although she was not entirely closeted, she preferred discretion. Harris was promoted to supervisor in 1987, but at the celebratory party her lover was absent. The everyday personal privileges of office life—the pictures on the desk, the spouse invited to social events—were not hers.

Plenty of gay workers never reveal themselves directly, but many others have described a gradual process of hiding themselves less and less. James Mitchell, the president of American Federation of Teachers (AFT) Local 280 in suburban New Rochelle, New York, taught high school history. He was unwilling to lie but was also aware of the stigma of pederasty in his profession, and he did not want trouble. So he avoided sharing much personal information, until 1966, when he gained tenure. Only then did he start dropping hints too broad to be ignored. "In September, when my co-workers were chatting about vacations, I mentioned my two weeks at Fire Island," he said. "They already knew I was single and that I lived with another man. It became clear to them." Word got around the school that he was gay, but it was not until 1971 that he really came out: "I didn't run off a ditto or anything, but I certainly let other people know, and when PTA and school board people found out, it didn't seem to faze them."[2]

Harris was represented by the American Federation of State, County, and Municipal Employees (AFSCME); Mitchell, by the AFT. Both of these public employee unions had worked with the civil rights and women's liberation movements, and both were among the first to endorse tolerance for gays in the workplace. Delegates to AFSCME's 1982 convention passed a gay rights resolution; in 1970, the AFT Executive Council published a denunciation of discrimination based on sexual orientation. But these official pronouncements did not protect individual members in their work lives. Even in the socially liberal cultures of their workplaces, Harris and Mitchell, two queer union members, still felt the need for circumspection.

Simple challenges to heterosexual assumptions can generate terrific friction. In the 1980s, Cliff Flanders, a secretary with the National Council of Churches in New York City, decided to personalize his cubicle by posting a snapshot of himself with his lover on the wall near his desk. This visual proof of his gayness was a sharp challenge to another worker's notion of propriety. "Dee came in and gave it a good look," he said. "Then she said, 'You know, Cliff, I wonder—do you really have to have that picture of you and your friend up there? You know, it really does offend me.' I said, 'Well, Dee, you know how your homophobia offends me.' I kept the picture up, and if I had been able to, I would have enlarged it."[3]

Flanders felt protected because the secretary in the adjoining cubicle, a lesbian, was an officer in the small, independent National Council of Churches Staff Association that represented both him and Dee. He knew he had the right to keep the picture where he wanted it, and he knew he had backup: his union's affirmation of gay rights in the workplace and his colleague's supportive presence.

Coming Out on the Job

The ethics of queer discretion have a rich heritage. For most queer workers, silence and the avoidance of exposure have long been the rule. But for the gay movement of the late 1960s and early 1970s, coming out became an essential first step toward general liberation. Freedom and pride could begin only with individual LGBT people affirming their queer existence. Activists argued that such primary acknowledgment and self-acceptance would follow ever more public paths of openness: coming out to kin, community, and co-workers. Each of these arenas bore intense risks: painful breaks in family life, social ostracism, loss of livelihood. However, in each of these situations, there was also the profound possibility of purging shame and finding respect where life matters most. It is the desire to continue being loved and to live with honor and authenticity in a hostile world that has eventually moved millions to assert their gayness at home, at work, and to society at large.

Coming out on the job has become a less dangerous choice for workers in the twenty-first century, but it can still bring trouble. How have people come to terms with the risks? How have they made coming out at work feasible? Elements vary: the nature of the job, individual temperament, the culture of a particular workplace. Jackie Harris, James Mitchell and Cliff Flanders—all white-collar employees living in liberal communities—became deft navigators of their workplaces' social flow. Importantly, all three were members of unions with strong records in minority rights. Still, once they had carefully considered their reputations and their choices, they took very different paths, each balancing peril with self-protection: Harris was reticent; Mitchell adopted a strategy of gradualism; and Flanders, knowing he had backup, was defiant.

Race, age, and individual temperament affected each of these workers' choices. Harris, an older black lesbian, was a rank-and-file civil rights and union activist who preferred to pick her own fights and who made a clear distinction between work life and home life. Mitchell was an extrovert, white, a well-known civil rights activist, popular throughout his school district, and consistently successful in union elections. Flanders, a mild-mannered white man and a generation younger than Harris and Mitchell, got along with almost everyone at his office. But his boundaries were clear: the cubicle decorations were his business, not Dee's.

Heterosexual workers regularly make the false assumption that all of their colleagues are just as straight as they are. Queer workers who do not come out—at least to one another—risk the pressures of that premise. For colleagues in the closet, ordinary workaday socializing becomes a wary negotiation of alienation and subterfuge, a convenient but painful masquerade that can be alleviated only by the inevitably awkward disclosure. But coming out can be dangerous. Many queer workers avoid doing so because they could be compromising their job security by telling the truth.

Workers who come out on the job have always risked dismissal, harassment, or being bypassed for promotion. The U.S. military adopted a policy of nondiscrimination when it rescinded its seventeen-year rule of "Don't Ask, Don't Tell" in 2011, but no federal statute protects queer civilian workers. In 2013, only 21 states and the District of Columbia banned discrimination against lesbian and gay workers, and only 17 and the District of Columbia included gender identity and expression as protected classes.[4] Some local union contracts explicitly defend workers from discrimination based on sexual orientation or gender identity and expression; unionized workers protected by such agreements have rights in the 29 states without nondiscrimination laws, as do jobholders in 190 cities and counties where local laws protect sexual orientation and gender identity. But these are rights on the books. Many are not enforced.[5]

Some applicants have been stopped at the initial employment interview. In 1974, Robert De Santis, an ordained minister in the gay Metropolitan

Community Church, applied for a clerical job at the San Francisco office of Pacific Telephone (Pacific Bell). He was questioned by a personnel officer about his training at the church's American Bible Seminary:

> When I told her what it was, she asked if I had heard yet about the "gay stink." She told me that Pacific Telephone was starting to have problems with its gay employees. She said that she personally didn't have anything against gay people; it was the company. And then in the same breath she told me to come back another time, that I hadn't been around long enough. I later met others who had been harassed until they quit or were fired outright.[6]

The next year, De Santis became a lead plaintiff in a class-action lawsuit against Pacific Bell. Investigations revealed a company policy of rejecting job seekers whose applications had been marked "code 48—homosexual." Pacific Bell, a public utility with its headquarters in liberal San Francisco, always denied the allegations and by 1980 was including sexual orientation in its official antidiscrimination policy. But De Santis and his 250 lesbian and gay co-plaintiffs persisted until 1986, when they won a $3 million settlement.[7]

Well before the settlement, dynamic new technologies were transforming corporate structures in the telecommunications industry. Pacific Bell merged with Southwest Bell in the late 1990s to become SBC and then acquired and took the name AT&T in 2005. Changes in policy accompanied each of these transitions. The "new AT&T" emerged as an enlightened corporate leader in workplace gay rights, a sudden shift in social values that surprised the older queer workers. They had experienced terrible discrimination in their years with the corporation, while a younger stratum of LGBT employees in newer facilities experienced the same company as a perfectly reasonable workplace.

Regional biases are also important when employees risk coming out on the job. Where laws have been established, there is some recourse. But unless queer workers hold jobs with "gay-friendly" companies or live in states or cities with secure antidiscrimination legislation, they are constantly confronted by the terrible paradox: to tell or to conceal.

Beginning in the late 1970s, the radical right mounted serious challenges to employment discrimination laws. Some of those efforts were spectacularly successful, the most notorious being the "Save Our Children" referendum in Florida that rescinded Miami-Dade County's gay rights ordinance in spring 1977. For decades to come, similar campaigns rolled from state to state and city to city.[8] Workers felt the threat wherever they were. Knowing that they were vulnerable, they pretended and hid. That may have functioned as an on-the-job survival strategy, but it damaged personal integrity.

Efforts to fight the political attacks on gays have slowed some of the right-wing momentum, and in many communities legal protections and corporate policies that encourage acceptance of openly gay people in the workplace and in society in general have diminished the stigma. But Jackie Harris, James Mitchell, and Cliff Flanders were not navigating civil codes or formal principles of tolerance. They pitched their choices of discretion and disclosure to the culture of their workplaces. They gauged the social climate, took their chances, and retained their self-respect.

Harris, Mitchell, and Flanders were also paying dues in liberal unions at the forefront of labor's advocacy of gay civil rights. As abstract as that history may have seemed to them in the workaday social fray of their white-collar jobs, it was their unions' explicit policies that set the tone of direct support for their civil rights so they could survive at work.

Queer Identities and Unionized Workplaces

The decisions that union members made about coming out at work were influenced by the quality of support they could expect from their unions, by the culture of their workplaces, and by their personal situations. Beginning in the late 1970s, lesbians and straight women alike endured vicious, sexualized hazing when they won coveted apprenticeships in the construction trade unions. They paid dues to "brotherhoods" that had no policies to address the rights of sexual minorities. Although all women were routinely dyke-baited, the insults had different effects on those who actually were lesbians. The women formed organizations across the trades to assert their basic right to make a living without harassment. Although they regularly sought help from union officials, real relief was rare, and leaders did not encourage male and female workmates to make peace with one another. Some lesbian tradeswomen did form bonds of mutual reliance with their male coworkers and came out on the job, with no real harm done to the honor of the craft.

Before women were admitted to the building trades, jobs opened up for them in the telephone crafts. Sexist hostility and dyke-baiting were just as dreadful as the torment that straight women and lesbians in construction jobs would later endure, but the union that represented these women offered a more flexible organization than the hidebound construction brotherhoods, and their one huge employer had to be far more accountable to the public than private construction contractors were. Lesbians in the telephone crafts found pockets of support, sometimes from male workmates who respected their skills and sometimes through union connections.

Male homosexuality and its public acknowledgment were taboo in the building trades and in the telephone crafts. Gay men in construction jobs had no networks of support and kept themselves as carefully hidden as possible, sure that workmates would never tolerate them at the work site or in the union hall.[9] Gay men in the high-wage, blue-collar crafts of the telephone industry were never open, though in service jobs such as billing and sales or as operators, the atmosphere was more tolerant.

Bus service was one blue-collar occupation in which gay men and lesbians were likely to find less prejudice in the work culture. Bus drivers perform their jobs separately from one another, alone in the driver's seat on their own routes; the common spaces of the bus yard are used for dispatching and downtime rather than for the tasks of transportation. Thus, friction among coworkers was typically less intense than on construction sites or among telephone crews. Bus jobs were plentiful in the 1970s, and queer workers formed a substantial and obvious minority in the workforce of several urban companies, where they led the organization and governance of bus drivers' locals.

The United Auto Workers (UAW) organized the auto industry in the 1930s and 1940s, and only since the 1970s have a few gay men dared to come out at work. Some were harassed to the point of quitting, but others persisted by finding allies and winning public respect both on the shop floor and in the union hall. A few queer UAW men have even achieved enough support from fellow workers to stand for election to union leadership, while others campaigned in their locals and at national meetings to put gay civil rights on the UAW's bargaining and social justice agendas. They were inspired at least in part by the democratic structures of the union itself. The UAW's vibrant history of militant caucus movements for minority workers' rights during the late 1960s and 1970s influenced a political and social culture that could bend toward tolerance.

Unionized shops with straight members in the minority offer the prevailing majority of gay workers a double advantage: comfortable environments and the likelihood of good wages and job security. Unions at queer workplaces have strengthened members' involvement by placing economic issues central to LGBT lives high on their bargaining agendas; members have supported those demands with labor actions that express their unique situations.

A Minority within the Minority: Lesbians in the Building Trades

"The boss said, 'I don't care who works for me, if they do the job, I don't care if they're a man or a woman or black or white or what color they are—as long as they're not gay! Somebody gay would be fired!'" recalled Nancy Brown, an electrician and a member of International Brotherhood of Electrical Workers (IBEW) Local 58.[10] In the 1980s, she was working as a foreman on a construction site in Detroit when the contractor got word that a state Labor Department inspector was coming. "He wanted a woman on the job, but what he said about gay was a warning. I thought I'd better keep to myself—they don't like you, you're gone." Paradoxically, through her connections in the gay community, Brown knew that this particular employer's right-hand man was gay. Once at a company social event, she came out to him. "I believe we have friends in common," she said, to which he quietly replied, "I believe we do."[11]

All women who have worked in the building trades have had to deal with sexist challenges, from discriminatory hiring practices to harassment on the job.

Their unions, the oldest in the labor movement and the most organizationally rigid, have been slow to come to their aid. Women who have continued their careers in construction have had to be stubborn. Lesbians, like their straight sisters, tell stories of exclusion and have a keen sense of themselves as women's rights pioneers. However, as a minority within a minority, lesbians like Nancy Brown have fought their battles at a much higher level of tension.

Union membership is no guarantee of safety for lesbians employed in the construction industry. Too often they have paid dues to unions that have done little to foster tolerance. The trouble was at its worst in the late 1970s and 1980s, when women were first coming into the trades. Isolated as women, and then as queer workers, few could rely on informal protection from workmates or more formal support from their unions. Despite decreases in harassment reported by a younger generation of female construction workers in some communities, since the mid-1980s the actual average of women's participation in construction labor has hovered close to 2 percent.[12]

During the late 1970s, the feminist movement encouraged many women to break into nontraditional careers. They were willing to face tough physical conditions in male-dominated workplaces in exchange for high pay, specialized training, and the security of a unionized workplace. Pride in a job well done was also a high priority in their career choices: like all construction workers, they thrilled at the sight of their glorious big buildings.[13]

In the decades that followed the end of World War II, it was all but impossible for any woman to find a job in construction. Executive Order 11246 (1978) and subsequent U.S. Department of Labor regulations required increased apprenticeships for women and the hiring of women on federally financed construction projects. Encouraged by these reforms, the pioneers of nontraditional work formed citywide organizations. Groups such as Hard Hatted Women of Cleveland and United Tradeswomen of New York City supported female carpenters and electricians through their rigorous apprenticeships and encouraged them as they achieved journey-level ratings.

From the start, female apprentices constituted a challenge to male traditions. The "brotherhoods" of the construction trades form the historic backbone of the labor movement and have always prided themselves on high wages maintained by their control of the labor supply. In a seasonal and project-driven labor market, unions such as the IBEW and the United Brotherhood of Carpenters and Joiners strictly limit apprenticeships and, therefore, job access. These rules have led to patterns of exclusion: the unions of the building trades are the least racially integrated in the labor movement. When women began applying for entry into the trades, the brotherhoods resisted ferociously, some with federal lawsuits against the new regulations.

Many of the pioneering women who crossed the gender bar were lesbians. "The work pays good money, so women who know they have to earn a living, they think about the trades," said Connie Ashbrook, whose blue-collar career spanned a variety of union experiences. She began as a school bus driver, drove a construction truck, apprenticed as a carpenter, and, in 1982, joined Local 23 of the International Union of Elevator Constructors in Portland, Oregon. "There is a higher proportion of lesbian tradeswomen than there are lesbians in the general public," she said. "There isn't the stigma about being strong and capable."[14]

Male construction workers perceived the encroachment of women into their domain as a terrible affront. The women were violating a masculine tradition in which actual tools and specialized techniques—for example, pipe bending or wood joining—were passed down from fathers to sons.[15]

Ashbrook became an elevator mechanic. She and other lesbians who succeeded in the trades thought the rewards were well worth the trouble. The pay was great, the skills built their muscles, and they enjoyed the work clothes: flannel shirts, tough overalls, heavy boots.

Dyke-Baiting

"I've been called a lesbian when it's not true and it's not fair, and I've been called a lesbian when it was true and they're gonna kill you if they find out," said Barbara Trees, a New York City carpenter who has identified herself as both gay and straight.[16] Another female carpenter observed that "almost every tradeswoman at one time or another is 'dyke-baited' by co-workers or other people in her life."[17]

The anthropologist Francine Moccio, who has studied female electricians, writes that "even today, dyke baiting is endemic. . . . Characteristics that can mark a woman as lesbian are assurance, assertiveness, physical strength." But any woman can be a target. Moccio quotes one journeywoman as saying, "You could be the most feminine woman on the job. But if they don't like you, the men will say you're gay. There is a constant discussion about which women are gay and which are straight."[18]

Dyke-baiting is a clear and frequent expression of male hostility when men's power and privileges are threatened by women's transgressions of traditional gender roles. Dyke-baiting pressures straight women to prove themselves as "real" women, and it pressures gay women to hide in the closet, thereby weakening women's solidarity. As a form of sexualized intimidation against the entire female minority employed at a construction site, dyke-baiting conflates sexism with antigay prejudice and so diminishes the status of all women in the trades, straight and gay.

Every lesbian construction worker has her own story of on-the-job hazing, and like her straight female colleagues, she has probably been dyke-baited. But the effects of this particular type of harassment are different from other types of bullying. While dyke-baiting reinforces the social isolation of lesbians, for straight women it encourages more traditional gender role behavior. For example, the custom of requiring women to do passive or "go-fer" tasks such as holding signal flags or fetching coffee "feminizes" them. Women who demand different tasks that involve heavier labor have to take a stand. Their aggression makes them fair game for dyke-baiting. Female construction workers, whether straight or gay, are thus caught in a bind: by looking for approval and deferring to the men, they are restrained from acquiring more sophisticated job skills. Ultimately, this diminishes their opportunities to master the trade.

For doing nothing worse than showing up for work, women in the trades have taken all sorts of harassment: pornography, profanity, violence, and other sexualized humiliation.[19] But women who have actually demanded equal treatment have been the targets of particularly nasty tricks. Barbara Trees, a member of the United Brotherhood of Carpenters Local 608 in New York City, tells the story of how she and another female carpenter ("who was straight as an arrow") demanded a shanty where they could change their clothes in privacy. Although the steward cursed them, they continued to complain to local officers until the order finally came to "send the bitches down to build the shanty." The women completed the task, took a break, and came back to find a mess. "The men shit in the shanty and wrote on the door 'Lesbians Local 69.'"[20]

Ann Jochems, another carpenter, was supervising a maintenance crew for the New York City Board of Education when she challenged coworkers about their pornographic posters and racist language. "They were screaming about Chinamen and niggers and fags and cunts," she said. "I told them that it's unacceptable. There were a couple of black carpenters in the shop, and I got along better with them." One day, when Jochems returned from a day off, her white coworkers had something new for her. "They brought out a black dildo and put it in the middle of the coffee table. They had whittled it and painted it, and they said, 'This is for Ann.'"[21]

Because of the divisiveness of dyke-baiting, women's solidarity has never been a sure thing, even within the safety of tradeswomen's support groups. Some lesbians have feared that their straight female coworkers might try to deflect men's antagonism by exposing them as "the real lesbians." Ashbrook described a tense climate of support mixed with suspicion during her apprenticeship as a carpenter in Portland in the early 1980s. "At the Tradeswomen's Network, we weren't that out to the straight women except the ones we knew were safe," she said. "The bond was to get through the day. We were so glad to be with other women who understood what it was like out there; being a lesbian was kind of irrelevant."[22] Karen Wheeler was one of fifty women among three thousand men when she apprenticed to be a welder in Local 5 of the Industrial Union of Marine and Shipbuilding Workers of America at the Fore River Shipyards of Quincy, Massachusetts, in 1976. This workplace was "scary for women" but treacherous for lesbians:

All of the women used to take breaks together. We mysteriously would go to the bathroom at the same time, and we would just hang out and share stories, say how our days were going. There would be ten women in the bathroom. Eight of us would be lesbians, and the two non-lesbians might be making some homophobic crack, and none of us would say anything.

It was so horrible, so closeted, the fear of giving the guys one more bit of ammunition. We would all go to the bar after work, and there would be a lot of eye rolling, talk about our ambivalence and hard feelings about not saying anything, feeling tempted to say something but also being scared.[23]

Irene Soloway, a carpenter and an organizer of United Tradeswomen, a support group in New York City, appreciated the "acts of solidarity" committed by straight women apprenticing with her during the early 1980s. "The heterosexuals would not admit to *not* being lesbians," she said. "They didn't want to have to prove themselves as straight. They just wouldn't say what they were."[24]

Building Trust while Coming Out

Some lesbians in the trades have managed the hostile workplace culture by developing buddy relationships with straight male coworkers. For Nancy Brown, the masculine code of loyalty worked to her advantage. "You develop close ties with a lot of these men, and if they really like you, anything bad that goes against their grain they're going to deny," she said. "One fellow didn't like women in the trade. He didn't like a lot of things. But when someone down at the union hall said they thought I was a lesbian, he wanted to beat that guy up—in my defense."

Coming out can actually neutralize sexual undertones and strengthen trust between job partners. The bonding of a lesbian and a straight man can function well when the woman has proved her skill and dependability. "I found that there are a lot of men who really like to work with me," Brown said. "I'm considered a good worker, conscientious, nobody has to carry me along. There have to be close ties, just from working together and talking, sharing thoughts and feelings, and trying to keep the day on the upside for everyone."[25] Karen Wheeler continued as a welder at the Quincy shipyard and eventually found a sense of sexual safety among male workmates. "My being a lesbian and very much of a tomboy made me some kind of in-between sex," she said. "There wasn't that kind of sexual dating tension. They could talk to me about sports, and we'd get along."[26]

In the building trades, trust cannot be casual. Construction workers have to anticipate trouble: their sensitivities to their partners' movements can mean life or death. They perform their jobs on precarious structures with heavy materials. They operate hazardous equipment, use dangerous chemicals, control torches, conduct live current. Brown worked on and off with the same man for more than ten years. Their closeness was important to both of them, even if she was not completely candid. "He considers me his best friend," she said. "We never discussed my relationships, but he's been to my house, and he has to be aware.

He's never asked, and I don't think he wants to hear. But I know if I was five hours out of town and my car broke down, if I called him, he'd jump in his car and be there. My sexuality isn't that important." With other coworkers, Brown dropped hints that were discreetly informative: "They'll say my wife and I did this and that, and then I'll say, well, my roommate and I, and so forth. It's up to them to read that phrase."[27]

Some lesbian tradeswomen became more overt, especially once they knew they were safe. In 1986, Irene Soloway took a civil service job in the New York City hospital system, working on interior repairs with a regular crew. She maintained membership in Local 257 but no longer had to report to the union hiring hall, where she had often been passed over. The security of her hospital assignment gave her the confidence to run for shop steward. She was elected, came out on the job, and then joined in the sex talk:

> They thought being a lesbian was the sexiest thing, because you get women. They wanted to borrow my lesbian porno magazines. But I said, I don't want it back after you've used it—go find your own pornography! My work partner, Arthur, was from Ireland, very sweet, very innocent. He never heard of a blow job until he came to New York. He wanted to know what we do in bed. I told him there, on the ladder. I said, "Arthur, I'll tell you in graphic detail—do you really want to hear it?" And he said, "No, maybe not."[28]

Connie Ashbrook came out at work in the early 1990s. For two election cycles, Oregon was a political hotbed. The ultraconservative Oregon Citizens Alliance (OCA) proposed Measure 9 (1992) and then Measure 13 (1995) to mandate the firing of LGBT workers in publicly funded jobs, including teachers, hospital employees, and social service workers. Wherever and whenever they could, queer citizens resisted by declaring themselves so that neighbors, coworkers, family, and friends would understand that these ballot measures would diminish the lives of people they knew and trusted. Although the elevator construction industry was nobody's target, Ashbrook came out at work merely by displaying a "No on 9" bumper sticker on her lunch box. She told her union business agent that the measure would harm her personally. "He said he already knew. Then he made some sort of joke. 'Well, I always said, you can't knock something unless you've tried it, and I'm not about to try it.' Another guy, we were talking about Measure 9 and bigotry in Oregon, and he said something about 'people like yourself' to let me know that he knew."[29]

At the end of four years, the OCA's efforts to codify homophobia failed. Indeed, the great furor roused during the two campaigns moved so many straight Oregonians to pay attention to the lives of their queer neighbors and coworkers that the LGBT cause ultimately emerged as a much stronger and more legitimate public movement than it had ever been before.[30]

Lesbians in the Telephone Crafts:
From Isolation to Community

Until 1972, the telephone industry's best-paid and physically toughest technical work was in installation, repair, and maintenance—job categories reserved for white men. A lawsuit filed by the National Organization for Women (NOW) and the Mexican American Legal Defense Fund against AT&T's sex- and race-based job classifications was resolved with a consent order to integrate those prized jobs. Change came slowly and was accompanied by much resistance. However, women's entry into the telephone crafts followed a different trajectory from what happened when women were first given access to apprenticeships in the building trades, six years later, with Executive Order 11246.

Construction unions are specific to particular trades (electricians, carpenters, painters, glaziers) and operate differently from the single large union that represents all telephone workers. Construction jobs are not permanent. Workers get their assignments through their unions' hiring halls, and work lasts only as long as is the project requires. The maintenance of high wages is the construction union's top priority, and unions sustain that principle by controlling entry to apprenticeships and, thus, the supply of licensed workers. Federally mandated integration of women and racial minorities into the trades pressured unions' control of that labor market. When women set up their citywide, multi-trade support organizations, such as the Boston Tradeswomen's Network, they did so beyond the purview of the brotherhoods.

By contrast, workers in the telephone crafts are represented by a huge central union, the Communications Workers of America (CWA). This union concentrates on industry-wide collective bargaining and leaves hiring, training, and promotions to the company. Although their hourly wages are not as high as those of construction workers, telephone workers are employed year-round by a public utility that is subject to strict regulatory oversight. When women integrated the blue-collar telephone crafts, it was the company, not a union-based apprenticeship program, that trained them to climb poles, splice cable, and repair equipment.

Women in the telephone crafts were often isolated and hazed as badly as any female construction worker who pioneered in the trades. Neither the company nor the union adequately prepared female entrants or their male workmates for the changing dynamics that the consent decree triggered. One or two women would come fresh from training onto a crew of as many as twenty experienced men who already knew one another very well. The consequences soon became evident, sometimes brutally so.[31]

One cold afternoon in February 1979, Faith Robinson, a probationary line technician at Michigan Bell, was dispatched in a utility truck to northwestern Detroit. She and two experienced male coworkers were assigned to install telephone poles. Robinson, a lesbian mother of two, was among thirty thousand workers at Michigan Bell, the fourth-largest employer in the state. She had passed the company's pole-climbing course, one of only 163 women in the company to hold an outside craft job. The men were supposed to be training her, but they called her names and cursed her. She ignored them and picked up a sledgehammer to break cement, but they kept baiting her. "They were laughing at me," she said. "They said I wasn't holding the hammer properly. They said I couldn't do the job." The abuse escalated:

> I said I didn't need a dick; they were the biggest dicks here. They started hitting their sledgehammers on the pavement, and with each crack as they hit the cement, they would call out, "This is for your dyke friend Sheila, and for your dyke friend Martha, and for your dyke friend Julie."
>
> One of them swung his hammer at my face and missed. Then he pushed the augur at me. It's a big, sharp tool at the back of the truck that can swing out on a boom, six feet long. This one only had a makeshift pin holding it together. Then they left me alone with the truck and went to lunch.[32]

The training program had left Robinson so unprepared that she did not know how to wield her tool. The next day she asked her supervisor for a transfer but was advised to stick it out. For a few weeks she did, while the men continued to harass her. Although she did not file a grievance, she did talk with a steward at CWA Local 4100. He sympathized and offered to set her up with a less challenging assignment. "But I didn't need an easier job," she said. "I needed them not to harass me and call me names and pick fights."[33]

Finally, Robinson walked off the job. Soon, she was recounting her horrific experience to officers of Detroit's chapter of NOW. The feminists immediately called the Equal Employment Opportunity Commission and a reporter from the *Detroit Free Press*. Now she had powerful advocates, and her discussions with the union and management became more substantial. Robinson agreed to return to work. The men would receive official reprimands but would not lose their jobs. "I didn't want money from a lawsuit," she said. "I had to support my two children. I wanted a job." Michigan Bell pledged to prevent further harassment and soon established mandatory companywide training programs, "and that started stopping the hazing and harassing."[34]

Women in construction learned their trades through apprenticeship programs administered by the very unions that had blocked their entry. Their citywide support organizations would never have been welcome at the union hall, and they did not expect their union delegates to take up their issues. Although the blue-collar telephone crafts were an all-male stronghold and significant in the CWA's power structure, there were other divisions of the union that were less rigid.

Michigan Bell was a publicly regulated utility, and the CWA, one of the country's largest industrial unions, had a substantial female membership. The CWA's National Women's Committee, founded in 1974, articulated working women's issues at union conventions and at other policy meetings. Robinson found her way to Detroit's branch of the Coalition of Labor Union Women (CLUW).[35] She was introduced to CWA women from other parts of the country who had risen in the union while working for the telephone company in traditionally female occupations. They supported Robinson in her quest for fair treatment, discussed her dilemma with officers of Local 4100, and pressed for her appointment to a committee that would examine the conditions that had moved her to walk off the job. Robinson transferred to a new technical job, splicing cable underground; the work was solitary and suited her better. "Now people have gotten to know me and they know I'm a worker and that I don't mess around," she said.[36]

Rosalie Riegel entered the telephone crafts in the 1980s, aware that the nature of telephone work was changing. Most workers were still climbing poles and ladders to repair equipment, and many women new to the industry were learning those tasks. But Riegel was not looking for hard physical work outdoors. Her focus was technology. She studied electrical circuitry and became one of the first women in CWA Local 1101 at New York Telephone to qualify for elite assignments in switching and testing, indoor jobs that required technical intelligence rather than physical prowess.

Riegel started her telephone career in her mid-forties. She understood that the technical skills necessary to perform her job had nothing to do with her gender. "These guys were the last word in macho, but their jobs were not macho jobs," she said. "If they were pulling cable, that would be macho, but here they were, sitting at a desk, doing wuss work." Riegel found friends on the job who were active in an opposition caucus of the union, CWA Local 1101. She contributed to the *Bell Wringer*, the caucus's newsletter, and in one issue published a protest against sexist images and dialogue in a training film. Suddenly she was transferred from the work site she liked to a new one where she had no friends. "It was punitive. The telephone company does a lot of that," she said.

> They hated me. It started out with pictures on the walls, disgusting sexist pictures with asses and breasts hanging out. Management is supposed to see that you don't have them up, so I would take them down. We eventually reached an arrangement where they could have whatever they wanted on their desks, but they couldn't keep it on the walls.
>
> You could send messages around with the desk computers, and everybody would get the same thing popping up. Their messages had my initials on Santa Claus's prick, or there were notes on my desk with penis stuff and always with my initials or name.

Riegel complained to Local 1101's chief steward, who helped her file a grievance for gender discrimination. "I could easily have gone to management, but I expected the union to clear it up," she said. "They waited until the steward wasn't there, and then they swept it under the rug." Riegel recalled the relief she found from working with the *Bell Wringer* caucus. "They had a fine political sense, and we had a women's committee, and that was influential," she said. She was out to the group, "but I never fought for lesbian or gay recognition or wrote any articles about it. I could have made it an issue, and they would have listened to me, but I never did."[37]

Sandra Lara, a young Puerto Rican and Italian lesbian in CWA Local 1101, avoided situations that could lead to confrontations. Even when the pressure was intense, she projected serene detachment. "The men could see that I wasn't available. I didn't allow them to do things for me. I just evaded their questions." She completed the technical training for a switchman position at AT&T and then learned fireproofing and other construction techniques. She was small and agile and skilled at repairs in tight spaces.

In 1975, a six-alarm fire severely damaged AT&T's central building, and Lara joined the emergency effort. "It was filthy work," she said. "Toxic materials were burning in that fire, explosive stuff. We were moving around and under the ceilings. One time I was stuck and couldn't see the light where the guys were because I had crawled over an air conditioning duct." Having proved herself worthy, Lara became part of the crew. The men showed her how to "work the job" during slow periods. "You put on your tool belt and walk around with a piece of paper looking at the ceiling and then back at the paper, trying to find something and nobody bothers you," she explained. The camaraderie suited her, and she grew less evasive. "On Thursdays, we would meet down at McSorley's [a saloon in downtown Manhattan], and we'd start drinking at noon until whatever time we decided to get up and leave," she said. "Often we left really drunk. Once, when it was really late, I said, 'I got to meet MaryAnne outside; she's probably been there for hours.' They said, 'Who?' I said, 'My girlfriend, MaryAnne.' And so then it was out."[38]

Regional telephone companies consolidated to form AT&T in the 1940s and 1950s, and the individual unions that represented telephone operators, mechanics, line workers, service representatives, and clerical workers merged to form one union, the CWA, in 1947. Some women who entered the crafts in the early 1970s had already built up seniority in the Bell System, in service positions, as switchboard operators, or as clerical workers. The men who trained them for their new jobs knew them from union meetings or from the workplace, and those connections eased their entry. While they did not altogether escape being hazed, they were better prepared than women who were newcomers, because the men tacitly accepted their right to be there.

Madelyn Elder's telephone career began in the early 1970s when she was employed as a switchboard operator in Michigan. She moved to Seattle, started out as an operator in 1977, and became a shop steward in CWA Local 9102. She trained for the crafts, took an assignment as a splicer, and was thrilled when her paycheck doubled. Her union experience as an operator gave her standing with the men at her garage, especially when she volunteered to be the shop steward. "Those guys were great," she said. "They hadn't had a steward for a couple of years." She was bold in her union work and popular with the men. They were flabbergasted, however, when she came out to them. "I had to tell them many, many times that I really was gay." What harassment she experienced came from the managers.

Shortly after Elder was elected chief steward of the Seattle splicers in 1980, she led a wildcat strike to protest hazardous conditions in the manholes. She knew that expanding the walkout would strengthen the strike, so she called on her former colleagues, the operators. They unplugged their boards, and three days later the strike was settled. "Once we got our improvement in safety, I made all those splicers go to the meetings and thank the operators," she said. "It was the beginning of the guys' changing from 'Oh, these operators, they're just in it for the pin money' to appreciating the women as valuable members of the local."

Six years later, Elder transferred to the Portland, Oregon, phone company and her CWA membership to Local 7901. Her reputation as an agitator preceded her. "My new crew expected me to jump on the table the first day and harangue the boss." At the garage, she easily took her place in the casual mix of lesbians and straight men. But then came the scandal: Elder took up with one of her coworkers, and the affair broke up an established relationship. The woman who lost out worked on the same crew, and "she just couldn't keep her mouth shut," Elder said. "Everyone knew our business. We all tried to be civilized, but people chose sides, especially the men. In Seattle, it had been, 'Oh, you're gay—no big deal.' Here in Portland, it's, 'She ran away with that gal from Seattle.'"[39]

A Very Gay Place to Work: Lesbian Bus Drivers

"It was a traditional lesbian workplace," said Shelley Crites, who drove for Seattle's Associated School Bus Company. Crites and her lover were both looking for work when they arrived in town in the early 1970s. They heard about school bus jobs at a lesbian bar where one of the regulars was a trainer for the company. "Maybe fifty workers in the shop were lesbians; some of them had been driving a school bus for years."[40]

Public transportation companies in other communities were similarly thick with lesbian drivers. When Connie Ashbrook was a school bus driver in Portland, she would hang out at the women's bar. She recalled seeing several coworkers, especially "this one older lesbian that I admired. It seemed like she had been around and knew a lot."[41] Shelley Ettinger, who drove a municipal route for the Ann Arbor Transportation Authority in the late 1970s, remembered how the veteran bus drivers, "mostly butch women," mentored younger female recruits.[42]

For mechanically competent women, the early 1970s were boom times for bus jobs. Few other lines of skilled work were then available: the Bell System's crafts and the construction industry's apprenticeships had not yet opened. This was an era of rising gas prices, and individual automobile use was expensive. To support alternatives, federal grants underwrote innovations in municipal mass transit. In Ann Arbor, the Dial-a-Ride system provided door-to-door van service. Other cities were increasing their suburban routes or updating their fleets with new vehicles. During those years, court-ordered school-desegregation plans required children from predominantly white or predominantly African American schools to be transported twice a day between their neighborhoods and schools across town. To bus the children, school boards in Boston, Portland, and Seattle contracted with privately owned school bus companies. Drivers were needed, and the companies eagerly hired as many capable candidates as they could, with little concern for whether they were racial minorities, female, or gay.

School bus driving was a convenient blue-collar job for women with children: the split shifts of the school bus day could be coordinated with home duties. Those rhythms also suited performers, social activists, and artists, who used the down times to fit in rehearsals, catch up on organizing projects, or do a bit of studio work. The jobs attracted people who did not mind solitude: drivers rarely encountered coworkers on their routes and knew that their passengers, even the most rambunctious, would eventually arrive at their destinations. For sociability, "a big thing was going out for breakfast, after you drop off the kids," said Tess Ewing of Boston:

> We'd all see who was in the drivers' room and go down to Posty's. There were clumps of dykes, but you would also see dykes with people who weren't dykes, maybe three dykes and one white guy from South Boston and a Latino guy and a couple of black women who were straight, whatever. We'd chat about driving conditions on our routes. Or we'd gossip—there was always somebody from the bus yard getting it on with somebody else.[43]

Throughout the 1970s and 1980s, bus jobs continued to draw women seeking nontraditional work. The wages were lower than those the construction and the telephone crafts were offering, but the qualifications were much less rigorous. Susan Schurman was hired at the Ann Arbor Transportation Authority in 1973 with no credentials other than her chauffeur's license, but a male trainer soon was sabotaging her attempts. She would never have passed probation had not two lesbian bus yard veterans advised her on the more complicated maneuvers. She learned to operate the vehicles in traffic after just a few weeks of practice.[44]

Five years later, when Ettinger was a trainee at the same company, the tone was completely different: it was ordinary for a woman to be sitting in the driver's seat. The men did not block the training, and the major challenge for Ettinger was the machinery. "This was before power steering," she said. "I was never an athlete or a big butch, and I never did relax into it. They gave you only one physical test. You had to get in the bus without it being on and turn the wheel, so I passed."[45]

A new wave of unionization accompanied expansions in mass transit. Some workplaces already had collective bargaining. AFSCME represented employees of some municipal bus agencies; other companies were organized by the Transportation Workers Union, the International Brotherhood of Teamsters, or the Amalgamated Transit Union (ATU).

The private contractors serving school boards involved in court-ordered busing were often nonunion. In Boston, the school bus drivers organized in 1977, with Ewing and two other lesbians at the head of the organizing committee. They wanted a union that would be open to the company's unconventional variety of workers—lesbians, gay men, artists, political activists. They first discussed affiliation with agents of the Teamsters and the ATU but were annoyed by the jurisdictional bickering that accompanied talks and dropped both offers. One afternoon, they called all of the unions they could find in the Boston telephone directory and got a friendly response from the district office of the United Steelworkers of America (USWA). "This isn't steelworker country," Ewing said. "The Boston district represented utility workers and came out of the old Mine, Mill, and Smelter Workers union. They could deal with us being leftists and militant and gay." The school bus drivers received their charter as Local 8751 of the USWA during the 1977–1978 school year.[46]

The social climate of the bus yards was casual, and coming out on the job was often a matter of everyday recognition rather than dramatic revelation. "We were in bull-dagger jobs. It never occurred to me to actually tell someone," said Susan Moir, a Boston driver.[47] "A job like that, managing large machines, that attracts dykes," concurred her coworker Tess Ewing.[48] "It was a very gay place to work," remarked Shelley Ettinger of Ann Arbor. "There was graffiti in the women's bathroom in the workers' lounge. It said, 'Oh how I love driving the big bus when you feel the motor throbbing against your clitoris on the seat.'"[49]

There would be occasional baiting, but the targeted lesbians took the hazing in stride and relied on one another and the good humor of their coworkers for support. On Friday mornings, Boston school bus drivers would line up for their paychecks, and one day, Moir, who was known for her quick temper, saw a note on the bulletin board. "It said, 'Lezzies work here.' Everybody was looking at me to see what I would do. I said, 'Hey, somebody left me a note,' and I folded it up and put it in my pocket, and everybody just laughed."[50] Janis Borchardt, who drove for Greyhound in San Francisco, ran for the vice-presidency of ATU Local 1225 in 1987 and won. During the campaign, "I had posters put up in all the terminals, and someone kept putting moustaches and beards on my face," she said. "This one guy who was working with me said, 'Well, Janis, looks like it's time for a shave,' and then he would put up new posters."[51]

Queer on the Line

Auto plants are huge structures where thousands of workers assemble heavy and complicated machinery on automated production lines. Each worker performs the same task repeatedly throughout the shift.[52] The production lines' constant rapid pace is physically harsh, a grueling and pressured monotony that determines a work life that is more restricted but also more continually and communally experienced than other blue-collar work cultures. Construction projects have their clear starts and finishes; the telephone workday is organized around assignments performed by small roving crews; and bus drivers, who transport passengers on set routes, operate their vehicles all by themselves. There are other work cultures that feature heavy equipment, close supervision, and tight timing, but the rhythm of the auto assembly line is a force in itself.

The UAW negotiated contracts that were models of progress in mid-twentieth century American labor relations. During the last two decades of the twentieth century, layoffs and contractual concessions in the declining auto industry severely damaged the union's gains. Even so, auto assembly jobs continued to rate as more highly paid, with better benefits, than almost any other employment available in working-class communities, especially in the Midwest.

At its best, the UAW sustained its power and tight organization by upholding the contract, maintaining generous benefit services, and asserting internal discipline on the line. In union politics, rank-and-file caucuses functioned as minority parties. Throughout the cycles of bargaining talks and union elections, these groups would campaign ferociously by questioning and resisting the authority of established leadership, both in the locals and union-wide.[53]

Factories created their own communities—"a city within a city," as one worker put it.[54] Although there was always plenty of turnover in the automotive workforce, many employees stayed put, performing the same job on the same shift, year in and year out, until they could retire on the "30 and out" pension plan. These were also communities that were overwhelmingly male. Women who had fought their way into assembly line jobs during the 1970s had lower seniority than most men; massive layoffs in the late 1980s decreased their number significantly.

Gossip moves fast in tight, stable communities. In his log of March 13, 1970, Ed Liska, president of UAW Local 3 at the Dodge Main plant in Hamtramck, Michigan, noted that "two black men were caught in the act in the body shop inside of a welding booth. One had his pants down, and the other man was intercoursing him from behind. . . . [T]he incident . . . is well publicized in the body shop areas."[55]

"You're straight in Windsor, but you're gay in Detroit," explained Jim Monk, who began working for Chrysler in Windsor, Ontario, in the early 1970s and was a member of UAW Local 444. When he was first coming out, he would cross the border to cruise gay bars along Detroit's Six Mile Road. "I'd see someone from work, and he'd smile and buy me a beer and sometimes hit on me. Then in the plant, it was as if he didn't know me." Monk remembered how a group of supervisors patronizing a downtown strip club spied a worker they knew leaving the Ritz, a gay bar nearby. "The next day, it was brutal. They told everyone about him, and he got really upset. He never admitted to being gay."[56]

The situation was no better a decade later, when Ron Woods began his four-year apprenticeship as an auto electrician at Chrysler. He committed himself to privacy and the achievement of excellent ratings. "I was totally closeted," he said. "I never missed a day of work, and I worked seven days a week, twelve hours a day. When I met gay people, I would never tell them where I worked. I would have been dead meat."[57]

In 1992, the UAW amended its constitution to include sexual orientation in the statement of unity, but to Keith Truett, a member of UAW Local 600 at the Ford Plastics Distribution Center in Milan, Michigan, this meant little. He worked the swing shift and kept his guard up. "I don't want one of these idiots to meet me outside the plant some night," he said. "There are people at work who feel that anybody who is gay should be shot and killed, so I am careful." But one Saturday evening in Ann Arbor, he ran into two co-workers at a gay club and enjoyed the moment: "We were all in the same place together." A clique formed, and then the circle widened. The men felt safe enough to eat lunch together and socialize on weekends. But shop gossip has its own energy. "One couple was together thirteen years, and they kept their secret pretty well," Truett said. "But when they broke up, one of them confided in the wrong person, and then everybody at the plant knew. One of them, you wouldn't know he was gay, he doesn't fit the stereotype. But the other guy is more flamboyant, and about him there was writing on the bathroom walls."[58]

Well into the 1990s, the scene could still be harsh, even for gay men with substantial straight allies. Richard Feldman was the plant chairman and a union delegate for Local 900 at Ford Michigan Truck. He intervened when a young worker was being harassed in the paint shop:

> The guys used this thick heavy sealing material from the shop and shaped the stuff into dildos, big ones, and put them in his lunch box and wrote "faggot" in chalk on his lunch box. It happened a lot, and I'd meet with them and scold them. We got him promoted to another shop, where more senior people were working and where he wasn't bothered. But during a layoff, they wanted to put him back in the paint shop, and he just went berserk. So we got him into a safer place.[59]

Bob Burrell, who had worked on the line with Feldman for decades, was well known throughout the three-plant system of Ford Michigan Truck. He lived in a nice suburban home with his wife and child. In 1997, he and his wife divorced. One summer weekend, he took his male lover to a wedding at which several co-workers were guests. "By Monday, everyone knew," he said. "There were some people who wouldn't look at me, but Richard said, 'Congratulations on your new life.'"[60]

There were men who never hid, even when the stigma of homosexuality was especially severe and the closet seemed to many the only sensible alternative. Long before the UAW ever considered the rights of sexual minorities, openly gay men worked side by side with straight men. They flirted; they cross-dressed; they had sex. They survived because they were tough enough to fend off physical attacks.

Harry Kevorkian was a college student in the mid-1960s who worked on the line at the General Motors plant in Pontiac, Michigan during summer breaks. He held temporary status in UAW Local 594. He said:

[Throughout the season] I would have sex with other students who were part of the summer crowd and also with regular workers. We did it in motels, in their homes, in their cars, in the parking lot—I was having fun. Some of them I knew from high school. I had had sex with them then, and now they were married and wanted to fool around, and I wasn't opposed to that. They didn't think of themselves as being gay. I was perceived as a queen, and they made certain assumptions that I was interested. And if they were cute, I was interested.

You heard people get called "faggot" and stuff, but it wasn't hostile, and I didn't have any trouble. That's because I'm five-foot-eleven and weigh 230 pounds and I look like a don't-fuck-with-me kind of guy.[61]

Jim Justen, a member of UAW Local 72, worked on the line for thirty-one years at the American Motors plant in his hometown of Kenosha, Wisconsin. As a teenager, he had moved with a tough gay crowd. He was a lightweight street fighter who knew the basics of boxing and jiu-jitsu. "We made up for the fact that we were gay by being strong enough to handle any situation. In the industry, it was known I was gay. There were fellows there I knew from high school. When they were younger, they were bisexual, and they had been tricks of mine."[62]

Dennis O'Neil took a summer job in 1968 on the graveyard shift at Chrysler's Eldon Gear and Axle plant in Detroit. There he met Buddy, a job setter and a member of UAW Local 961:

We were welding the gears and halves of axle housing, and it was mostly black guys on the line. Everybody called Buddy "she." Buddy was very strong—she had these great big biceps. She wore a do-rag like Little Richard, color-coordinated to her outfit, and cheap perfume you could smell eight feet away. You had to wear leather shoes at the plant. Buddy's were white go-go boots. People who had seen her at parties in a dress said she was a knockout.[63]

When he first came to Ford Michigan Truck in 1971, Bob Burrell knew a male worker who always came to work in a dress. He worked in "the pit," below the assembly line, where workers installed heavy parts in units passing above them. "This was before ergonomics, and you had to be very strong," said Burrell. "There was no women's room, and the men didn't like him. They didn't think it was right to share a bathroom with this individual, but they left him alone."[64]

Changing Gender at the Point of Production

Johnny Cisek was one of thousands of white men in their twenties who started out in 1968 at the brand-new, highly automated General Motors plant in Lordstown, Ohio, "the Woodstock of the workingman."[65] He was a member of UAW 1112 and was married, the stepfather of one daughter and the natural father of another. For Cisek, working on the line meant "great wages, and that seemed to be a wonderful way to finance my music."[66]

Cisek took a leave from work in 1975 for gender reassignment surgery and returned with a new identity and a new name: Joni Christian. "The company would have fired me in a minute," she said. "But because of the union, I survived and kept my job."[67] Cisek's gender transition began with an experimental course of hormone therapy at the Cleveland Clinic for special surgery: "Everyone at the plant wore jeans and T-shirts. With the estrogen, my body changes were becoming noticeable, but my shop coat hid what was going on. I told my wife that I was changing my sex, and she tried to cope, and then much later I told my drug buddy, the guy who worked across the line from me. They were the only ones who knew."

Throughout her transition, Christian kept working, sanding Chevy Vega bodies on an assembly line that ran at the crushing speed of 101 units per hour. She abused drugs and alcohol "rather than deal with what was happening with me," she said, and twice quit the Cleveland Clinic. Treatments were expensive, and she was paying out of her own pocket. She eventually had the surgery in Youngstown. "My marriage dissolved after the operation. For a while, I lived at a halfway house. Then I had to deal with the reality of General Motors."[68]

The bosses harassed her with an ugly glee. "Line supervisors and people higher up were after me. They made lewd gestures when I wasn't there, motions pretending to cut the penis off." Coworkers gave her trouble, too. The aggression was never physical, but the hostility was palpable. A petition circulated to bar her from the women's restroom.[69] Gary Bryner, the president of UAW Local 1112, was furious: "We had only started having women working on the line in 1971, and we had to get tough then with how some of the men were acting. So women alone were a scarcity, let alone what Joni was doing. Some of the workers were acting like animals, but there were other brothers who were pretty embarrassed. She was paying dues. She had the right to do whatever she wanted."[70]

That year, 1975, the union was offering a new benefit: attorneys' services for everyday legal cases such as real estate filings, divorces, and workmen's compensation. Bryner and the lawyers encouraged Christian to sue General Motors for invasion of privacy. Eventually, she won a satisfactory out-of-court settlement. She transferred out of the paint shop to a job in quality assurance, an assignment that allowed her to move around the plant. Her confidence grew. "I learned how to look people in the eye and say good morning, whether or not they said anything, and it was five years and then ten years and then they started to respond," she said. "Some didn't want to make contact, but that was OK, because I still had my allies. If they said hello, that was enough. We didn't have to like each other, but we learned to live together."[71]

In spite of Bryner's advocacy, Christian's relationship with union leadership was never an easy one, but she regularly attended local meetings and once ran for alternate committee person. The support she got from workmates was far more dependable than what she found in the gay community of Youngstown. The lesbians rebuffed her, and she felt strange among the female impersonators and other gay men she met at the local bar. She also found solace and validation with her church, where her musical offerings were warmly received.

Having completed thirty years at the Lordstown plant, Christian retired in 1999. She had never intended to make her gender identity a political controversy; her simple goal was to keep working, but for that she had to fight hard. "The union and the company and I all grew up and evolved," Christian reflected.[72] Bryner added, "It was a pretty radical departure for people in that part of the world."[73]

UAW Politics and Queer Identity

At first, Jim Monk said nothing to his coworkers about his gayness. He was active in a radical caucus within UAW Local 444 at the Chrysler truck plant in Windsor, Ontario, where he worked on the engine assembly line.[74] He had a reputation as an agitator, was respected among his coworkers, and gladly stood up to both managers and union officials: "I would force them either to discipline me or to concede the point without my going through the grievance procedure."[75]

On the shop floor he enjoyed the horseplay and "affectionate physical contact" that helped relieve the factory's pressure and monotony. In an interview published in Toronto's gay newspaper, the *Body Politic*, he described the scene he encountered when he started working at Chrysler in the early 1970s: "Guys rubbed each other's backs, kissed—mainly on the cheek but sometimes on the lips—grabbed each other's balls, did dry runs at a bumfuck. . . . You know, when you're uptight and somebody grabs your balls some of it's gotta go. . . . If you suggested that it was homosexuality to these guys, they'd vehemently deny it and get really upset."[76]

Then, in the spring of 1978, Monk decided to make the union his platform for coming out on the job. Windsor Gay Unity was circulating a petition for civil rights, and Monk agreed to solicit at Chrysler's plant gate. "Then I realized that the only ethical thing to do was to come out before we did the petition," he said. An article about the campaign in *The Guardian*, the UAW newsletter distributed to every unionized autoworker in Essex County, Ontario, reported that he was campaigning for autoworkers' support.[77] The next day, when he arrived at work,

> people had clipped that page and put it up on the bulletin boards by the punch clocks. I started working on the lathes with my work partners, and it's like nothing happened, like the hockey game last night. They didn't say a word about it to me, and this goes on for two days.
>
> At first, they assumed that it was one of my causes. Then there was a different reaction. There was this intense discussion going on about me and my sexuality. People would ask me questions—like, "Have you ever been with a woman?" or "How did you figure out that you're gay?"[78]

Everyone knew about Monk's successes as an amateur wrestler, so he was not worried about being beaten up. Moreover, this unionized workplace was in Canada, where the national government had legalized homosexual behavior between consenting adults in the 1960s, and where the religious right had little influence in social policy debates.[79] Still, it took another few months before Monk was included again in the back rubs and ball squeezes. Meanwhile, he maintained his sense of humor. "Once in a while, there would be graffiti about me on the bathroom walls, or a cartoon of me being bum-fucked," he said. "But usually those kinds of cartoons would show a supervisor fucking a worker. A fair number of people kept on respecting me. Just the gay people were scared silly. They stopped talking to me."[80]

Things were different at Chrysler's engine plant in Trenton, Michigan, where Ron Woods, a member of UAW Local 372, came out in 1991. The religious right was mobilizing a severe antigay backlash, and in the public at large, expressions of hostility were growing vivid and volatile. Woods had been at the plant since 1986 but had kept silent for the four years it took to complete his apprenticeship in the skilled auto electrician's trade. Woods's safety was in jeopardy once he became known for leading demonstrations against the Cracker Barrel restaurant chain and its antigay employment practices. At his request, he received a transfer of his electrician job to the Chrysler Tech Center and a transfer of his union affiliation to Local 412.[81] But the move brought him no peace.

In 1992, a union-wide debate began in the UAW about the rights of sexual minorities. A motion to amend the union's constitutional unity statement to include sexual orientation was proposed by Local 1981, the National Writers Union, and supported by an alliance of other white-collar units. The 1992 biennial convention adopted the amendment, and the national newsletter, *UAW Solidarity*, ran a feature in the spring of 1993 about Woods's role in the Cracker Barrel campaign and the prejudice he had encountered at Trenton Engine.[82] Reactions, both positive and negative, were very sharp.[83]

Among his coworkers at Chrysler Tech, Woods found two important allies: Terry Kremkow, his work partner and a union leader, and "Big Bill" Witmer.

They took heat simply for befriending and defending Woods. Gradually, his sense of safety improved. He took classes in union leadership and began to channel his indignation into union activity. When a manager took up tools that belonged to union workers to perform a task assigned to those workers, Woods rebuked him vigorously and then lodged a grievance. His fellow electricians congratulated him for his "defense of the trade."

For a while, Woods was popular. He ran for delegate to the 1995 constitutional convention against a former committeeman who had been one of his worst tormentors. During the energetic campaign, his rival accused Woods of sexually soliciting him in the men's room. The ploy backfired: no one believed the charge; the complaint was dropped; and Woods won the election by a wide margin. He represented Local 412 as a delegate to the next two UAW national meetings, the constitutional convention, and the 1996 Chrysler bargaining convention.

At the 1996 meeting, two other gay Chrysler workers—Jim Justen, retired from Local 72 in Kenosha, Wisconsin, and Martha Grevatt, a tool-and-die maker from Local 122 at Chrysler's plant in Twinsburg, Ohio—helped Woods prepare a stirring speech for the addition of sexual orientation to the equal application section of the contract. The speech was well received, and the proposal was adopted. But at the bargaining table, negotiations for sexual orientation protection were less successful. Rarely does a proposal make it into the contract the first time it comes up. Chrysler insisted on excluding the provision, and late in the negotiations, the union acquiesced. Woods took the exclusion as a personal betrayal.

Meanwhile, Chrysler was encountering substantial pressure from other quarters. Consumer groups, a stockholders' initiative, and a new gay and lesbian salaried employees' organization were calling for the company to make an explicit declaration that it would treat all workers fairly, regardless of their sexual orientation. Late in 1996, Chrysler publicly affirmed sexual orientation nondiscrimination as company policy. A few months later, the corporation signed a side agreement to the contract, a de facto victory for the equal application proposal that had been passed over during negotiations.[84]

Queer Work

At some unionized workplaces, LGBT employees do not worry about coming out, because straight employees are in the minority. "Certain jobs seem to call gay people more than other jobs," said Bill Roberts, who spent his entire career in queer workplaces. He started as a ballet dancer and a member of the American Guild of Musical Artists and then retired from the stage to represent other unionized performers for the American Guild of Variety Artists. In the 1970s, he joined the staff of Local 30 of the Office and Professional Employees International Union in Southern California and negotiated contracts for hospital staff and clerical workers. "I wouldn't even guess the number of gay workers in our union," he said. "There's an awful lot of gay male nurses, and computer work, male secretaries—that's the kind of work that attracts gays."[85]

In his research on gay identities and working-class communities, the historian Allan Bérubé explored the notion of "queer work," occupations in workplaces that are "restrictive but are places where queers can feel they belong and which queers have shaped to meet their needs."[86] Queer work, he argued, "is performed by, or has the reputation of being performed by, homosexual men or women. . . . Many but not all of these jobs are filled by people who are crossing gender roles: jobs where men do women's work and women do men's work, or where effeminate men and masculine women can make a living."[87]

Queer work for men typically is in the service sector, where they perform "feminine" tasks that entertain and nurture, that improve personal appearance, and that enhance indoor spaces. The drift of gay men toward those occupations has had economic consequences: for most of the twentieth century, service work was less likely to be unionized and therefore was more poorly paid than jobs in typically blue-collar masculine occupations. However, a steady increase in union density in the service sector during the late twentieth century meant that men who performed queer work—as nurses, as workers in food and building services, as sales specialists—began to see their socially comfortable jobs improved economically by contractual guarantees of wage hikes and job security. Still, even in those unionized workplaces, queer pay remained consistent with what women typically earned—overall, about 75 percent of compensation for male-dominated job categories.[88]

Some gay men have accepted the economic disadvantages as an offset to creative opportunities and social amenities provided by primarily queer workplaces. With heterosexual men in the minority, the pressure is less intense to mask one's self in ways that will permit fitting in with the straight world. Bill Roberts entered show business as a young ballet dancer in the 1940s and found a work culture that encouraged his sexual awakening:

> At first I was committed to being the only straight dancer in New York, because that way I would give my family the sense of, 'Yes, he's a ballet dancer, but he's straight.' I got married at seventeen, just so I wasn't queer.
>
> My first ballet job was with the Metropolitan Opera. Putting on tights and getting up on stage and doing things that other people couldn't do, I just loved it. Most of the guys were gay; several of them were in relationships. I would see them kissing each other, in the dressing rooms and in the showers, and I would want that.[89]

Peter Tenney waited tables and cooked in restaurants, both fancy and ordinary, in Boston, San Francisco, New York City, and New Orleans. He loved the vivid gay jokes and swift gossip, the yelling and open flirting. "Part of the fun was that I was always out," he says. "I wasn't putting a lot of energy into not being myself."[90] When Scott Reed was an organizer for Local 8 of the Hotel Employees and Restaurant Employees Union (HERE) in Seattle, he observed that the restaurant industry encouraged "a certain congregation of queer people. The radar is out and we're looking. Being queer always helped my work with the membership, because that was an extra reason for members to trust."[91]

Sidney Sushman waited tables in Boston's hotel dining rooms and was the creator of his own raunchy drag act, "The Sylvia Sidney No Talent Review," which played to gay audiences in Provincetown and Boston throughout the 1960s and 1970s. "Sylvia" could not support him, but his union job did. "I like to eat, and I always got meals where I worked and good tips," he said. "I did lunches, dinners, breakfasts. For banquets, I had a tuxedo with a white shirt and white bowtie." Late every Monday night he would dash out of the hotel to the Other Side, a gay club, where he would change into fabulous, vulgar costumes and trade insults with the audience. "I'm the Bitch of Boston, one of the oldest living female impersonators," he bragged.[92]

Sushman enjoyed camping it up with hotel guests in fine dining rooms. "I wait on tables, I let my hair down and they all have a ball. I even wind up with a few dollars more." But he saved his best hijinks for the kitchen. "When you have to wait an hour for the banquet to start, it gets dull, so I would start carrying on, keeping everybody happy until we'd go in and set up."[93]

Sushman joined Local 26 of HERE in 1963 and remained faithful to the union all his life. He attended the monthly meetings and wore full drag to social events, picket lines, and demonstrations. In 1981, he was en route to Washington, DC, with Local 26 for the Solidarity Day rally, but the bus broke down, and the group was stranded in southern New Jersey. "So I changed into my burgundy sequined pants suit and a hot pink headdress, with feathers and full face makeup," he said, and he entertained the crowd until another bus picked them up and took them home.[94]

Union Action in a Queer Environment

Barneys in New York City, in the 1990s, was the gayest union workplace ever.[95] The store began as a popular, dependable destination for conventional men's clothing in 1923, added more expensive lines by stylish designers in the mid-1970s, and was being celebrated as a top destination for men's and women's couture by the mid-1980s. Glamor flourished; profits were high; and pay rose with the good times.

Two branches—downtown in Chelsea and uptown on Madison Avenue—employed more than six hundred workers. The Amalgamated Clothing Workers of America first organized the store in the 1930s, and Local 340 continued to represent the workforce through its own changing affiliations: the Amalgamated Clothing and Textile Workers Union in the 1970s, the Union of Needletrades, Industrial, and Textile Employees (UNITE) in the 1990s.

"The whole store was out," said Irving Smith, who was hired at Barneys Chelsea in 1993, in the children's clothing department. "The older guys who sold the traditional suits, and the stock and security workers, they were straight. But the sportswear guys and the men selling ladies' fashions and the designer-designer stuff in the Penthouse department—all gay." Smith transferred to the Madison Avenue store, where the sales culture was even more dazzling and elite. As the most successful salesperson in his department, he felt free to encourage his coworkers to loosen up. "I told everybody, 'We can't have all that attitude. These people who come in, they're spending $5,000 but we're the salesgirls, we buy at 35 percent discount.'"[96]

One aspect of the fabulousness of Barneys was the annual deluxe employees-only "kick-off" breakfast to start sales for the high-volume fall and Christmas seasons. Staff members donned designer outfits and vamped down a runway. Smith performed as Michael Jackson during his final season at the Chelsea store. A year later, uptown, he was Dionne Warwick:

> I decided we'd go total glam. I wore this size 8 Vera Wang gold strapless gown with a long brown chiffon coat and a wig, jewelry; it must have been $10,000 worth of stuff. One of the girls from cosmetics did my makeup. I started out lip-synching "I Say a Little Prayer," and the straight guys from alterations were yelling, "You look really good!" I don't think you'd be having that at Saks or Bergdorf's, not even Macy's—no, somehow I don't see it.

In January 1996, Barneys filed for bankruptcy. Local 340 commenced negotiations, and Smith joined the team. The union's top priority became maintenance of a clause that was already in the contract, a successor statement, a standard provision that would bind any future owner to pre-existing agreements. This would be critical to the bankruptcy deal because it would retain union membership for all positions, no matter who owned the business. "I saw what the union was doing for people," Smith said. "You were protected, you had your sick days, and I thought, 'Wow, we like unions, and we want any company that comes in to honor our union.'"

With the contract set to expire in late March, the staff decided that a job action would be necessary but did not want the usual informational picket line or everyone showing up for work with union buttons and T-shirts. These unionists wanted a stylish event, one that would interest faithful customers. "Barneys was a store known for its non-color; everybody always wore black," said Smith. "So we did Red Days, on Tuesday, twice." Men in cosmetics painted their nails red while sales staff in the traditional suits department wore red ties or pocket squares. Smith sported a red jersey turtleneck tunic.[97] The flashy touches captured customers' attention, as did the raucous pickets outdoors, with salesmen in $2,000 suits distributing flyers next to stockroom workers, all chanting for the union.[98] But management would not budge, and the contract expired.

The union then staged a fashion show. On April 6, Local 340 set up a runway on the corner of Seventeenth Street and Seventh Avenue, outside the Chelsea store. Music and lights attracted a crowd that cheered the workers as they camped on Barneys' seasonal kickoff with their own labor-themed drag fashions.[99] "We showed our union T-shirts underneath our outfits, and we all carried signs like 'No to the No Successor Clause,'" said Smith. "That cinched it for us, and we were able to close the contract."[100]

The business took three more years to emerge from bankruptcy. New owners came in, closed the Chelsea store, and set a different tone for uptown. When the contract came up for renewal in 1999, bosses demanded pay cuts and reductions in commissions. "They had insisted on the new commission system in the 1996 contract," said Smith, "but now we were making goo-gobs of money, and we had gotten used to living a certain way." Then management worsened its position by trying to tamper with the sales culture, "and we had a fight-and-a-half," said Smith.

> The new CEO came onto our floor, and we're all in black, and he says, "Oh, we're going to have to teach you guys to smile." He wanted Bloomingdales. So we did Yellow Day. That's not one of my colors, but I got this yellow, white, and gray plaid shirt and a tie in the same colors, gray pants, and gray boots.
>
> We leafleted outside with big yellow smiley-face balloons. We wrote our message about their pay cut proposals on the back. Customers took the balloons into the store and let them float to the ceiling.

One contract demand was quickly won: the adoption of same-sex domestic partner benefits, which had been proposed and then dropped in the 1996 negotiations. "We are the people that make Barneys what it is," said Smith. "They didn't fight it."[101]

"It All Begins with Coming Out"

In cities where public employee and other service sector unions have negotiated nondiscrimination and domestic partner benefits, and where gay rights have been established by municipal law, slow but substantial pressure has influenced less liberal elements of the labor movement to keep pace with community standards. Reform caucuses have pushed some of the most conservative-thinking trade unionists to pay attention to the rights of women and ethnic minorities. Queer workers have taken advantage of that attention. Even in the construction industry, with its straight male, blue-collar culture, queer workers have come out on the job and made their issues part of the union's agenda.

In San Francisco in the mid-1990s, a rank-and-file caucus in Carpenters Local 22 battled nonunion contractors and then ran a slate in the next local election that placed a few reformers on the executive board. Women who had participated in the insurgency demanded a revival of affirmative action in the local's apprenticeship programs and hiring hall. A group of young lesbians who had recently entered the trade became regulars at monthly meetings.

Donna Levitt, a business agent for Local 22 and a straight feminist, had always advocated for her lesbian coworkers. But these young dykes were something new. "They're out and obvious about their lesbianism," Levitt said. "They have short hair dyed in bright colors. One of them asked the local to donate to the 1996 Pride at Work convention in Oakland. That made me very nervous. We had never discussed anything like this in the union, but it was nothing to the woman who made the motion. And then it passed—unanimously."[102]

The next bold move was initiated by a women's coalition of carpenters, both lesbian and straight. They passed a motion at the general membership meeting to request that the Carpenters Trust Fund, the labor-management body that administers benefits in Northern California, make domestic partner benefits available. Trustees tabled their letter forthwith, but the issue did not die. In 1997, the City of San Francisco passed an ordinance that would require benefit equity of all contractors doing business with the city. The debate at the Carpenters Trust Fund then focused on the feasibility of a lawsuit to resist the measure.

Explaining that domestic partner benefits would actually cost the fund very little, Levitt lobbied trustees to approve the benefits and avoid a battle in court. Grudgingly, the trustees implemented a program in accord with the ordinance, a move that turned out to be both thrifty and wise. Meanwhile, United Airlines, one of the biggest corporate opponents of San Francisco's ordinance, was going ahead with its lawsuit to halt the law. Local 1781 of the International Association of Machinists and Aerospace Workers (IAM), which represented the airline's mechanics, supported the airline's suit, and the IAM's San Francisco district lodge and its national office joined the case. The court upheld the ordinance, and a storm of protest arose from pro-gay consumers, who persuaded United that its best course would be an abstention from any further appeal. United retreated and made the benefits available not only in San Francisco but also throughout its national workforce.

Fewer than one hundred members of Carpenters Local 22 applied for the benefits in the program's first years. Both same-sex and opposite-sex couples received the coverage. As Levitt had predicted, the reform was not expensive; however, its breadth was huge.[103] The Carpenters Trust Fund covers not only Local 22 of San Francisco but also other carpenters' locals throughout Northern California. Thus, since 1997, domestic partner benefits have been available to fifteen thousand working carpenters and ten thousand retirees.

Unions cannot control individual members' personal reactions to sexual diversity in the workplace. However, they can make queer identities part of their civil rights agendas, and they can educate their memberships about contractual safeguards for sexual minorities.[104] Local leaders who pay attention to these policies and encourage members to do the same have given individual

LGBT workers good reason to come out on the job and participate in the union. This is an essential first step toward integrating LGBT politics into the lives of their locals.

"It all begins with coming out," writes Desma Holcomb. "Coming out is a necessary precondition for any joint work because unions can't collaborate with an abstraction—invisible lesbian and gay workers."[105] Most unionized workplaces, though far less macho than the construction sites of San Francisco and far less swish than the sales floor of Barneys, have become safe for LGBT workers to come out with dignity.

Coming out is only the beginning. A wide range of LGBT trade unionists have struggled to balance queer identity with union activity as they move from the edges of their union's social world into positions of central leadership. They have come out while serving as union officers, as insurgent activists, or as staff organizers and educators. Their lives are public, but the decisions that move those open statements have been personal, dramatic, and sometimes quite painful, and some union leaders who fear compromising their positions have held back. But those who have revealed themselves have integrated their queer identities with their public responsibilities in a process that has turned out to be very much worth the trouble.

2

Outsiders as Insiders

Sexual Diversity and Union Leadership

Marcy Johnsen, a registered nurse at the Fircrest School for developmentally disabled adults, near Seattle, was out at work. But when she stood to address her union's delegate assembly, she felt "so strange." As a vice-president of the Service Employees International Union (SEIU) Local 1199 Northwest, a regional union for health care workers, she often gave speeches; however, at this meeting she was revealing her lesbianism. She knew that the 150 delegates would be reporting back to 7,000 constituents and that many of them would be uncomfortable with her message. "It was like telling people how you have sex," she recalled. "They really don't want to hear about it."[1]

Johnsen and three other panelists were presenting their life stories as part of a program on discrimination and diversity. The union was considering an appeal for support from the Hands Off Washington coalition, which was fighting a petition drive to put two antigay proposals on the November 1994 ballot. Initiative 608 would prohibit the legislature from making sexual orientation "a protected class" and would bar public school teachers from describing homosexuality as "positive, healthy or appropriate behavior." Initiative 610 would forbid state recognition of domestic partnerships and would restrict public libraries from giving minors access to books that discussed homosexuality. It would also ban gay men and lesbians from adopting children or providing foster care and from being granted custodial rights in divorces.[2]

SEIU's constitution had guaranteed sexual orientation protection since 1984. The Executive Board of Local 1199 Northwest, preparing for the delegate assembly, discussed the Washington initiatives and Hands Off Washington's request. Johnsen argued to the board that fighting bigotry was essential union business; some board members disagreed. The board decided that a panel comprising various minorities would explain to delegates why their concerns were union concerns. Johnsen volunteered to make a presentation about sexual diversity: "I felt that it was time. I said, 'Of course I'll speak on the panel, because by the way, I'm gay.'"

Johnsen told the assembly that she would be a likely victim of the discriminatory measures, should they ever become law. Some delegates agreed that the union should oppose the initiatives, like the nurse who declared that she "didn't agree with people's lifestyles, but it wasn't her decision; God made everybody."[3] However, Johnsen felt the chill once the meeting adjourned. "I went to the ladies' room during lunch, and there were some people in there, and not one of them said a thing to me," she said. "Later, one nurse resigned her position as a delegate. She felt that the nurses in her chapter couldn't support this activity."[4] The motion to endorse Hands Off Washington carried; the petition drive for initiatives 608 and 610 failed to collect enough signatures to place the proposals on the November 1994 ballot, and Johnsen continued to serve Local 1199 Northwest, now as an openly lesbian officer.

Acceptance of gayness in union leaders was, in the 1990s, a new commitment with inconsistent antecedents; SEIU, however, was well known for its strong record of advancing queer activists to leadership positions. Mary Kay Henry, director of SEIU's national health care division, was a founder of the union's Lavender Caucus in 1993. She rose to SEIU's executive vice-presidency in 2004, was elected president of the union in 2010, and became the third openly lesbian union leader to be seated on the Executive Council of the AFL-CIO.[5]

Before the Stonewall Rebellion in 1969 and the rise of the modern gay liberation movement, queer labor activists who served as local officers, staff members, national officials, and insurgent leaders were seldom out in their unions.[6] Many in leadership positions would shield their gayness and subdue their personal lives, not only to avoid direct harassment, but also to protect the reputation of their organizations. In sacrificing openness, they often lived lives of detachment, if not duplicity.

Unions during the 1950s represented 36 percent of the U.S. workforce and upheld culturally conservative values, even as they leaned toward liberal politics. Homosexual labor leaders did not come out. Many gay union staff and elected officials feared blackmail, and many others became targets of smear campaigns or were fired or turned down for promotions. Unions then were no safer for queers in leadership than the Democratic Party, liberal churches and synagogues, universities, or IBM.[7]

Jim Justen grew up gay in Zion, Illinois, in the 1950s. His father, a locomotive engineer and a union officer, had befriended lesbian co-workers on the railroad. Justen remembered well his father's advice: "He said, 'This is not something you ask for. Accept yourself as an individual.'" Justen said he decided "not to hide myself from anybody. I want them to understand where I'm at. There will be no blackmail." After high school graduation in 1962, Justen began working on the American Motors assembly line in nearby Kenosha, Wisconsin.

"In our heyday, we had 12,000 workers over three shifts," he recalled. He was elected and reelected shop steward of United Auto Workers (UAW) Local 72 from the mid-1960s to the early 1970s:

> We were a rebel local. If we had to pull a safety strike, we would shut the line off and tell the people don't go back to work until the problem is resolved. When we hit that button, we got attention.
>
> One guy got injured from a spring clamp. It slipped and exploded in his face—could have killed him. It was the second injury in two weeks. One of our board members asked me, "What do you think," and I said, "Shut it off."
>
> We told management we're not going back to work on that particular job. Until you get a safety clamp that is safe enough to operate, you can take your two supervisors and put them on the line; we're not putting another union person on that job until the problem is resolved. The next day, every engineer and every master mechanic was out there to solve it.[8]

Justen lived with his mate in Kenosha, a one-company and one-union town, where UAW awards banquets and charity activities were central to community life. But even at the height of his union involvement, Justen did not mix socially with UAW colleagues. He and his mate were never invited to couples parties, and they avoided the dinner dances. Instead, they enjoyed a cozy social scene with lesbians from the shop and older male couples in town. "There was Don Nolan and Jim, his lover," Justen said. "We called him Mother Nolan, and we'd have dinner at Mother's on Sunday night. The girls, the guys—Mother would serve everybody."

The long years of mutual disregard did not matter much to Justen. He maintained his dignity and did not worry about the prejudice. "I'm not going to pry into your life, and you don't pry into mine" was his creed, and it functioned well enough.[9] He straddled two worlds: union mainstream and gay subculture.

Many queer labor leaders did not come out in their unions until the 1970s and 1980s, when the gay liberation movement was gathering power and gay culture was flourishing. Some did so joyfully and fully; others revealed themselves gradually among trusted friends; and many others, convinced that prejudice was still thicker than tolerance, took precautions to avoid detection, declaring themselves only with reluctance if they were exposed. Closeted union officers and staff members were concerned that openness would risk their campaigns or damage their careers and therefore divided their public lives from their sexual identities. Their fears were not unfounded. Not until the 1990s did many of their organizations adopt explicit antidiscrimination policies for sexual minorities.

When labor leaders came out, their individual temperaments made a difference in how well they integrated their queer identities with the better-known facts of their public roles. But there were other important influences, such as the actual nature of the leadership positions they held. Rank-and-file leaders who were elected by fellow workers to serve as volunteers wondered how they would fare with their workmates and in their communities. Full-time elected officers considered diverse political climates within their national or regional constituencies, as well as their reputations among colleagues in allied organizations. Staff specialists appointed to their positions operated in "a different reality," said Bailey T. Walker Jr., director of leadership training for the American Federation of State, County, and Municipal Employees (AFSCME). They functioned at the pleasure of the officers, unlike "local people who get elected and have their own political identities."[10]

From the 1960s through the 1990s, rank-and-file leaders, national officials, and professionals appointed to union office came out in their unions. Their LGBT identities were not central to their achievements, but the way they experienced being different did affect how they functioned in the movement. Their actions and influences were profound: from Bayard Rustin's articulation of the Civil Rights Movement as an essential cause for economic justice during the 1960s through Judy Mage's leadership of a public employees' strike in 1965, to Bill Olwell's representation of labor's opposition to the Vietnam War during the late 1960s and his involvement in a major union merger in the late 1970s. Jeanne Laberge and Ruth Jacobsen, a couple who were out in their blue-collar union, advocated for the training of more women in an elite mechanical trade. Teresa Rankin in the 1970s and Martie Voland in the 1990s participated in the last great industrial organizing drives in the textile towns of the South. From the 1970s to the 1990s, Donna Cartwright, Ed Hunt, Gary Kapanowski, and Kim Ramsey led local insurgencies that challenged union officials on unsatisfactory contracts, weak leadership, and plant closings.

Union Staff, Union Closet

Bayard Rustin's story is more widely known than are the stories of most other gay people who have worked for labor's cause. Rustin never stood for election but was prominent for fifty years in movements for labor, peace and civil rights. He was a charismatic speaker, a thoughtful negotiator, a brilliant organizer. He was right-hand man to A. Philip Randolph, founder of the Brotherhood of Sleeping Car Porters, and lead strategist for the March on Washington for Jobs and Freedom in 1963. But Rustin's illustrious career was forever tarnished by the stigma of an arrest in 1953 on "morals charges." The scandal was known to both his allies and his enemies, a queerness that was tacitly forgiven by some and condemned by others.[11] Only shortly before his death in 1987 did Rustin address a wider public about his life as a gay man in the movement.[12]

Less famous union staff members of that era coped the best they could. "You couldn't be openly gay and expect to maintain a job in the union," said Gary Deane. As a labor educator for the Amalgamated Clothing Workers of America's midwestern region in the 1960s, Deane specialized in union-sponsored cooperative housing. He said:

> [As a staff member] I never lied, but I did sometimes change genders in a conversation. Once I was driving to an assignment with another guy from the Education Department and Frank Sinatra came on the radio with "Strangers in the Night." We listened to the song, and he turned to me and said, "You know, they say this song is about homosexuals." I almost wrecked the car.
>
> I would go to union socials as a bachelor, but there was this assumption that I wanted to get married. People would angle to see if I was interested in dating their daughters or their sisters. Sometimes at union retreats there would be a woman who would steal my room key.

Deane was turned down for a high-profile job and later found out that rivals were gossiping "that I was something less than a man." In the late 1960s, he moved from Chicago to New York City to work for the union-sponsored United Housing Federation. Here, too, a promotion was blocked with the comment, "No, not that fag."

It was in New York City that Deane met Connie Kopelov, the associate national director of education at Amalgamated headquarters. He had heard about her in Chicago, "a whispered conversation about her sexuality, so that was a tip-off."[13] Deane and Kopelov would cover for each other at dinner dances and other union functions. Kopelov had been on guard about her sexual identity since the late 1950s, when she realized that she was a lesbian. "I refrained from relationships with colleagues because I wasn't comfortable bringing them home to meet my partner," she said. "I couldn't really be a friend. I'm sure many people must have had some idea."

Kopelov, like Deane, stuck to the rule forbidding sexual liaisons between union staff and union members. But a lesbian organizer for the Textile Workers Union of America, a friend of Kopelov's, risked an affair with a factory worker. Kopelov recalls that when it came to the attention of the lead organizer, "He dealt with it professionally. He took her aside and said, 'I really don't care what you do, but I don't think it should happen in the organizing campaign.' He said what he would have said to a man."[14]

Deane eventually left the labor movement. He co-founded Brooklyn's Gay and Lesbian Independent Democrats, an influential political club, and in 1977 became New York City's first openly gay candidate for City Council. Kopelov continued to work as a labor educator for the Amalgamated Clothing Workers and in the late 1970s for District 1199, the National Union of Hospital and Health Care Employees.[15] For a younger generation of union staff, the strictures began to loosen. As the movement for gay rights gained political respect and cultural force, unions, like many other civic, religious, academic, and corporate establishments, reformed their policies at headquarters and in the locals.

The limitations and whispers that had halted Deane, Kopelov, and many others were fading. Queerness stopped being a reason to deny promotions.

Van Alan Sheets, AFSCME's associate director for political action, rejoiced that he could integrate his sexual identity with public service. He recalled a holiday party at national headquarters in the mid-1990s with same-sex dancing and "two men who came not with their lesbian friends but with their male partners as dates." Sheets traveled widely for political campaigns and noticed that life in the field was changing for the better, too:

> I used to remain closeted when I traveled to Alaska, New Hampshire, Florida, all those places. I didn't know the territory. Sometimes I'd be there a month or two, working seven days a week. I would hear "faggot" and other stuff behind my back. But gradually I got to know the people out there, and somewhere along the way it became a political cause. Nowadays when I go to the field, I'm still wearing both my earrings, like I do at headquarters, and I'm not at all covering up that I'm a gay man.[16]

Coming Out to Save the Day

Tom Privitere, a union staff member, came out only because a tense situation made his declaration necessary. For fifteen years, his public circumspection had served him well. At the beginning of his career as a field agent for AFSCME District Council 66 of Rochester, New York, he was a married father of two children. Then he fell in love with another married man, and both marriages broke up. Privitere remained cautious among the workers he served: "I never even told the lesbians—a couple of truck drivers, a draftsman—but I think they figured."

In 1985, Privitere took a job with the Public Employees Federation (PEF), the union of fifty-five thousand technical, professional, and scientific employees of the State of New York. The federation's LGBT culture was more political than the one Privitere had known at AFSCME. "I still only told people about myself on a need-to-know basis," he said, "but at my first convention I sat at the gay and lesbian table and was staff liaison to the gay rights task force."[17]

New York City, Buffalo, Albany, and Rochester enacted domestic partner registration in the 1990s, and gay rights organizations soon were forming coalitions with public employees' unions to negotiate partner benefits into state workers' contracts. In 1994, Governor Mario Cuomo enacted coverage for gay and straight employees by executive order. However, the benefits were not contractually protected. Governor George Pataki's Republican administration took over during the first year the coverage was available and proposed to do away with the benefits during contract negotiations. "This was nothing we didn't expect," said Privitere, PEF's chief negotiator. "They were trying to court Republican conservatives."

Privitere was not the only gay person at bargaining sessions. Another gay staff member from PEF joined him, but neither man was out to anyone at the table—not to the openly gay and lesbian officers who were participants in the talks or to the rank-and-file queer PEF activists who were monitoring the process. The union team came to the table with an analysis of how members had used the benefits in the previous year. They found a substantial constituency of heterosexual PEF members whose unmarried partners were enrolled in the plan, many more than the domestic partners of gay and lesbian members. Clearly, the benefit had broad support. The team insisted "at the table, in caucus, and on the record" that without continuation of the coverage, there would be no settlement. "And we wanted it in the contract, not as an executive order."

But the queer rank and filers were wary. "They worried that we were going to lose what the gay community had fought so hard to win. They wanted assurances that this issue was going to be fought for at the table with our full resources." Privitere and his colleague knew that the talks could be compromised if such a pledge were made. They set up a separate meeting in a public place:

> We told them that this was critical and that we weren't giving up. But we had to be very careful not to say to the other side, "Either we get this or there is no contract." That borders on bad-faith bargaining and could jeopardize the whole deal.
>
> They kept on grilling us, so I finally said, "Look, I think it's really important for you to know where we're coming from. I sense that a lot of you don't trust us to go to the wall. So I'm going to share with you something that may help you believe that we're not letting this go. I am a gay man. I'm as sympathetic as anybody can be on this issue. I want to see domestic partner benefits become a reality in New York."

Privitere's colleague came out next. Their revelations broke the tension. The caucus pulled together with the negotiating team for a final push. PEF had been running a public campaign that emphasized how the coverage would be both fair and fiscally responsible. "On billions of contract dollars," according to Privitere, "the benefits meant pennies."[18] The financial argument made continuity of the program much more appealing to the State of New York. Labor and management had a deal.

With the contract ratified, PEF found new allies, especially among advocates for seniors. Among unmarried heterosexual partners already enrolled in the coverage were many retired state workers who were widowed and whose Social Security benefits would be diminished if they remarried. Unions, LGBT organizations, and other liberal groups throughout the state also admired how neatly PEF's campaign had clipped the governor's political intentions.[19]

Breaking Through: A Strike and a Smear

Labor leaders who first attempted the integration of their sexual identities and labor movement commitments did not see themselves as pioneers of gay liberation. Their politics were anchored in their union work. In the 1960s, Judy Mage, an idealistic social service caseworker and activist in New York City, and Bill Olwell, a popular local president in Seattle, led their unions during critical times while living queer lives on the edge of coming out.

Mage, an organizer, vice-president, and later president of New York City's Social Service Employees Union (SSEU), risked herself regularly, both politically and personally (often simultaneously), many years before gay liberation was a movement and coming out was a political act. In the midst of a driven life unionizing caseworkers, she was sexually adventurous, often with union colleagues. It was her political intensity that sustained her romantic excitement, her sexual charisma that energized her union-building devotion.

Mage returned to her hometown of New York City in 1959, bachelor's degree in hand, with a clear goal: to end poverty in America.[20] She got a job at the municipal Department of Welfare's Amsterdam Center near Pennsylvania Station. The vast workplace reminded her of a factory. "Caseloads were huge. You either hardened or you left," she said. "You'd go into the women's bathroom, and there would be young caseworkers in tears." Throughout the city's public sector, workers were beginning to form the complex and powerful municipal unions that have since set the pace for how the city and its employees do business with each other. AFSCME Local 371, an established union in the Department of Welfare, was attempting to organize caseworkers, but after her first few meetings, Mage was disappointed. The rules of the civil service system predominated, and supervisors controlled the agenda. "I wanted fundamental changes, for us workers as well as for the clients."[21]

Mage joined the independent SSEU. With her radical proposals to involve clients in decisions about welfare reform and her willingness to speak out, she quickly rose to leadership. Throughout 1963 and 1964, her group agitated and organized, boosting recruitment through daring job actions. A formal complaint to the federal Department of Health, Education, and Welfare about excessive caseloads drew sixty-day suspensions for Mage and three other ringleaders. The four activists used those two months to agitate full time. 'Social work, not paper work,' that was one of our slogans," she said.[22]

During her first year at the Amsterdam Center, Mage had found herself with a deep crush on a co-worker: "Being in love with her and doing union work together was so exhilarating. I'd see her on that gray factory floor in her lilac suit, and it would inspire me. But we never became lovers. She did not want the lifestyle." Mage, a married woman, was becoming more and more curious about the gay life. She read *The Ladder*, the publication of the lesbian advocacy organization Daughters of Bilitis; she visited a lesbian bar; she went to a

Daughters of Bilitis social; and she had a few affairs.[23] "It was a double life. My husband covered for me," she said. "It wasn't that I was ashamed, but it would have been political death. So even if it was used in a whisper campaign, which it probably was, people could say, 'Nah, you know, she's married.' I'm sure that people close to the inner circle of the union suspected and were sympathetic, but they respected my secrets."[24]

The SSEU overcame AFSCME Local 371 in an election for citywide bargaining rights in October 1964, and Mage took leave from her job to organize and negotiate. The city balked at the crucial issue of workloads; a newly reformed Local 371 joined the battle; and on January 4, 1965, both unions—eight thousand welfare workers—walked out. The Condon-Wadlin Act prohibited strikes in the public sector, so the city obtained an injunction and then fired the workers. For the next twenty-eight days, strikers encircled City Hall and picketed welfare offices; two-thirds of the city's centers closed down for the duration of the strike.[25] "We put out leaflets every day, from a secret place where we kept our mimeograph machine. It was just night after night, two to three hours' sleep, and then I'd be back on the picket line. I couldn't have done any of this if I hadn't had exceptional energy and the ability to get along on very little sleep."[26]

The social workers' strike was a call to solidarity throughout the city's labor movement. The Congress of Racial Equality, the National Association for the Advancement of Colored People, Dr. Martin Luther King Jr., and other civil rights advocates tried to intervene with city and state officials; deans of six schools of social work attempted to broker a settlement. The national AFL-CIO did not sanction strikes by public employees, but in this crisis, leaders of New York-based affiliates defied national policy. They contributed to the strike fund (the recently formed and rapidly growing United Federation of Teachers donated $34,169), and they urged members to join the social workers on the picket line.[27]

Mage was arrested and jailed during the strike's final days, along with eighteen others from both the SSEU and Local 371. "It was such a relief. I could eat! I could sleep! And we all began to appreciate each other." Behind bars, she found a special connection with one of Local 371's top officers. "Before the strike, we had been enemies, denouncing each other, but in jail we wrote a poem together and sat on each other's bunks touching toes."[28]

Caseworkers returned to their jobs the first week of February while the union continued bargaining. By June 1965, they had a contract with substantial economic improvements and broader rights for all unions in the municipal system.[29] The agreement also spelled out a reduction in caseloads, a priority for caseworkers as well as for clients. Community and civil rights activists who had participated in the strike were now better connected to militant union members who were already engaged in the emerging movement for welfare rights.[30]

Mage continued to see her jail companion during the next few months. "Nobody blew the whistle, so we could pretend to ourselves that people didn't know, but they did," she said. The secret affair did not last, and neither did the crisis alliance of their rival unions. "Both of us were so loyal to our organizations. We couldn't keep it going."[31]

In Seattle, Bill Olwell was similarly committed to his causes. His rivals so thoroughly detested him and his vision of labor politics that they tried to oust him with gay smears. Although it was union reform he was advocating, and not sexual freedom, he found himself, like Mage, maneuvering on both fronts.

Olwell had no problem being in the closet. In the 1960s, he was the business representative and then president of Local 1001, one of the biggest in the Retail Clerks International Association. Its twelve thousand members were employed at Seattle supermarkets and department stores; the only local union in the region that was larger represented machinists at Boeing. When Olwell made the rounds of union social events, a lesbian schoolteacher was his regular date. "It wasn't that often, but I used her for years, and it took the heat off," he said. But as he prepared to run for reelection in 1969, he came up against a campaign of defamation that challenged his future as a union leader, as well as the general direction of labor politics in Seattle.[32]

Olwell was also president of the King County Labor Council. He advocated racial integration in the construction industry, and he represented the council at antiwar rallies, where he spoke against military escalation in Vietnam. Conservative leaders of Seattle's building trades council decided that Olwell had to be stopped.[33] They put up $15,000 to finance an opposition candidate. "They would ask, 'Have you ever seen Bill Olwell with a woman? Doesn't it seem strange to you that he's thirty-five years old and not married?'"

Olwell was scared. His rivals were exploiting his gayness, so he focused on what really mattered to members—his service—and visited every store under contract, mornings, evenings, weekends. "I always knew that if I could get the election on my experience and my delivery, I would win," he said, "and as it turned out, I did. Once I put my contracts up front, the gay thing just wasn't an issue. I don't think it cost me ten votes out of the four thousand that voted. We had 121 polling places, and I won every polling place but one, and the day after the election, I started working on that one."[34]

Women constituted 75 percent of the Local 1001's membership, and they were Olwell's enthusiastic supporters. Just a year earlier, the contract Olwell had negotiated with Seattle's best department stores ended long-standing patterns of gender-based wage differentials and dramatically increased female workers' income.[35] With the election won, Olwell never looked back. "Those members could have cared less about me being gay," he said. "From that day on, there was a huge change in me. I stopped worrying about what people knew. I stopped taking the schoolteacher to the parties."[36]

Olwell rose in the bureaucracy of the Retail Clerks to serve on the national executive board during the 1970s and then moved with Eddie Miller, his partner, to Washington, DC, where he worked on the consolidation of the Retail Clerks with the Amalgamated Meat Cutters to create the United Food and Commercial Workers International Union (UFCW), chartered in 1978. During talks, opponents in the Meat Cutters denounced Olwell for his homosexuality, but he would not take the bait, nor would his allies. He was elected a national vice-president, in charge of negotiations; then, in 1981, he became executive vice-president and assistant to the president, William Wynn. The UFCW became the first of the aggregated mega-unions; by 1985, it was the largest in the AFL-CIO, with more than a million members. "People would dismiss me as a lightweight because I'm gay, and then when they saw my influence, they figured that Bill and I had had an affair," he said. "I was a trench fighter, a real political operator. The question of my gayness only came up when people couldn't think of anything else to say against me."[37]

Since Olwell's time, other activists have found themselves with similar dilemmas: are their public positions so vulnerable that coming out would interfere with effective leadership? Is the world of the union tolerant enough to integrate public office with private reality?

Outsiders on the Inside: Breaking Up, Burning Out, Fitting In

To Steve D'Inzillo, the heterosexual business agent of New York City's Motion Picture Projectionists Local 306, the lesbian relationship of two new apprentices was a plus. Within the International Alliance of Theatrical Stage Employees (IATSE), D'Inzillo was a well-known maverick and advocate of civil rights. In the early 1970s, he wanted to see women surmount his union's gender bar. They would have to be skilled enough to learn a complicated trade and brave enough to deal with the flak. In Ruth Jacobsen and Jeanne Laberge he found a lesbian couple willing and able to accomplish the breakthrough. Jacobsen, a textile artist, knew a few things about hard times from her life of privation as a "hidden child" during the Nazi occupation of Holland. And the brash Laberge loved a challenge; she had a union background.[38]

D'Inzillo sponsored Jacobsen's apprenticeship in 1972; she received her license a year later, becoming the city's first female booth man. Laberge applied and was admitted to the trade in 1974. D'Inzillo saw how the couple supported each other on the job and at the union hall, and when they proposed that Local 306 sponsor pre-apprenticeship training for women, he agreed. Many who signed up were already members of Local 306—the sisters, wives, and daughters of booth men who worked at less skilled jobs. "We got several licenses out of that first class," Laberge said. "It was the first crack of having not just fathers and sons in the trade. We were into the feminist thing. We had the union change how they addressed the letters, to get rid of 'Dear Sir and Brother.' The men could be pretty derisive at meetings, so our women's group dealt with their disruptions."

D'Inzillo wanted Jacobsen to join the Executive Board, but she was not willing to promote herself politically. In Laberge, however, he found his avid volunteer. She came onto Local 306's board, started a local newsletter, and wrote most of the articles. Laberge became D'Inzillo's right-hand woman as he rose in IATSE politics. He ran twice for the national presidency and was elected to a vice-presidency with a seat on the executive board. There he continually pushed "the only proposals at conventions that addressed larger social and political issues," said Laberge, who assisted him through many years of controversy.[39]

Laberge and Jacobsen were as out in the union as any lesbians could be. Local 306 added "sexual preference" to its antidiscrimination articles during the late 1970s "out of deference to us," Laberge noted, and they turned the union's attention to other gay issues of the day. The union made regular donations to lesbian and gay charities, supported three gay members who were sick from AIDS, and mourned them when they died.

It was not the closet but their prominence that pressured the relationship. D'Inzillo's campaigns took up more and more of Laberge's time, and Jacobsen was often upset. During one period of especially sharp conflict, D'Inzillo apologized to Jacobsen. "Perhaps I take too much advantage of Jeanne's abilities and dedication to union objectives," he wrote. "I often feel I call on her time and effort too frequently. . . . I fear it promotes disturbance between you. This should not be. Her work in the union is vital but the love between you is more so."[40] But their strife continued; after ten years together, the couple broke up.

Teresa Rankin, by contrast, knew that union work would be a complicated field, though not because colleagues might be prejudiced. "I felt that because I'm gay, I could not trust the union to take care of me," she said. In the early 1970s, she went to Washington, DC, with a college degree but no interest in a conventional career. Instead, she was enjoying lesbian downward mobility: a communal house with other women and a job at First Things First, a feminist bookstore. She kept an eye on working women's issues through the National Organization for Women's labor task force and soon got involved with the campaign to unionize the J. P. Stevens textile company, one of the most powerful southern labor events of the decade.[41]

In 1974, the Textile Workers Union of America won an election to represent employees at Stevens's central plant in Roanoke Rapids, North Carolina. However, following certification, the company shook off the union's bids to bargain collectively. In 1976, the Textile Workers Union and the larger, more solidly financed Amalgamated Clothing Workers merged to form the Amalgamated Clothing and Textile Workers Union (ACTWU). The J. P. Stevens contract was its first priority. The union deployed an old-fashioned AFL-CIO-wide consumer boycott of the company's sheets, towels, and home products—"Don't Sleep with J. P. Stevens"—with a new strategy designed to isolate the textile giant from the greater business community: the corporate campaign. Union analysts charted the financial connections of Stevens's trustees; targeted corporate boards on which they served; and then pressed religious organizations, union pension funds, and other large stockholders to demand dismissal of these officers from their board positions.[42]

Rankin joined the boycott staff and was assigned to ACTWU's Joint Board in Baltimore. The union's business agents were old-school Italian American tailors from the men's clothing trades, and Rankin knew that they would be watching how she dressed. "So I bought business outfits—camouflage—and I shaved my legs. I didn't talk about being gay with anybody. But I didn't invent a man in my life, either." Her reticence worked well with both the older, more formal men at headquarters and her aggressive younger colleagues who staffed the corporate campaign and ACTWU's other organizing projects. "There was a culture of not talking too much about your life," she said. "These guys were all going through relationships at a rapid clip, sleeping with people they technically shouldn't be sleeping with—members. They didn't get into talking, because it is tricky territory, and that worked to my advantage. I didn't get into it, either."

In the field, Rankin worked hard for the Stevens campaign; in nearby Washington, she could fall back on her lesbian scene. "A lot of organizers rely emotionally on other union people, and then they burn out. My support base was always my home, not the union. We were political, and this was my thing for the cause, and I think that helped me with the labor movement."

When the J. P Stevens contract was settled in 1980, ACTWU offered Rankin an assignment in Stuart, Virginia, not far from Danville, her hometown near the North Carolina border. She turned it down. The territory was familiar, and she was a talented organizer, but she understood that the isolation would be too much. "I already knew how hard it is to be gay in a small town, and if you're trying to organize a union there, it's going to be even harder."[43]

Instead, she stayed in the city and kept living at her communal house. She took a secretarial job at George Washington University's medical school. She was there as a "colonizer," a worker with a union assignment, and reported to SEIU's new clerical division, District 925.[44] Rankin's office employed two other clericals, one of them an openly gay man. "The other worker was a straight woman. She loved him and his gay sensibility, so I could be out as a lesbian. But she didn't like the union. Him I could talk to about the union, but not her."

Rankin returned to ACTWU's Baltimore Joint Board in 1983 and teamed up with a male organizer; together they won a few shops. Gradually she came out to colleagues from the Stevens campaign. Nobody was surprised. "They just said, 'Teresa, this is old news.'" Still, when the Metro DC Labor Council honored her with its community service award in 1985, she arrived at the banquet alone. Between public work and private lesbian identity she maintained her sharp divide.[45]

Like Rankin, Martie Voland came from the South. She joined ACTWU's Organizing Department only a few years later, in 1989. "I assumed that the labor movement would be welcoming of lesbians and gays," she said, and she came out to fellow staff members as a matter of course. Voland was looking for tough assignments and found them in ACTWU's textile drives. For the next ten years, she participated in the union's most important campaigns, always out to colleagues but only rarely to workers.[46]

By then, southern textile employers were paying for advice from antiunion consultants, who told their clients to fire known worker-activists. Such dismissals were illegal, but the Reagan and Bush administrations enabled denials of court orders to reinstate with back pay and delays long enough to weaken the court's remedies.

One of Voland's first campaigns was in Martinsville, Virginia, home of the Tultex T-shirt and fleece mills, a huge operation that employed five thousand workers in several plants over three shifts. ACTWU was deploying its new multiphase program of counterattack. It began in stealth with intense training of a small core of activists. Voland came to town just as the committee shifted from tactics of caution to an aggressive "blitz" phase. Workers were canvassing, and ACTWU signs were everywhere. "We would get a majority to sign up quickly, before the company could react and discipline the leaders," she said. "We could go to the NLRB [National Labor Relations Board] early and aim for a quick election. That would protect workers from the eventual crap that came down."

Once the petition had been filed with the board and a date had been set, the union would retreat. "You stabilize with only a few people in the office, and you keep a low profile in town." Expecting energetic activity from the union side, the company would drop its guard. Then, on the very eve of the election, staff would return with officials and other supporters to rally the workers. Activists would show up for work the next morning wearing ACTWU T-shirts. Victory was still not sure, but if election results showed a close loss, the union would withdraw with plans to try again. The 1990 tally at Tultex came in with the union winning only 45 percent of the vote, a margin thin enough to encourage another shot. ACTWU returned four years later with enhanced support and won, 1,321–720.[47]

Voland returned to the South in 1991, to her home state of North Carolina and the town of Kannapolis. There ACTWU was engaged, as it had been since the 1970s, in its "holy war" to organize the huge industrial complex of Cannon Mills. The company changed owners, corporate goals, and names three times: from Cannon to Fieldcrest (Fieldcrest Cannon) to Pillowtex. The union petitioned for certification elections four times: in 1981, 1991, 1997, and 1999. Everyone knew that the 1991 campaign would be tight. The company was violating basic labor laws blatantly and often.[48]

Voland was assigned to one of the main factories and learned from another lesbian on staff that one of the workers there, a towel sewer, was also lesbian. She was part of a couple; her lover worked in the weaving division. Voland said nothing to either of the women until the day she found out that a male organizer had made a pass at one of them. Voland and her lesbian colleague attempted to calm the woman down. "She was shaken, and I was pissed, out of lesbian solidarity, and also that any of our guys was trying it with a worker." Voland eventually drew the couple more deeply into the campaign, and they became dependable rank-and-file organizers. "For them, doing union work was not social justice. It was a part of the job. It was seeking a better life."[49]

ACTWU lost by 199 out of 6,267 ballots cast, contested at the NLRB, and won an order to overturn the vote. On appeal in 1995, the U.S. Court of Appeals for the Fourth Circuit upheld the NLRB's findings of 150 unfair labor practices during the organizing period and penalties of $3 million in back pay. Chief Judge J. Harvie Wilkinson III wrote, "Fieldcrest simply adopted a scorched earth, take-no-prisoners approach to stop unionization without regard to statutory limits."[50]

But the company would not correct itself. The Fourth Circuit ordered the next vote to be supervised by the NLRB itself. Once again, ACTWU lost. On appeal, the board joined with the union, and the court once again overturned the results. At that point, Fieldcrest sold out to Pillowtex and left town.[51] ACTWU itself reorganized in 1995, when it merged with the International Ladies' Garment Workers' Union to become the Union of Needletrades, Industrial and Textile Employees (UNITE).

Voland returned to Kannapolis again and again, usually during the summer. She saw the lesbian couple "almost always together," at committee meetings or hanging out at the union hall. "They were comfortable with me. They were closeted, not out to anybody but each other. They did not live together. The older one was taking care of her parents." Union staff members—perhaps some workers, too—respected the relationship. The mill town became part of Voland's life. Throughout the years of turmoil, families who had worked all their lives in those mills, some over generations, kept the union faith. "Some of the women I first met in 1991 had little kids," Voland recalled. "By the last time I came back, one of those kids was having a baby of her own."[52]

ACTWU was running another campaign in nearby Gastonia, and Voland was finishing a project at the office one evening and had time to spare. She went out on a house call with Joe, a fellow organizer. This time she paid attention to her instincts.

We only had the name and address for this one gentleman. It was dusk, and a woman answered the door. When we asked for the man, she said, "Now what has he gotten himself into!" She talked with us through the screen door. In any house call, you have to make a quick assessment, and I remember that it just hit me: this was our worker. She was dressed in a skirt and blouse, but it was clear to me that this was a man.

We talked about the issues at work. She said, "You know, I have trouble sometimes, but they let me be who I am." Something like, I'm not rocking the boat, because the company does not hassle me. As we left, Joe said, "Well if you see him, please tell him we came by."[53]

Outsiders on the Inside: Union Insurgencies

During labor's strongest years, unions were often headed by leadership groups that held on to power term after term. Incumbents remained in charge and sustained the system's strength through routine contracts negotiated placidly with cooperative managers. However, as new technology, global trade, and plant closings challenged that stability, rank-and-file members organized to confront leaders' decisions. Negotiations became flash points. Reformers' questions ranged from the distribution of raises to how work would be performed and compensated and how the workforce would fare in the future of the enterprise.

From teamsters to teachers, insurgents tested leaders and campaigned to replace them. Some unions, plagued by corruption and racketeering, became the focus of civil or criminal investigations and were taken into trusteeship, either by their internationals or by the federal government.[54] Other unions, though weakened by static leadership, required less stringent correctives and reformed themselves by electing new leaders. By agitating through word of mouth, newsletters, and websites, reformers mounted substantial challenges to entrenched establishments. Their efforts required the courage to follow the union's own democratic principles as delineated in its constitution and bylaws, as well as knowledge of basic rights codified in labor law.[55]

Campaigns for labor reform usually are not friendly events. Activists have risked their livelihoods, if not their lives, to clean up their unions.[56] Although notorious crimes are not the case in most union halls, the fight to disrupt a poorly functioning administration can highlight the worst of labor politics. Few incumbents would willingly forfeit longtime perquisites such as released time from regular assignments, sometimes at full pay, or general political influence in the wider community. And workplace familiarity can breed especially rough tensions when electoral opponents or their supporters work side by side in the same shop.

LGBT unionists have participated in opposition caucuses and advocated for the status quo. But it is the political outsiders who have been most open about their queerness. Having already put their status on the line as dissidents, some have found that openness about queer identity has actually given them the political edge—shows of honesty in tense contests when personal integrity is at stake. "I was always willing to be a minority of one," said Donna Cartwright, a loyal oppositionist in Local 3 of the Newspaper Guild. Cartwright lived as a man, on the job and in the union, until 1998, when she had sex reassignment surgery. For twenty years, she had edited copy on the foreign desk of the *New York Times*. She was a shop steward, a regular on the Executive Board of Local 3, and, for a while, general grievance chair of the paper's 1,500 member unit. "I took complaints and I explained the contract. I knew the formal processes and understood how the deals were done. I was known as Mr. Union."[57]

Cartwright began hormone therapy and electrolysis in 1997. She broke the news to family and friends, dressed as a woman in her neighborhood, endured harassment and assaults.[58] But what worried her the most was the future of her livelihood. She knew the stories of people in transition losing their jobs. There was nothing in Local 3's contract, or in any federal or state legal codes, that would safeguard her employment. "I thought, at first, that my life was going to change totally, that I'd have to go away and come back as somebody else," she said. "Nobody had ever changed sex at the *New York Times* before."[59]

Those concerns did not stop Cartwright from organizing protests against ratification of the recently negotiated contract, just around the time that she was alerting managers of accommodations she would need after surgery. "Management could have made life so much harder for me. The *Times* was not good about labor, and I was a thorn in their side." But the conversation went well, "and I knew I wasn't going to go away; I was going to keep my job."

Cartwright announced her transition in March 1998 through a letter posted on bulletin boards, with copies in mailboxes. "Then I logged into my computer, and right away there were twenty-five messages of support, and they kept on coming." That week, her female colleagues set up a lunchtime welcoming party. Cartwright was surprised; then she reflected on her years of leadership. "I had helped members understand what was in the contract, and I was willing to challenge management, to say respectfully but firmly, 'No, you can't do that,'" she said. "Hundreds of those people had voted for me. I was always known as a stand-up person, and now, when I had to stand up for myself, it made a difference."[60]

As a union dissident, Cartwright sometimes had to operate solo, but she preferred support and advice from reliable collaborators. When Ed Hunt joined a union reform movement among co-workers at Boston City Hospital in 1978, the political dynamics remixed his gay identity and a new romance with family loyalties. The insurgency in AFSCME Local 1489 became the first in a series of rank-and-file challenges to topple an old guard and empower new leadership in Boston's growing service sector.

Local 1489 represented 1,200 nurse aides, cooks, pharmacists, security guards, and other workers at Boston City Hospital. Boom times in the health and hospitality industries were opening more and more unionized positions, and workers who took those jobs were often Latino, African American, or Caribbean. New activists emerged and formed alliances with young Irish American and Italian American workers, many of them, like Hunt, veterans of recent civil rights battles to integrate Boston's public schools.

Hunt began working in the hospital's laundry room in 1972, when he was still in high school. "The loads were 110 pounds, and we worked on huge conveyor belts," he said. "The full-timers were mostly women from the Caribbean. Our crew was young white kids like me who were relatives of other hospital workers. We were lots of trouble." Hunt had grown up with the local, one of AFSCME's largest in the State of Massachusetts. His father, a vice-president, was part of the leadership clique. "He was much sought after as a grievance representative," said Hunt, "though he never actually wrote a grievance in his life. But he was so intimidating, he could just make the managers back down because they were scared shitless of him."

The father urged his son to attend union meetings, but for two years he would not, until his job was upgraded to full-time housekeeper. Part-timers on the laundry crew were not being paid their contractually secured bonuses, so Hunt urged his workmates to join him at a local meeting, and they raised a ruckus. His father's powerful ally, Joe Bonavita, executive director of AFSCME's Massachusetts Council 93, took the complaints as a personal attack. He insisted that the bonuses were prorated, but Hunt had read the contract. "There was nothing about prorating the bonuses. My father started to see how sleazy this guy was. That was the beginning of the end of their friendship."

Hunt senior had long known about his son's homosexuality. He introduced him to John Ingemi, a dashing young hospital security guard, "never intending for us to get together, but we did, and then he accepted it. One night John came to my place, and that was it—he never left. Right away we became an item at the hospital." The love affair developed into a political partnership. Hunt and Ingemi collaborated as caucus organizers and then stood for the reform slate in the election of 1978:

> I ran for the executive board, and John was the presidential candidate. The opposition put out flyers saying that the Communist Party is about to take over your democratic union local.
>
> They kept on defacing our flyers, writing on them "fag" and "queer." On my posters they crossed out "for Executive Board" and wrote in "First Lady." The opposition was handing out the anti-commie flyer every day, openly. The queer stuff they were doing at night.
>
> But this wasn't news to anyone. People would have had to be totally unconscious not to know about us. In the end, it didn't matter because I was a fighter and had stood up for them.

Just before the election, Hunt's father, running for vice-president as an incumbent, shocked his allies by jumping to the dissident slate. "He was pretty popular, so whoever had his backing stood a good chance of winning," Hunt said. "We took it by a landslide." Family loyalty was one factor in the father's decision, but so was his political sense that the fresh new caucus was a harbinger of reforms to come.

During the next decade, similar insurgencies arose in Hotel Employees and Restaurant Employees Local 26 and in two SEIU affiliates, Local 285 (health care workers) and Local 509 (state employees). The reformers reshaped their unions to become more inclusive and responsive to the needs of a changing multiethnic and queer workforce. And Local 1489's caucus kept its momentum strong by running winning slates "until the right wing of the union eventually became no threat at all."[61]

Union Insurgencies: A Tale of Two Plant Closings

Insurgencies are by no means exclusive to unions in expanding economies. Union rebellions marked many of the closings that devastated working-class communities during the late twentieth century. From Newark to Seattle, employers "ran away" from northern industrial centers with high union density to relocate in southern locales where tax breaks and right-to-work laws would enable lower wages, higher profits, and union avoidance. From Charlotte to San Antonio, a new southern industrial base emerged but did not stabilize. By the mid-1990s, the trend toward deindustrialization was giving way to globalization.

Union leadership attempted to stanch the closings but moved too slowly, and membership diminished by the millions over thirty years. Some unions tried to mobilize wider communities to support state-sponsored job retraining schemes and the regulation of manufacturers' timetables. Some leaders advocated contract concessions, hoping for deals that would save jobs and maintain memberships. But there were no lasting solutions. Employers left town, selling off machinery and abandoning their employees, sometimes with only a few months' notice.

Rank-and-file rebellions challenged concession bargaining by targeting companies, as well as union leaders. Gary Kapanowski, a gay man, and Kim Ramsey, a lesbian, were leaders of significant insurgencies in their manufacturing shops—Kapanowski in Detroit in the early 1970s, and Ramsey in Seattle in the early 1990s. Seeing their shops threatened, they challenged established leaders while organizing community alliances. They were up against industrial giants: Kapanowski's local union fought the Chrysler Corporation, and Ramsey's members opposed General Electric (GE). They fully expected forceful opposition from the bosses, but not from the highest councils of their unions, the UAW and the International Union of Electrical Workers (IUE). The majority of Kapanowski's and Ramsey's constituents were older white men who had no idea that their young local leaders were gay. Kapanowski and Ramsey focused on salvaging the last remnants of their constituents' economic security. Neither of them saw much point to telling the sexual truth, yet that truth was eventually revealed, though very uncomfortably.

In the late 1960s, Kapanowski was a young gay man in Detroit, a civil rights activist, and a part-time student at Wayne State University. He worked alongside his father and two uncles at the Briggs Beautyware factory in Sterling Heights, where seven hundred workers produced enameled bathtubs and other plumbing fixtures. From the 1920s through the end of World War II, Briggs, a leader in the manufacture of auto parts, had pitted itself against the union, UAW Local 212, often with bloody consequences. When Briggs sold out to Chrysler in 1953, all employees, including those at the Sterling Heights factory, remained members of Local 212.[62]

The workforce was white, male, and aging—mostly southerners, Polish Americans, and Italian Americans. The younger men worked on the shipping dock. They would load 140 bathtubs per hour, catching each tub by the drain hole with a big hook and moving it down the line. In 1970, Kapanowski's workmates elected him shop steward, and he quickly won their respect for his handling of grievances.

More central to Local 212's mission than its 700 Beautyware members in Sterling Heights were the 14,500 autoworkers of Chrysler's Mack Avenue stamping plant, a huge, old factory on the east side of Detroit. Here and at other inner-city shops, militant black union members were mounting increasingly tough challenges to the UAW leadership: unauthorized "wildcat" strikes, plant gate rallies, even pickets of Solidarity House, the union's national headquarters. In 1969, the Mack Avenue Revolutionary Union Movement (MARUM) joined with other "RUMs" to form the League of Revolutionary Black Workers.[63]

Kapanowski was one of many white radicals who worked with the United National Caucus (UNC), an insurgency of black and white activists that was especially powerful among UAW skilled trades workers. Back at his factory, he led a caucus of younger white workers who sympathized with Local 212's black militant wing, in opposition to a conservative faction of George Wallace supporters who held the shop's three committeeman (delegate) positions.[64]

Kapanowski, known in the shop as "Beetle" because of his long hair and Beatle-style bangs, fell in love with a co-worker who was married and devoutly Catholic. "We would have oral sex in the stockroom, during breaks," said Kapanowski. "I always knew when he had gone to confession, because that's when he wouldn't want sex. For special occasions, we would have beers and go to the motel on the corner, a half-mile from the factory." As for the other men at the plant, "I would do it with anybody that I was attracted to, and I wouldn't get turned down." The older men were ignorant, including his father and his uncles, "but the guys who did know about me didn't harass me. There was a lot of overtime, so after work we would go out to somebody's trailer and drink, and sex would follow. I was the one for sex. Those guys didn't usually run into people like me."

Nevertheless, the combination of dissident union politics and sexual freedom was bringing Kapanowski closer to danger. "Someone from the opposition came and asked me for oral sex in the frit room, where they made enamel. It was a setup. There's a roof with windows, and we were being observed by the committeeman."

But it was not until 1972 that Kapanowski's troubles really began. Rumors were starting that the factory would soon shut down. Kapanowski began with his contacts in the UNC; soon he was talking with black militants in Local 212 about coordinating his shop's issues to their challenge of Chrysler. The contract was about to expire, and a shop election was coming up. Kapanowski ran for chairman, campaigning on his intention to fight any attempt to close the shop. The incumbents assured the rank and file that no problems were pending, and Kapanowski lost by a narrow margin in what he considered a stolen election. The winning faction quickly negotiated a new contract, loaded with concessions. The dissidents recommended a "no" vote, but the deal was ratified.

Three weeks into the agreement, Briggs announced the sale of the plant to a conglomerate based in Tampa, Florida; the Beautyware operation would be relocated to Knoxville. Jobs would be available in Tennessee for the workers at Sterling Heights, but "they would be paying $2.40 per hour, and our wages were averaging $5.00—I was making $4.70." The runaway scheme included steep increases in mandatory overtime, to build up stock prior to the move. For the older men who would not relocate, Briggs offered pensions.

Kapanowski had been concerned about the pension plan well before the closing was announced. He wanted to review the figures. He made repeated requests to the UAW, but he had no standing and was refused. Only after he and his caucus began preparations for a federal lawsuit to challenge the closing did they receive permission to review the documents. Their examination revealed a drastically low pension fund that would just about cover the company's meager offer: one year of benefits for 250 working and vested workers and 141 retirees.

The insurgents filed suit, which focused on depletion of the pension fund. Only then did the UAW's negotiators raise any objections to the company's proposals. A new termination deal was proposed: deferred benefits after sixty-five, with a range of lump severance payments, none larger than $5,000. For older workers, including Kapanowski's family members, "this would be a disaster. The average age was forty-five, the average seniority was twenty years, and there were plenty of diseases and injuries, lots of fingers cut off." Kapanowski decided to run for shop chairman again so he could be involved in the next round of negotiations. He knew that this time he would have to keep a sharper eye on the ballot box. But his vigorous opposition to the UAW's sign-off on the pension agreement was a hard push. His rivals would do anything to stop him.

In the heat of the campaign, Kapanowski leased a room at the nearby motel to meet with supporters and to be closer to the action. One Friday night, after workers were through with a shift of mandatory overtime, "some of the stewards came over to the room to play poker. Then a new guy came in, a foreman from Briggs. He had a projector and several short porn movies, and there was pot. I drank until I passed out." Kapanowski rose early the next day to work his Saturday shift and then walked back to the motel. Three detectives from the Sterling Heights Police Department were at his door within five minutes. "They found the porn films and the projector and an ounce of marijuana, not mine. They also found my stack of flyers for Monday morning, about the plant closing. One of the cops said: 'You're a communist. We know all about you.'"

Kapanowski went to jail for two nights, until his father bailed him out and took him home. Macomb County prosecutors and the judge offered him a deal: the porn and marijuana charges would be thrown out if he would quit his job and blame the other caucus members. Appalled, Kapanowski found two radical lawyers to defend him, and the charges were dropped. But the pressure kept up. The election was scheduled for May 11. The day before, Kapanowski found out that the federal lawsuit against the pension deal had been dismissed, on the grounds that it would interfere with an already standing agreement between the company and the union. That same day, the opposition put out its most devastating flyer. "It was all over the plant, everywhere," he said, "in huge letters, black against orange, 'BEETLE IS A FAGGOT—DO YOU WANT A FAGGOT TO BE YOUR CHAIRMAN OF THE SHOP COMMITTEE?' They were saying that as a steward I had had sex with people, that I was not a good steward. At dinner, my father took the flyer out and asked me in front of my sisters and my mother, 'Is this true?' I said, 'Is it true that I'm gay? Yes.'"

This confrontation was the hardest of all. "I didn't even know if I was going to go to work next day," he recalled. But he did, and then the votes came in with a 2–1 margin of victory for the reform slate. Kapanowski was thrilled: "Now I had a right to all the documents." Immediately his shop committee took a hard position, starting with refusal of any more overtime unless the company paid $1 million more into the pension plan.[65]

This was the summer of 1973, when Detroit was popping with wildcat strikes, many of them protests of safety violations and speedups. On August 14, workers at Mack Stamping shut down the plant. A group of approximately two hundred stayed inside, while others picketed the four plant gates. The wildcat held, around the clock, until daybreak on August 16, when one thousand UAW officials and retirees gathered at the Local 212 hall. Many were armed with baseball bats or pipes. They advanced on the gates, beat up the pickets, and then penetrated the plant and broke up the occupation.

Kapanowski and his shop committee had been taking food to the rebels and later that day attempted to enter the Local 212 hall for a meeting. When UAW officials would not let them enter, they rallied on the street in front of the hall and approved a resolution against the violent actions of their union leadership.[66] Less than two weeks later, the UAW International Executive Board charged Kapanowski and his shop committee with not upholding the collective bargaining agreement, specifically with refusing overtime work. The shop committee, its lawyers, and forty Briggs Beautyware workers drove to Solidarity House in downtown Detroit to respond to the charges. They ended up in a parking-lot melee with UAW sergeants-at-arms. The entire unit was then put into receivership, to be governed by two regional trustees.

Eventually, the UAW, the company, and the rebels struck a deal. Kapanowski would represent the workers at all meetings between the company and the union. Mandatory overtime would stand, but the company would pay $1 million into the pension fund. When the Sterling Heights factory closed in early 1974, it was Beetle Kapanowski, the twenty-seven-year-old gay shop chairman, who handed out severance checks to his fellow workers. He was the last to exit the plant.[67]

Plant closings such as Briggs Beautyware were the beginning of the end of the postwar industrial boom. By the early 1990s, the downward trend was dominant. Unions attempting to contain the ravages of plant closings negotiated pensions, schedules, and relocations and worked with communities on schemes for economic renewal. But the net loss was disastrous.

Twenty years after Kapanowski's battle to win an honest pension settlement at Briggs Beautyware, Kim Ramsey was organizing co-workers and community to halt the closing of a GE shop in Seattle. Kapanowski battled through two years of turbulent politics in the UAW—a police setup, a stolen election, street fights. Ramsey's local endured the shutdown and the move of jobs south and abroad with less drama but no better response from the IUE than cold passivity.

During those twenty years, many blue-collar workplaces had become more tolerant of queer people on the job. Kapanowski's supporters at the shop included family and friends, but his gay life was separate from his union work. Ramsey, by contrast, relied on a network of gay and straight allies. "There was one gay guy who wasn't out to me. But it was satisfying just to have lunch with him, especially when I'd just had too much heterosexual crap—the girly stupid birthday sex cards, the jokes." Temperamentally, she leaned toward restraint, but she would not hold back from confronting bigotry: "This guy who had been my lead man for a couple of years was making nasty remarks about one of the lesbians, so I said, 'Look, buddy, *I'm* a lesbian, OK? I'm just like her, so if you want to criticize her, criticize her for something else besides her sexual orientation, because you're criticizing me, too.' And he backed down."

Ramsey learned the machine trade at her brother's shop in Ypsilanti, Michigan, before she and a lover moved to Seattle in 1984. She found a job at a GE jet engine factory. Local 1002 of the IUE represented the two hundred workers at the shop and at another GE unit nearby. Ramsey joined Seattle's lively chapter of the Coalition of Labor Union Women and edited the Local 1002 newsletter. She ran for local vice-president in 1985 and won easily; the incumbent had not bothered to campaign. She was the board's first new face in years.

A few of Ramsey's allies won positions in the next round of elections and formed a caucus, with education of the members a priority. "The previous board was always saying, 'We can't spend any money,' but the coffers were full, and the money was just sitting there," she said. Local 1002 sponsored women members' attendance at leadership seminars, "but some of the other programs we tried were contentious, like the speakers from Nicaragua and the Philippines."

When Ramsey was elected president in late 1991, "the plants were still profitable, but we knew something was up." The contract required a six-month warning of any layoffs due to plant closing, and in June 1993, GE gave notice. Ramsey's local was the only chapter of the IUE in the State of Washington. She called the union's contract department in Louisville, Kentucky, to ask what Local 1002 should do. "There was dead silence on the other end of the line," she said. "They weren't going to help us. They wanted to act like we weren't there. We knew then we would have to get out there and help ourselves."

Ramsey had been to national union conventions where she met insurgents active in larger GE plants; they guided her as she sought information for the fight to come. She was sure that top IUE officials had already agreed with their corporate counterparts that the Seattle operation would be shut down without formal protest. So she and her caucus circulated a petition throughout Seattle's labor community. They wanted the IUE's president, Bill Bywater, to support their bid for legislative hearings to investigate connections between GE's business practices and job losses. "The message from headquarters was really clear. Bywater wouldn't support us. I don't know what the other side of that bargain was."

Working with local labor economists, Ramsey's team researched GE's stake in scuttling the shop. An international deal would allow the company an offset contract with the government of Turkey. GE would sell engines to equip Turkey's F-16 fighter jets; in exchange, GE would export some of Seattle's machinery to maintain a plant in Turkey. From sympathetic staff members at the IUE's Washington, DC, headquarters, she learned that the Seattle closing was part of GE's overall antiunion strategy: the company was transferring production from unionized factories, large and small, to manufacturing centers in right-to-work states. A brand-new plant in the Southeast would take on what was left of Seattle's jet engine work.

To workers in crisis, the information provided little relief. "Nobody was thinking about anything except, 'Where am I going to get another job?'" said Ramsey. "All kinds of stress and sad stories, new babies, divorces. We had older women not knowing what they were going to do with the job market so poor." The King County Reemployment Project provided job retraining programs and referrals, but most union members were too panicked or depressed to follow through. "People just wanted to keep on working as long as they could, and GE was offering tons of overtime to get everything squared away." In July 1994, one year after the announcement was made, GE locked the doors.

Early in her local presidency, Ramsey had proposed domestic partner benefits for GE's national contract but made little headway. Just before the plant closed, however, she attended a district-wide Executive Board meeting and got a bit of satisfaction. IUE's national board had just passed a resolution that would prohibit discrimination within the union based on sexual orientation. "In that room of maybe thirty union leaders, you could hear a pin drop," said Ramsey. "I was sitting in the back, and my inclination was to jump up and cheer. Then I looked around the room at all the dead, expressionless faces, and I knew we had a long way to go."[68]

Union Leadership and Sexual Diversity

During a twenty-year period of union retreat and corporate retrenchment, Gary Kapanowski and Kim Ramsey stood up for their members. They could not stop their plants from shutting down, but their leadership in the fight made a difference. Kapanowski found smart, militant allies; trumped his rivals' smears on the eve of an election; and achieved an urgent goal: decent pension settlements. Twenty years later, Ramsey researched GE's maneuvers for a global runaway and understood, just as Kapanowski had, that the union's compliance was part of the problem. Her ferocious advocacy for members whose livelihoods were being destroyed was controversial; her queerness was not. For both Kapanowski and Ramsey, constituents were far less concerned with their sexual orientation than with the effectiveness of their leadership.

LGBT union people participated in queer communities during the early years of gay liberation, but they did not fit in politically. The cultural scene of individual expression and sexual freedom was not so easily balanced with union processes that favored economic progress through solidarity, and the queer world's spontaneous, community-oriented organizing style did not work smoothly into labor's more formal modes of national resolutions, collective bargaining cycles, and conventional electoral campaigns.

Nevertheless, as early as the 1970s, when queer people were first articulating their unique political visions for justice and democracy, the two movements did attempt to find common ground. There was nothing about the process that was inevitable; at first, few in the labor movement could even imagine such a connection. But lasting and effective partnerships did form and did function because creative leaders on both sides were intent on practical paths. Meaningful alliances that began with focused organizing against discrimination in the workplace led to sustained collaborations of the gay movement and the labor movement to confront countermovements determined to weaken them both.

II

Coalition Politics

3

From Common Enemies
to Common Causes

The Labor Movement and the Gay Movement
in Action and Coalition

Coors: it was nothing more than beer, but a favorite in taverns and a best seller in package and grocery stores throughout the American West. Coors beer topped a very competitive market—and made an excellent object for a boycott.[1]

The Coors beer boycott was not a single, isolated campaign but a series of protests that rolled through American working-class and ethnic communities for more than three decades, starting in 1967. For each of its constituencies, the boycott held different meanings and resulted in different outcomes. Some groups achieved their ends; others fell short. Tactical gains aside, however, the campaign was a superb coalition builder. Organizers of the boycott shared a long-term goal: to discredit the Adolph Coors Company by exposing its conservative ideology and anti-minority, antiunion policies as "an injury to all."

At its beginning, the boycott was focused on employment discrimination at the Coors brewery in Golden, Colorado, and was led by Chicano community activists in nearby Denver, members of the American GI Forum, a veterans group and the largest Latino civil rights organization in the United States. At the time, 3 percent of Coors employees were black, 6 percent were Latino, and 7 percent were female.[2] Organizers patterned their strategy on "La Causa," the grape boycott supporting the United Farm Workers' union drive in California.[3] Over a ten-year period, the Coors campaign spread to other Latino communities in the West, keeping pressure up and driving sales down.

Organized labor began its boycott in 1973. Beer truck drivers in San Francisco, members of International Brotherhood of Teamsters (IBT) Local 888, struck distributors for two years as they campaigned for renewals of their contracts. A second boycott by unions, to support a strike by brewery workers in

Golden, started up in 1975 and lasted until 1987. This time the union was an independent unit directly affiliated with the AFL-CIO, Local 366. Although the campaigns by Local 888 and Local 366 damaged Coors's reputation and profits, neither of the unions succeeded in signing another contract with Coors.

However, it was San Francisco's gay community that raised the ante for the boycott and eventually commanded national attention. Launched in 1974, this gay phase sustained labor's protests while exposing patterns of antigay discrimination in Coors's employment practices. The gay-labor boycott spread and stayed alive for the next fourteen years. Its militancy stirred new respect for a previously despised minority as it defined the gay community in action and in coalition.

Since those first heady years of boycott, the LGBT and labor movements have continued to collaborate on vital common causes. Differences between the two movements have made the formation of coalitions sometimes surprising, but not impossible. Since the early 1960s, unions have formed coalitions with civil rights groups, the women's movement, and local community organizations, and those alliances have strengthened organizing drives and collective bargaining. By defining and developing mutually important issues, both movements have enhanced their political influence on American society.

LGBT activists in the ranks of organized labor who have observed the political effectiveness of unions' alliances have urged their own community leaders to seek labor's support on issues where there is common ground. What unites the interests of both movements is their shared constituencies. Queer communities in America have always included a large working-class element. Whether out or not, lesbian, gay, bisexual, and transgender people have earned their livelihoods from unionized jobs.[4] But historically and structurally, the labor and gay movements have developed along distinctly different trajectories.

There is much that the labor movement accomplishes that is not central to gay liberation. Labor's primary program is economic: to organize workers in all industries and better the material lives of all Americans. The gay liberation movement focuses on civil equality and freedom of sexual self-determination. LGBT people benefit materially from collective bargaining; however, issues of sexual identity and gender expression do not inspire union drives. Even when workers in the sex industry have organized and bargained collectively, they have balanced conventional improvements to wages, hours, health, and safety with contract demands particular to their workplace.[5]

As early as 1973, labor-gay coalitions influenced some of the nation's mightiest unions to adopt the denunciation of antigay discrimination as a constitutional principle. Those policy resolutions came alive during the late 1970s, when cities from Miami to Seattle were rocked by right-wing referendum campaigns to legalize dismissals of LGBT teachers and social service workers. During the 1980s, the trend expanded to statewide initiatives. The unions that had already resolved to defend queer workers set the example for other unions.

The Coors beer boycott initiated four decades of organizing partnerships between queer communities and unions, alliances that continue today. Labor-gay coalitions have promoted innovations in collective bargaining and have supported labor-gay political campaigns. As regional groups, they coalesced in the 1990s to promote gay caucuses in local unions. Discussions of common interests among LGBT unionists at regional and union-wide conferences led to the formation of a national organization of labor-gay groups: Pride at Work.

In 1997, Pride at Work was welcomed into the AFL-CIO as an allied organization. That acceptance was the product of many battles to withstand attacks from common enemies and many campaigns to build support for shared reforms. For the labor movement of the twenty-first century, the inclusion of Pride at Work in the federation's everyday projects seems like a necessary inevitability. But it took the unlikely collaboration of unionized truckers and gay bar patrons to set the motion forward.

The Coors Boycott and How It Grew

Of all unions, the International Brotherhood of Teamsters would have seemed to be one of the least likely to promote a consumer boycott based in San Francisco's flourishing gay Castro neighborhood of the early 1970s. For decades, the union had been the target of federal investigations into labor racketeering, and members were not much inclined toward advocacy of gay liberation. Nor did the IBT's regional governing body, the Western Conference, improve the union's reputation among liberal activists when organizers tried to take over the United Farm Workers' recruitment campaigns in California's vineyards and lettuce fields.[6] Nevertheless, when the union called for help to extend its fight with Coors, gay activists were willing to listen. Gay liberation and the Teamsters: the combination proved to be a great surprise and then a steadfast and creative collaboration that successfully challenged a common enemy.

In the fall of 1973, Local 888, the Bay Area beer truck drivers' union, was put into trusteeship by the powerful Western Conference, and Allan Baird, an officer of newspaper truck drivers' Local 921, accepted the administrative assignment of running the local. His first task was to win contract renewals from six independent beer distributors in San Francisco. They had nonunion drivers delivering the beer, so Baird devised a plan to interrupt all business along regular routes. "Our cars would follow the scab truck. As soon as it stopped at a store to make a delivery, we'd jump out with our picket signs, and we'd go into the stores and talk the owners into not taking their product," Baird said. The tactic worked well with five of the distributors. After two months, Local 888 had a settlement, and union drivers were back at work.

But Coors distributors in San Francisco and other distributors in Oakland and the wider East Bay held out and hired a private security company. When Local 888 members attempted to hinder deliveries, they were met with armed guards in uniform. "They had short-wave radios; they were licensed to carry clubs and pellet guns; they had German shepherds," said Baird. "They would shoot our tires, break our windshields. They'd have one of their goons riding in the cab of the truck with the scab; another would be in a car behind them. Sometimes there would be a car in front."

Baird wrested renewals from the conventional distributors and then turned to community-based grocers' associations to focus on Coors, the holdout: "I explained to the Arab grocers' association that when the word goes out to ninety thousand Teamsters and their families that you're still taking Coors beer, they're not going to come into your stores." After the Arab grocers pledged support, he turned to the Chinese American grocers and then to Huey Newton and the Black Panther Party in Oakland. "They heard about Coors's racist employment practices," he said, "and helped us with stores in the African American neighborhoods."[7]

Baird had lived all his life in or near the Castro, a working-class neighborhood in central San Francisco that in the 1970s was becoming a residential and commercial destination for gay men. The new migrants renovated Victorian homes and opened small businesses, with a network of lively bars at the hub of it all. Baird visited Harvey Milk, an up-and-coming community organizer, who agreed to publicize the boycott in the gay press and got a pledge against Coors from the Tavern Guild, a citywide association of one hundred gay bars. For his part, Baird would hire openly gay applicants to drive Local 888 beer trucks.[8]

Gay men in the Castro bars were not looking for political action. A ban on Coors would be a business risk to Tavern Guild hosts because the brand was popular. But Milk's arguments for gay sanctions were based on more than sympathy for the union and objections to Coors's racial prejudice. Particularly galling to bar patrons were reports that the company sought out gay workers for dismissal. The company had been administering pre-employment lie detector tests since the early 1960s. Among the 178 items on the test were queries about political views, religious commitment, and sexual proclivities. Whether registering as the truth or a lie, a yes or a no answer to the question "Are you a homosexual?" could be grounds for firing. Since 1958, Coors's contract with Local 366 (at the time a Brewery Workers affiliate) had banned "conduct on company premises which violates the common decency or morality of the community."[9]

"They wanted to screen out anyone with a brain larger than a pea," said Howard Wallace, who had migrated from Denver to San Francisco in the late 1960s and then come out. He worked on the night shift at the Planters Peanuts factory in Oakland and was a rank-and-file Teamster in Local 856. Wallace brought the Coors issue to the attention of Bay Area Gay Liberation (BAGL), a new political group in the Castro, and invited Baird to one of BAGL's first meetings in early 1974. Baird's tales of Coors's bigotry stoked the group's anger. That spring, BAGL's packed weekly meetings regularly concluded with direct action in the bars where Coors was still available. "We had our leaflets, and we'd go in there with, 'Hey, get rid of that shit,'" Wallace recalled. "The bar owners didn't like this, but you didn't have to threaten them that much. We told the patrons about the lie detector tests, and so we just got Coors out of the Castro bars. Then we took it to other parts of the state."[10]

For all of its rambunctious solidarity, the Coors campaign worked no major miracles in transforming the union or gay culture. No gay or lesbian beer truck driver suddenly came out of the closet to persuade fellow Teamsters about the importance of gay liberation. Nor did masses of gay beer drinkers from the Castro eagerly volunteer to support other labor movement campaigns. But the Castro "gaycott" did become the talk of the San Francisco labor scene, inspiring curiosity and respect. "The gay campaign just steamrolled, and I started telling people, once the gay community locks into something, they can stop any product they want," Baird remembered.

Local 888 never settled with Coors distributors. In the summer of 1975, Baird walked a picket line with the United Farm Workers at Safeway stores, against orders from the Teamsters, and the Western Conference moved quickly to punish him. Local 888 was disbanded, and members were reassigned to two other Teamster affiliates. By year's end, the beer truck drivers' strike was over.

Nonetheless, gay people kept faith with the boycott. The campaign broadened to grocery stores and bars beyond the Castro as word spread that the largesse of the Coors family, derived from beer profits, was being directed against the gay movement. Throughout the 1970s, substantial donations by the Adolph Coors Foundation and individual Coors family members ran the gamut of conservative politicians and organizations and fortified the right wing of the Republican Party. In 1973, Joseph Coors provided initial funding to establish America's leading conservative think tank, the Heritage Foundation. The emerging visibility of the family's ideological generosity intensified the company's already terrible reputation.[11]

In April 1977, a new labor dispute flared up, this time at Golden, in a conflict far more critical than the Bay Area battle over beer distribution. Members of Local 366 who went on strike were the actual workers who produced the beer. Contract negotiations had been tougher than usual. The union wanted an end to the lie detector tests. Although Coors had stopped asking job applicants about their sex lives, polygraph tests were still routine. On its side, the company wanted to nullify the union shop agreement, an article in the contract negotiated in 1935 that required all workers to join the union and pay dues.

On the strike's first day, Coors canceled workers' health benefits. That pressure scared the strikers, as did the company's rapid deployment of replacement workers. Before the walkout was a month old, at least 20 percent of the 1,430 union members had crossed picket lines. Local 366 called for a renewal of the labor-wide boycott. With the blessing of George Meany, president of the AFL-CIO, Local 366 organized union support throughout the sixteen western and southern states where Coors beer was sold.[12]

Labor's return to the boycott refreshed efforts of the gay community while spreading the protests beyond California. The AFL-CIO placed Coors on its "please do not buy" list, a shoppers' advisory posted on workplace bulletin boards and published in union newsletters. Back at the brewery, enough scabs were on the payroll to secure a "no union" majority in an election supervised by the National Labor Relations Board (NLRB), and just before the election, the company raised wages 10 percent. In December 1978, Local 366 was officially decertified.[13]

Loyalists from Local 366 and the AFL-CIO joined forces with civil libertarians, feminists, advocates for ethnic minorities, and gay activists to continue the campaign against Coors's ideology. The first wave of boycotts had been effective, in the gay communities of the Bay Area and beyond. In black and Latino neighborhoods where grocers had cooperated since 1974, the beer was rarely available, and when it was in the stores, it sold poorly. By 1975, overall sales in California were down 4 percent. As the national phase of the boycott took hold and consumers turned to other brands, Coors's share of the California market fell from 40 percent to 14 percent; between 1977 and 1984, national profits decreased from $67.7 million to $44.7 million.[14]

These losses had several causes other than the boycott. Coors executives had responded late to market trends, had bungled decisions about packaging and distribution, had quarreled over advertising campaigns, and had resisted introducing new products—for example, a low-calorie "light" beer. Finally, in an increasingly crowded market, they underestimated their rivals' strengths, believing that competitors' more modern sales schemes would be trumped by their own product's innate purity.[15] But even that reputation was called into question: Coors beer, brewed without pasteurization, was being publicized by the AFL-CIO as "unsafe to drink."[16]

To raise money, Coors, hitherto a family-held concern, made its first public offering in 1975. Shares at first represented only 10 percent of ownership and were designated strictly nonvoting. When first quarter earnings in 1977 fell by 70 percent, some stockholders questioned the company's antiunion ferocity and pressed for expansion into new markets.[17] But an eastward move would prove difficult. Consumers in Chicago, Detroit, Boston—target cities—typically sympathized with the union cause and already had their favorite brands among Coors's rivals.

Coors began exploring cracks in communities that had been strongholds of protest. Latino civil rights groups had roused the first boycott in 1967 and had settled their discrimination lawsuit in 1977. The company then hired Latino community leaders for its Public Relations Department. It also developed a scholarship program, and the company and individual family members made donations to Latino community projects.[18] Some groups returned the checks; others did not.[19] To court the gay community, the company included "sexual orientation" in its nondiscrimination policy in 1978. This was the first such statement by any brewery in the country and enough to persuade some gay bars to put Coors back on tap. San Francisco's Tavern Guild withdrew from the boycott in 1980, and in 1984 Coors made donations to AIDS charities sponsored by the guild.[20]

Despite Coors's many attempts to repair its reputation, sales continued to sag. Then a scandalous speech by Bill Coors triggered a more precipitous drop. Addressing black and Latino business leaders in Denver in February 1984, he declared, "The best thing they did for you was to drag your ancestors over here in chains." He went on to say, "In Rhodesia, the economy was booming under white management. Now in Zimbabwe, under black management, it is a disaster. . . . It's not that dedication among the blacks is less, in fact it's greater. They lack the intellectual capacity to succeed and it's taking them down the tubes."[21]

No national black organization had ever formally joined the boycott, but now heavy sanctions seemed imminent. Coors executives hastily negotiated an elaborate series of "covenants" with the National Association for the Advancement of Colored People: a five-year hiring program from production jobs to middle and top management, franchise opportunities in distribution, investment plans with black-owned banks and businesses, targeted advertising campaigns, and charitable donations. The concessions, subject to regular audits, would cost Coors $325 million. Latino organizations, their longest-lived boycott opponents, agreed to a similar set of deals, again worth $325 million. But sponsorship of Latino literacy drives and Black History Month events bought Coors neither approval nor peace. Many community groups disavowed the covenants and kept up the boycott.[22]

Continued agitation against Coors in the mid-1980s was more than a response to Bill Coors's stupid remarks; by 1984, the boycott had become an essential vehicle of protest against the growing influence of conservative ideology in national politics. Endorsements of the boycott came in from the 1.5 million member National Education Association (NEA), a frequent target of conservative attacks on the teaching profession and public education; from the National Organization for Women (NOW) because of right-wing threats against reproductive rights and equal opportunity; and from Mothers against Drunk Driving (MADD) because Coors was promoting Halloween as a beer holiday.[23]

By 1986, Coors was at a commercial crossroads: the company needed to expand, but new markets were not opening up. Detroit's City Council endorsed the boycott with an official proclamation, and union members picketed bars and party stores to block sales. Boston's boycott was coordinated by the AFL-CIO in cooperation with gay and lesbian political groups. The Gay and Lesbian Labor Activists Network (GALLAN) persuaded more than two hundred bars in the greater Boston area to reject the beer, and David Scondras, an openly gay member of Boston's City Council, sponsored an official anti-Coors resolution. Food service workers at Fenway Stadium, members of the Hotel Employees and Restaurant Employees (HERE), notified management that they would not handle Coors at the ballpark; then they persuaded Fenway's beverage vendor, who also served prime sports venues in the New York area, not to carry the beer to Yankee Stadium and the New Jersey Meadowlands.[24]

Nevertheless, Coors was serious about cracking the huge New York and New Jersey market, which constituted 10 percent of national beer sales. Early in 1987, Coors deployed twenty members of its public relations staff to prepare the way. The Lesbian and Gay Labor Network (LGLN) coordinated its campaign to block Coors with New York City's Central Labor Council. An alert went out to local union leaders, and the boycott was advertised in union newsletters. Union members posted stickers all over town, and activists picketed taverns and halted deliveries to stores. One warm spring evening, Googie's bar in Greenwich Village became the center for a boisterous "Dump Coors" demonstration at which the proprietor, planning no refills, donated his last half keg to the cause. Frontlash, an AFL-CIO youth group, lined up with queer activists and construction apprentices to pass full pitchers out of the bar, into the street, and down the sewer.[25]

That fall, Coors negotiated a truce with the AFL-CIO. The Teamsters had been planning a renewed contest at the brewery in Golden. The company agreed not to violate labor laws during the organizing process, and the AFL-CIO agreed to end its boycott. The truce weakened labor's pressure on the northeastern markets, the Teamsters lost their election, and Coors gained in sales.[26] But the boycott was far from over, and the brand name itself seemed to be souring the beer's flavor.

Coors reorganized as a corporation in 1992 and then began a new round of public relations projects in preparation for another foray into the lucrative queer market. An employee advocacy group, the Lesbian and Gay Employee Resource (LAGER), included Scott Coors, an executive of the company. In 1994, Coors hired Mary Cheney, former Congressman Dick Cheney's lesbian daughter, to work as a liaison with lesbian and gay communities. In 1995, the company implemented domestic partner benefits for lesbian and gay employees, a first for the industry. Cheney distributed grants to local organizations for cultural projects, sports events, political action, and pride festivals. Coors's biggest contribution of $110,000 went to a high-profile national organization, the Gay and Lesbian Alliance against Defamation (GLAAD).[27] By the time Cheney left Coors in 2000, it was no longer unusual to see banners and neon signs with the Coors trademark on display in gay bars.

The coalition that built the Coors beer boycott started with one local union and one gay neighborhood and then developed the protest, layer by layer, into a national movement that was later dismantled, piece by piece. Still, when protests were at peak potency, they were brilliant models of mutual defense. Evolving over several years and in many regions, the Coors boycotts enabled gay and labor activists to take measure of the others' political strategies and moral stamina. Coalition partners got the picture: Coors was just the beginning, because the ideological right was not just selling beer.

Convention Politics, Queer Proposals

The Teamsters' boycott of Coors, a quick and forceful fight-back campaign, had nothing to do with the union's policy on sexual orientation and civil rights, which, until 2005, was nonexistent.[28] The notion of such a policy had been mentioned, however, one spring evening in 1975, when Allan Baird sat down in San Francisco with Jimmy Hoffa, president of the Teamsters. Baird told Hoffa about the discipline and militancy of the Castro boycott and urged Hoffa to consider further coalitions with gay and lesbian communities. For a sustained social base of solidarity, he argued, the street could be only the inspiration, not the venue, for negotiating a solid alliance.[29]

Labor's participation in social movements is guided by policies adopted at national union conventions. By federal law, unions elect their executive officers at least once every five years. By union constitution, the requirement is usually fulfilled more by meetings of delegates that occur more frequently than that minimum. Typically, delegates consider goals for organizing and collective bargaining; they make recommendations for social policy; and they endorse political programs and candidates. They also propose resolutions or amendments to the union's constitution, which may arise from an agenda set by leadership, from initiatives important to individual local unions or caucuses, or from a group allied to the union in coalition. On the convention floor, advocates of individual resolutions lobby leaders and delegates well before their proposals come up for debate and vote.

Union conventions, at their best, provide delegates with a forum for public debate about members' concerns and affirm those issues with resolutions from the convention floor. Delegates take resolutions back home to their locals and are supposed to encourage rank-and-file members to apply the ideas to their everyday work lives. A resolution that has not been proposed by a caucus of delegates committed to its implementation will simply be recorded and forgotten, and with some early resolutions for gay rights, that is what happened. But queer delegates who were set on keeping their issues viable and visible learned how to maintain the pressure on the plenary floor. A thirty-five-year record of union policies on LGBT rights reflects dynamic floor debates as well as top-down decrees at national meetings.

In the private sector, the first policy statements to acknowledge the rights of sexual minorities came from unions in industries where gay people often made their living: entertainment and fashion. In 1970, the American Guild of Musical Artists, the union for opera singers and dance artists, amended its constitution to defend "affectional preference" in principle, and in 1983 the union made that protection binding in all of its contracts.[30] At its national convention in Los Angeles, also in 1983, the International Ladies' Garment Workers' Union unanimously approved a resolution proposed by Frank Monti, the openly gay education director of the union's Western region, which supported the inclusion of "all persons without regard to sexual orientation" in the union's civil rights policies. It furthermore stated that the union should "guarantee that workers shall be judged on the merits of their work and not by irrelevant criteria of what they do in their private lives," and that the union would "protest any personnel actions . . . merely on the basis of sexual orientation."[31] In 1995, when the union merged with the Amalgamated Clothing and Textile Workers Union to form the Union of Needletrades, Industrial and Textile Employees (UNITE), the resolution was carried into UNITE's founding constitution.

In the public sector, the American Federation of Teachers (AFT) and the NEA were the first to pledge protection of queer members. For gay male teachers, who remained vulnerable to charges of pederasty, the adoption of this safeguard was especially important, but lesbians were similarly fearful for their jobs. Queer teachers had opportunities to socialize with one another more openly at national conventions than they would among colleagues in their communities. Some did come out at school, but to select co-workers only, and almost never to administrators, school boards, or students.

James Mitchell taught history at New Rochelle High School in suburban New York and was a frequent delegate to the AFT's annual meetings. During the 1960s, he attended in full western drag—big hat, boots, and a fringed leather vest. Mitchell's outfit was a signal to other queer delegates, who joined him for socializing and politicking. Authorized by New Rochelle's Local 280, Mitchell introduced a gay rights resolution to the 1969 convention in Washington, DC. "It went to the Human Rights Committee, and the chair killed my proposal by loading the committee against it," he said. "Then the resolution was referred to the Executive Council."[32] That convention ended with no floor vote on gay rights. But in 1970, the AFT's Executive Council did quietly release its own resolution, differently worded and less stringent than Mitchell's, titled, "Discrimination against Homosexuals Denounced." It stated, "Whereas professional people insist that they be judged on the basis of professional and not personal criteria; and whereas it is the responsibility of trade unions to provide job protection from all forms of discrimination that is not based on performance, such as race, color, sex, religion, age or ethnic origin; be it resolved that the AFT protests any personnel actions taken against any teacher merely because he or she practices homosexual behavior in private life."[33]

As gay liberation developed to become a political force during the 1970s, cohorts of openly gay and lesbian teacher activists emerged in both the AFT and the NEA. A resolution at the AFT convention in 1973 called for the repeal of state laws and School Board regulations that punished "acts committed by teachers in the course of their private lives unless such acts can be shown to affect fitness to teach." The next year, the NEA amended its constitution to include sexual orientation in its nondiscrimination articles.

But AFT locals did not support national policies. When leaders of the recently formed Gay Teachers Association of New York City met with executives of the United Federation of Teachers (Local 2 of the AFT) in 1974, the union's record was not part of the discussion.[34] Newsletters did not publish gay rights resolutions that had been adopted or post alerts to workplace bulletin boards. Thus, queer teachers in the ranks had no indication that their union was ready to back them, and local AFT officials did not feel bound to heed what the conventions had approved. The Gay Teachers Association lobbied the union leadership for ten years before gaining the union's endorsement of a controversial and sweeping gay rights bill before the New York City Council.

In San Francisco, the Gay Teachers Coalition, formed in 1975, was similarly stymied. This group included educators in both public and private schools, among them many who paid dues to AFT Local 61, the union representing employees of the San Francisco Unified School District. The coalition fully expected the School Board to reject their requests for inclusion of sexual orientation in the district's nondiscrimination policy. What infuriated them was that their elected union leaders were refusing to back them up. It would take a major attack on teachers in California, later in the decade, to bring the union to the side of its gay members.[35]

After Ronald Reagan won his landslide victory in the presidential election of 1980, gay and lesbian organizations and liberal unions became more serious about the need for allies. Political analysts in the Gay Rights National Lobby observed that union membership was diminishing in the private and manufacturing sectors but growing rapidly in the public and service sectors. They wanted an explicit endorsement of gay rights by a big national union and targeted the American Federation of State, County, and Municipal Employees (AFSCME), which by 1980 numbered 1.2 million members and was expanding.[36]

Tom Stabnicki and Barry Friedman, a couple from Chicago, were both employed at the Illinois Department of Children and Family Services. Out at work and in their union, each had served as president of AFSCME Local 2081 and had held district-wide offices in Council 31. Like Jim Mitchell in his cowboy outfit, Stabnicki and Friedman dressed queer for national meetings. At a leadership conference in 1981, their matching black leather outfits caught the eye of Bailey T. Walker Jr., a staff organizer. Walker, Stabnicki, and Friedman called a meeting for queer people at that conference and at later national meetings. "The first time, no one showed up," Walker said. "The next time, the people who came would say 'I don't want anybody to know I'm here.' Still, at each meeting they got a few more."[37]

Among the most avid activists were Russell Cardamone of Philadelphia and Victor Basile of Washington, DC. Cardamone, secretary of District Council 47 and a child abuse investigator, had seen colleagues fired because of their homosexuality. Basile, a recent president of both Local 2027, which represented Peace Corps staff, and federal employees' District Council 26, was a volunteer consultant for the Gay Rights National Lobby. In the spring of 1982, Cardamone, Basile, Stabnicki, and Friedman prepared to introduce a gay rights resolution at the national convention to be held during the summer in Atlantic City.

Basile discussed the resolution with William Lucy, secretary-treasurer of AFSCME and the president and co-founder of the Coalition of Black Trade Unionists. Lucy pledged his support to the passage of the resolution and prepared his allies for an intense debate. As the convention got under way, a cadre of lesbian and gay activists lobbied sympathetic AFSCME leaders and pinned them with buttons that declared, "Another AFSCME Member for Gay Rights."[38]

"They were steeling themselves for what they thought was going to be a horrible battle," Walker recalled. "The first speaker supported the resolution. But then, all of a sudden, some other guy had the floor, and he started talking about sexual perversion, and what would be next—would AFSCME start having resolutions endorsing the rights of people to have sex with animals?"[39] Lucy was the next speaker: "He said, 'These are members of the union, working men and women,' and emphasized that the resolution squared with the union's tradition of civil rights, [Dr.] King and Memphis, and the women's movement. Not another negative thing was said. The resolution was passed by voice vote, and that was that. Every convention since then has renewed those rights."[40]

Lucy's affirmation of the common ground shared by the civil rights, labor, women's, and LGBT movements set a new standard for the labor movement. A few months later, Lucy extended AFSCME's message in speeches before two governing councils within the AFL-CIO: the Building Trades and the Industrial Union departments. He won approval for strong gay civil rights resolutions— again to unanimous acclaim.[41]

A year later, in October 1983, the AFL-CIO convention adopted its own gay civil rights resolution and added a second resolution urging the federal government to increase funding for AIDS research in consideration of "a history of discrimination against the people in the high risk groups."[42] But in the increasingly conservative American political and cultural climate of the 1980s, lasting alliances would need more than simple goodwill.

Bigotry on the Ballots: Miami-Dade and Seattle

Intense political campaigns shook working-class communities from Florida to California during the 1980s, and in the course of those fights, labor's recognition of the rights of sexual minorities changed profoundly and necessarily. During the 1970s, gay and lesbian advocates had peacefully achieved municipal antidiscrimination ordinances in forty cities and towns. Those laws became a provocation to political groups on the far right whose fears energized a rising movement of backlash at the ballot box.

The gay movement's first electoral confrontation with the organized right was a spectacular loss. A special election in June 1977 overturned Metro Ordinance 77-4 in Miami-Dade County, Florida, a gay civil rights statute that the city had adopted just six months earlier.[43] Anita Bryant, the entertainer and former beauty queen who led the movement to repeal the ordinance, called her campaign "Save Our Children." Bryant received generous financial backing from religious conservatives around the country. Ordinance 77-4 banned discrimination in housing, employment, and public accommodations based on "affectional or sexual preference." Bryant, however, narrowly framed her campaign as a referendum on the employment of gay teachers. She declared that gay men's sexuality was by its very nature predatory and insisted that "since homosexuals cannot reproduce, they must recruit." School boys would thus be the likeliest objects of gay men's lusts.[44]

"It was the first time that homosexuality was really in the news, and the context of that topic was that we molest children and we're horrible," said Hank Wilson, a teacher who traveled to Florida that spring, along with other activists from San Francisco.[45] Gay and lesbian groups across the nation were trying to halt Bryant's momentum. Her wealth and much of her fame derived from her position as the official spokesperson for Florida orange products. Gay activists called for a Coors-style national boycott of Florida orange juice and raised a campaign that was economically punishing enough for the citrus growers to threaten Bryant's contract.[46] But she persisted.

AFT Local 1974, the United Teachers of Dade, represented eighteen thousand Miami-Dade school workers. "We were concerned that Save Our Children would result in a witch hunt against gay teachers and against gay students," recalled Annette Katz, a union staff member. Local 1974 advertised its objections to Save Our Children on the basis of its constitutional and contractual policies on human rights and reminded members and the general public of the union's stand against racial segregation in Miami's public schools during the 1960s. The union wrote that "any teacher inflicting their sexual, religious or political preferences or activities on children and students" would be fired, but five hundred teachers still quit the union in protest.[47]

The rest of the labor movement kept its distance. "We were being attacked, and we didn't have predictable allies," Wilson said.[48] Florida had always been a right-to-work state, with unions wielding little influence on public policy. The AFL-CIO of Florida took no position, and institutional support did not come from unions important to the local economy—for example, those representing hotel and restaurant workers in Miami's robust tourist industry.

Then as now, Miami was thickly populated with retired people who had worked in unionized jobs in northern industries. Their lives in Florida were supported by their pensions, and they could have been an influential voting bloc. But for this special election, there were no alerts from national organizations, not even from the AFT or the NEA. Well before 1977, both of these organizations had recorded policy statements against sexual orientation discrimination. But in this crisis, the Political Action departments of these organizations did not make recommendations to their Miami-based retired constituents to vote "no."

The repeal carried, with 70 percent voting "yes." Bryant took her cause on a national tour. By the spring of 1978, Save Our Children groups in Wichita, Kansas; Eugene, Oregon; and St. Paul, Minnesota had won reversals of ordinances for gay rights. "We knew that Miami-Dade would have a ripple effect. It mobilized a powerful antigay backlash that drew national attention," Wilson said. "I was following the national statistics on teen suicide, and in February 1977, when the Save Our Children campaign was launched, the numbers jumped off the scale. People don't know why, but I think I do. When the topic surfaced, it affected young gay people. All of a sudden, their parents, the people they counted on for support and love, weren't there. Their parents were agreeing with the hate."[49]

In the fall of 1978, Dennis Falk and David Estes, two police officers in Seattle, led a referendum initiative for Proposition 13 to repeal their city's gay rights ordinance. Their campaign, "Save Our Moral Ethics," was substantially compromised when Falk shot and killed a burglary suspect, a young mentally retarded black man. Well before the shooting, political activists in Seattle's gay and lesbian communities had organized a broad coalition of civil rights and liberal religious groups dedicated to retention of the ordinance. Seattle's labor movement was divided. The city's construction unions favored affirmation of Proposition 13, but unions in the service and public sectors were leaning toward "No on 13." Local 9102 of the Communication Workers of America (CWA) represented employees of the Seattle telephone company, a mix of service and skilled trades workers, with the industry's typical gender division: most women staffed the operator boards; most men held crafts jobs.

Madelyn Elder was a former telephone operator now working in the crafts as a splicer. She had endured the hazing common for all women in nontraditional jobs and been elected by her co-workers as shop steward. She achieved an excellent grievance record and was confidently out at work. "The men may have called me a dyke and stuff, but it wasn't to my face, and they weren't hostile," she said. Elder wanted her union to join the "No on 13" coalition. The president of Local 9102 "was a very conservative guy, but a very strong unionist. He hadn't had such a good shop steward in a long time, so he backed me 100 percent."[50]

Winning support from the wider membership was less easy. The first time Elder asked for backing for the "No on 13" campaign, she was ruled "out of order." However, in an effort to consolidate a rank-and-file caucus in Local 9102, she had been meeting with a group of installers recently transferred from New York City. The newcomers had voting rights in Local 9102 and agreed to support Elder at the next meeting. But other crafts workers had heard that there would be a gay item on the evening's agenda and came in with a less friendly attitude. Elder said:

> I don't think the New York guys were interested in the gay thing at all, but they were pissed at the local leadership, and they saw it as a union democracy issue. Then there were two gay men who came, telephone operators. And then some white male installers showed up, guys from Seattle, with their crew cuts. They were going, "Where's the gays?" And there I am with my little hand raised. It was frightening to get up and talk about gay rights.
>
> I urged the local to take a resolution against Proposition 13, that this was a job discrimination issue, and we were for equality for all workers. The vote was close, so we had to have a division of the house.

That meant that you literally had to get up out of your seat and get your butt up to one side or the other and they physically count you.

The two gay men abstained. They were scared shitless of the guys who were saying that they were going to beat up any gay men who were in the room. And we lost by two votes.[51]

Although she was not an official delegate from Local 9102, Elder attended general meetings of the King County Labor Council when Proposition 13 was on the agenda. AFSCME initiated a "No on 13" proposal supported by other service and municipal unions. But the secretary-treasurer of the labor council, James K. Bender of the Cement Masons, led an adamant opposition. "The fight was intense," Elder said. "We didn't get all the unions on our side, but it was important to neutralize the ones that were leaning toward actually endorsing Proposition 13, like the construction trades. But the way we fought them, they realized that it wasn't cool."[52]

In November 1978, 63 percent of Seattle voters voted "no," and the city's gay rights ordinance was retained. After a harsh season, Seattle's Proposition 13 became the nation's first repeal referendum to be voted down.[53]

The State Finds a Compelling Interest

Seattle's campaign to stop Proposition 13 ran parallel to California's statewide battle over Proposition 6, also known as the Briggs amendment after its author, the ultraconservative State Senator John Briggs. The Briggs campaign became a crisis of transformation for the gay and labor movements, and on November 7, 1978, its resounding defeat sealed their alliance.

The campaign to pass the initiative drew its antigay rhetoric and organizing style from the Save Our Children movement. But Proposition 6 was a significant break from Bryant's successful crusade. It was not designed as a repeal of a municipal gay rights ordinance; rather it sought to amend the education code of California's constitution with new discriminatory rules for all school workers, complete with an elaborate apparatus for investigations and penalties.[54]

The campaign to pass Proposition 6 was modeled on the Helm Act, enacted in Oklahoma earlier that year, which had been overwhelmingly approved by the state's legislature.[55] Senator Briggs attempted to move his version of Oklahoma's law through California's legislature and failed; his appeal to the general electorate was his second option. His supporters collected enough signatures to place a referendum question on the November ballot.[56] His Proposition 6, section 1, asked voters to consider that

as a result of continued close and prolonged contact with schoolchildren, a teacher, teacher's aide, school administrator or counselor becomes a role model whose words, behavior and actions are likely to be emulated by students coming under his or her care, instruction, supervision, administration, guidance and protection. For these reasons the state finds a compelling interest in refusing to employ and in terminating the employment of a schoolteacher, a teacher's aide, a school administrator or a counselor, subject to reasonable restrictions and qualifications, who engages in public homosexual activity and/or public homosexual conduct directed at, or likely to come to the attention of, schoolchildren or other school employees.

Proposition 6, section 2A, stated:

"Public homosexual conduct" means the advocating, soliciting, imposing, encouraging, or promoting of private or public homosexual activity directed at, or likely to come to the attention of schoolchildren and/or other employees.[57]

Other sections of the amendment restated California's education code on sexual misconduct, regulations that applied to homosexual and heterosexual acts alike. What was new was the broad topic of "public homosexual conduct." The new law would not only punish queer school employees for public or private declarations of their sexual identities; it would also penalize any school worker, gay or straight, for advocating or affirming gay existence. Its complicated process of inquiry required formal charges and hearings at the local School Board, to be followed with votes by a majority of the board for suspension and then dismissal.

Labor's response to Proposition 6 was sharp and sure: trade unionists were familiar with Senator Briggs's consistent legislative record of opposition to union issues and understood his proposition as a bold attempt to disrupt the contractual process while legalizing workplace discrimination. The amendment would give precedence to its own rules of investigation and penalty over "any other provision of law regarding dismissal procedures." Unionists correctly read that provision as a plan to undermine collective bargaining agreements.[58]

Many gay people took Proposition 6 as a personal threat. "Briggs was both a terror and an opportunity," said Peter Tenney, a gay cook who often worked as a waiter and an activist in San Francisco's HERE Local 2.[59] The opportunity was to be found in organizing. Especially in the Castro, the fight to stop Proposition 6 seemed like a natural extension of the Coors boycott, now in its fifth year and evolving into a substantial political alliance. In 1975, activists from BAGL campaigned against a set of municipal referenda that proposed cuts in city workers' salaries and pensions. In 1977, Harvey Milk won a seat on San Francisco's Board of Supervisors, solidly endorsed by union leaders who were rewarding his involvement in the Coors boycott and his support for the municipal workers. Now, with Proposition 6 looming, blue-collar unions—locals of the Construction Trades Council, the American Postal Workers Union (APWU), the Teamsters, and the International Longshore and Warehouse Union—joined public and service sector unions to constitute the labor subcommittee of the Bay Area Committee against the Briggs Initiative (BACABI), a vigorous coalition of religious, political, neighborhood, and civil libertarian groups.[60]

Many gay activists were surprised that any straight people cared at all, but labor leaders who spoke out against Briggs cast the issue in terms that made sense to their members. Walter Johnson, president of Local 1100 of the Retail Clerks International Union and an ordained Lutheran lay minister, was a much respected member of the San Francisco Labor Council. He urged his colleagues to endorse BACABI's campaign, telling them, "It's a matter of equal rights. They're all people; they were all babies once."[61] Late in June, a huge Gay Freedom Day rally filled the streets of downtown San Francisco; three days later, the labor council announced its unanimous opposition to Proposition 6.

Earlier that spring, a multiethnic insurgent coalition in the seventeen thousand member HERE Local 2 captured the presidency, the vice-presidency, and a minority of Executive Board seats. At the celebratory party, Peter Tenney discussed the possibility of a gay caucus with his union friends. They were confident that the new president, David McDonald, would agree that Briggs was a threat to individual workers and to the union process. Local 2 was one of the first unions in the private sector to endorse BACABI, but caucus members wanted more: they insisted that McDonald speak on behalf of his queer constituency at the next anti-Briggs rally. The new president wavered. "There was a lot of inner conflict within the union—old guard, new guard," Tenney recalled. "McDonald said, 'I don't have time to write a speech.' So we wrote it. Then he said, 'I can't read this!' But we held him to it."[62]

California's AFL-CIO council recommended a "no" vote in early July, and other municipal and regional labor councils soon followed. Statewide organizations such as the California Teachers Association and the California Federation of Teachers (affiliates of the NEA and the AFT) made their own declarations as did the California Nurses Association and other unions in the public and service sectors.

A grassroots campaign spread through the cities and suburbs. Gay and lesbian volunteers knocked on doors, introduced themselves as homosexuals, and then explained to neighborhood residents how deeply Briggs menaced their lives and the civil liberties of all Californians. Squads of activists traveled to rural communities and spoke frankly at churches and union halls about homosexuality and queer identity, now and then debating local fundamentalists in what the sociologists Ruth Milkman and Diane Ehrensaft called "probably the fullest public debate over homosexuality and homophobia ever to take place in the United States."[63]

Still, by late August, polls showed Proposition 6 ahead by a wide margin. Anti-Briggs forces tried a new argument, appropriate to the values of conservatives: the amendment would simply be too expensive and too difficult to enact. They published cost estimates and warned of bureaucratic messes that the law's investigative processes would generate, and these arguments persuaded many municipal Boards of Education and Chambers of Commerce to oppose the proposition. In late September, former Governor Ronald Reagan, a right-wing rival of Senator Briggs, shifted the balance. He affirmed the fiscally conservative, anti-expansion-of-government themes and recommended "No on 6." By mid-October, polling differentials were emphatic enough to pull anti-Briggs statements from other nationally renowned politicians.[64]

In late October, labor got out the vote—phone banks during the last few weeks, a front-page editorial in the state AFL-CIO newsletter a few days ahead of the election, 2.3 million cards to be handed out at the polls.[65] Virginia LaGasa, a founder of the American Civil Liberties Union's gay rights committee in Orange County, Briggs's home district, was an intern in special education at a local public school. "I was in one of the professions that would have been hit by Briggs," she said. "There was no union for us student aides, but for the teachers there was, and the teachers' union was really working hard against Proposition 6. If they hadn't been involved in the school during that time, making their facilities available for the phone banks and all of that, I don't think we would have defeated the initiative."[66]

Proposition 6 was rejected by 58 percent of the voters. Reagan's timely warning about big budgets and bureaucracy strengthened the reversal in public opinion, but seeds for the turnaround had been planted earlier that season through intensive, positive community organizing. Well before Reagan's statement, disciplined collaborations among liberal religious groups, civil libertarians, and gay and lesbian activists were sustaining the basic moral opposition. As for organized labor, the contributions arrived early and late and always dependably: generous financing, strong endorsements, a full-throttle release of the political machine. The gay movement and its allies had studied the failures of Miami, St. Paul, Eugene, and Wichita and chose to think and act differently. A potent coalition emerged, inspired by the fresh, angry voices of gay liberation and shaped by labor's essential commitment to fairness and equality.

From "Making Love" to Making Politics

San Francisco, New York, and Boston were union strongholds with large, politically sophisticated queer communities. In the 1980s, they became the proving grounds for creative organizing projects led by labor-gay alliances. Success with the Coors boycott and anti-bigotry electoral campaigns had demonstrated to coalition partners the strengths and quirks of queer political cultures. Some of the new projects were protests; others were celebrations. As the years went by, structures and themes varied and mutual concerns shifted, but organizing itself reinforced cooperation and continuity.

In San Francisco, queer-labor coalitions that had arisen to boycott Coors, elect Harvey Milk, and defeat Briggs continued to encourage gay support for labor issues and union principles. In February 1982, the cause was a strike by janitors who cleaned movie theaters. They were members of Local 9 of the

Service Employees International Union, and their wages averaged $6 per hour over a thirty-hour workweek. Local 9 hired Sal Roselli, a janitor and vice-president of the Alice B. Toklas Lesbian/Gay Democratic Club, to lead the strike, and Roselli chose the United Artists theater chain as the strike's target.

Action focused on the Metro Theatre, where *Making Love* was the premier attraction. The movie featured Michael Ontkean as a married man who leaves his wife, Kate Jackson, for another man, Harry Hamlin. These were popular stars playing gay bedroom scenes in a romantic plot with a happy ending, a first for Hollywood. On opening day, Local 9 led three demonstrations at the Metro box office, right before show time, and picket lines were up for every screening that followed. Union groups and four gay and lesbian political clubs pledged not to cross. But Roselli would have to deal with a wider community if he wanted to keep the lines strong. Gay moviegoers were yearning to see the picture; it was not showing anywhere else in the city; and 20th Century Fox was spending $5 million to promote its San Francisco run.

Local 9 set up a reasonable alternative for film fans, with the help of Local 1741 of the United Transportation Union, which represented school bus drivers in San Francisco. The drivers set up weekend convoys of school buses to transport moviegoers to unionized theaters in suburban Hayward, San Mateo, and Concord, where *Making Love* was playing at the malls. The assembly point was the picket line at the Metro. "It was a party," Roselli recalled. "We'd have lines of people getting on the buses with their signs, 'Alice B. Toklas Lesbian/Gay Democratic Club Supports Local 9.'" The steady protest continued for several weekends, but management held out throughout *Making Love's* run. The party died down, and Local 9 never reached a settlement. But the janitors appreciated the effort. "These were middle-aged guys with families," said Roselli. "They were so surprised to be getting that kind of support."[67]

The Lesbian/Gay Labor Alliance (LGLA) of San Francisco was formed in early 1983 and typically operated as an ad hoc support squad. Activists joined union picket lines throughout the city and assisted unionization attempts at businesses in the Castro. In the spring of 1984, LGLA sponsored a public meeting on domestic partnership benefits and then joined with NOW and the Coalition of Labor Union Women (CLUW) in a forum on lesbians in the labor movement. Later that summer, the alliance organized meetings and rallies to welcome delegates, both gay liberation-minded trade unionists and pro-labor queers, who were in the city as delegates to the Democratic National Convention.

New York City's gay-labor group was sparked by a migrant activist who arrived in town from San Francisco in 1986. Peter Tenney landed a job as a line cook at Union Square, a fine new restaurant, and then began to wonder, "With numerically more queers in New York than probably anywhere else, where are the gay and lesbian trade unionists?" He met Vivienne Freund, an examiner of unemployment claims for the State of New York and a member of the Public Employees Federation. Together they tried the field. The first time they posted notices at the Lesbian and Gay Community Center, they got a 100 percent no-show. "I was very discouraged," Tenney said, "but Vivienne said we should try again before giving up. The next time, ten or twelve people came out of the woodwork—much better."[68] Other queer labor activists were interested, and the idea caught on, especially among the city's white-collar unionists. In June, LGLN hosted a garden party at the community center in time to form a contingent in the Gay Pride Parade. After a season of meetings, LGLN led its first action, the splashy "Dump Coors" demonstration at Googie's in the spring of 1987.

As a matter of course, LGLN activists visited picket lines with gay-labor support signs. They were also avid consultants. In 1990, the network published its one hundred-page handbook *Pride at Work: Organizing for Lesbian and Gay Rights in Unions*, the first publication to study union-based AIDS work and union-negotiated domestic partner benefits.[69] Queer unionists around the country read the book and got in touch, eager to find others fighting their kind of fight. They wanted advice on how to develop their AIDS discrimination grievances, negotiate partner benefits, and formulate nondiscrimination resolutions.

LGLN worked with gay caucuses in New York City unions such as the Gay Teachers Association (after 1990, the Lesbian and Gay Teachers Association), whose lawsuit for domestic partner benefits was crawling through the state courts. In 1991, they encouraged queer activists in AFSCME District Council 37 to launch their own Lesbian and Gay Issues Committee. The group, LAGIC, quickly achieved status as a standing committee of the council and then made attaining domestic partner benefits through collective bargaining its top priority. In 1993, Mayor David Dinkins settled both the teachers' lawsuit and the municipal workers' contract by issuing an executive decree. For a workforce of 250,000, benefits would be available to all domestic partners, gay and straight, in all city employment contracts.

Boston's GALLAN has been the longest-lived of the citywide coalitions. The group started up quietly in the mid-1980s with at-home potluck suppers for lesbian trade unionists, "just to talk," according to Karen Wheeler, a medical equipment technician and a steward at Boston City Hospital.[70] Along the way, a few gay men joined the circle.

GALLAN has always kept the conversations personal. More than similar groups in other cities, the organization sustains itself through longtime friendships, such as the collaboration of Susan Moir, who handled grievances, and Tess Ewing, who served as the president of Steelworkers Local 8751, the school bus drivers' union. Moir and Ewing eventually left the bus yard and got involved in other sectors of Boston's busy labor scene, but their bond continued. Other organizers have layered political and workplace projects with loyalty and intimacy. Ginny Cutting, an officer in SEIU Local 509 and an AIDS claims examiner for the State of Massachusetts, described the community and the kinships: "We have had deaths from AIDS in our families—my brother, Susan's brother, my partner's brother, so we've all gone through a lot together. Having come from here, the class stuff, the way you talk about your history, remembering what it was like—it's comforting, like a safety net. Things don't have to be spoken."[71]

That sense of support similarly touched Tom Barbera, Cutting's colleague in Local 509, who was employed at a state facility for mentally retarded adults. In the late 1980s, managers accused him and ten other queer mental health workers of sexually abusing clients. Local 509 took up the defense, and they were exonerated. Through it all, "GALLAN people were backing us up," Barbera said. "In many ways they are my family. I've shared my whole life with them."[72]

For some of the activists who came from Boston's Irish working-class South End, the union actually *was* the family. GALLAN's political debut in October 1989 was a special occasion for several queer sons and daughters of leading union officials. Most had already come out to parents, siblings, and co-workers but had not come out yet to the family's union.

The event was an ambitious fundraiser, "Allies for the 90s: United for Health," to benefit two organizations, one labor and one gay. Labor's focus would be the United Farm Workers. Cesar Chavez would give the keynote speech about the recently renewed boycott of California table grapes. Half of the evening's proceeds would go to a new building for Boston's Fenway Health Center, a full-service agency for the gay community. A gay male multiracial a cappella group, "The Flirtations," was coming from New York to sing for the crowd. "We were ready to see what you could do with all these gay folks who also knew organizing," said Wheeler.[73]

Old-timers in HERE Local 26 had known Janice Loux, the benefits director, and her mother, an organizer, "since I was a little kid," Loux said. "So when I asked the local to support the event, I wasn't directly saying, 'Hey, I'm queer,' but it did go through the Executive Board, and we talked about it at the union meeting, and I did say, 'we' instead of 'they.'" Loux was nervous about the poster she put up in her office. "But then, after the event, I got more involved in the AIDS movement," she said. "As the benefits director, I could help members who had AIDS."[74]

Preparations were going well until GALLAN learned that the new Fenway facility was being built with nonunion labor. "We basically shut down the planning for the event for a couple of weeks and sought to convince Fenway of the value of using union labor," said Susan Moir. Although the two sides came to an agreement that the unions would refer jobs to "any out gay and lesbian construction workers who wanted to work on that site," once the party was over and the funds had been allocated, "Fenway reneged. They built the building nonunion, with scab labor. Substandard wages, no benefits, extremely cheaply. It was a real betrayal," Moir said. When Fenway's reversal became widely known, the Building Trades Council laid no blame on its allies in GALLAN, who had tried so hard to bridge the two communities.[75] GALLAN, for its part, saw the controversy in terms of a growing divide between labor-oriented queers and the gay community's rising entrepreneurial class.[76]

GALLAN played an influential role in campaigns of opposition to the state's Republican power structure. The network's endorsements became successful predictors in statewide and municipal contests, and its reputation for disciplined political action grew.

Through most of the 1990s, GALLAN publicly examined the class-based politics of William F. Weld, the moderate Republican governor of Massachusetts. His support of the state's gay rights bill and his approval of same-sex partner benefits for top administrators made him a hero to some sectors of the LGBT community. But Weld would not grant partner benefits to the state's unionized workforce, and GALLAN pointed out that this divided gays in public employment. GALLAN also protested Weld's plans to curtail government agencies that served people with AIDS and other LGBT clients from working-class communities. The cuts would directly affect members of GALLAN who were employees of those agencies.

The first of GALLAN's many get-out-the-vote drives in 1990 was directed at Question 3, a referendum on cuts in social services. Question 3 had been placed on the ballot by Citizens for Limited Taxation the same year that Weld was elected, and he supported the measure. Ed Hunt and other union activists campaigned in working-class neighborhoods against Question 3 and Citizens for Limited Taxation. The activists took their truth squad, "Lick CliT," to gay neighborhoods. "When we began, Question 3 had a 70–30 chance of passing," said Hunt. "We put out the word that this would hit AIDS services and everything else that got state funding, and we talked about how it would hurt gay and lesbian workers. And we killed it. It was voted down, by 70 percent. We licked that CliT."[77]

Weld maintained his antiunion focus and eventually had his way. By the time he left office in 1997, approximately fifteen thousand state jobs had been eliminated.

"When You Knew You Belonged": The Labor Movement Comes Out

The AFL-CIO celebrated its own gayness during a cool, clear weekend in October 1987. Huge crowds were gathering in Washington, DC, for a National March for Lesbian and Gay Rights. Queer people arrived with families, friends, and union buddies to participate in the weekend's offerings: parties throughout the city, religious services, college reunions, concerts. A mass wedding was assembled at the doors of the Internal Revenue Service building, with two hundred same-sex couples, some of them union members, pledging their troth. The National Mall was covered with the bright oblongs of the AIDS memorial quilt, its first national display. Among the 1,920 patches were memorials to members of SEIU Local 250, the union for workers at San Francisco General Hospital. Surviving co-workers had sewn an entire section for their own.[78]

The AFL-CIO formally welcomed queer unionists the day before the march. Five hundred rank-and-file union people crowded into the front hall of the federation's national headquarters and were joined by labor and political luminaries, among them Bill Olwell of the United Food and Commercial Workers International Union, Anna Padia of CLUW, Norman Hill of the A. Philip Randolph Institute, and Congressman Barney Frank of Massachusetts.

A national gay rights march on Washington in October 1979 had gathered seventy-five thousand people. Although that event had no labor contingents or official labor signs, LGBT union people were at the rally, and Jerry Wurf, president of AFSCME, was one of the speakers. Eight years later, public and service sector unions were still foremost in the crowd, but labor's situation was drastically changing. Union membership, especially in the private sector, was decreasing sharply, and political influence was diminishing accordingly. The right's continued political dominance was pushing some labor leaders to examine new approaches to organizing and coalition building. They were hoping, as never before, that gains in the public and service sectors might slow the movement's waning.[79]

The demonstration on Sunday, October 11, drew 500,000 people to Constitution Avenue. Labor's contingent, sometimes twenty, sometimes forty marchers, led their line with a "Gay Pride at Work" banner. Union members on the sidelines called out their organizations, their local numbers, their hometowns. "We supported lesbian and gay rights when it was just a crowd of 10 people," Cesar Chavez told the assembly. He vowed loyalty to the gay cause and reminded marchers to hold true to the boycott of table grapes. He concluded with a round of the United Farm Workers' chant, "Viva la Huelga, Viva la Causa."[80]

LGBT unionists made simple plans to stay in touch while maintaining local union caucuses and citywide coalitions. Organizers chatted on conference calls, circulated newsletters, and traveled to each other's regional meetings. They looked to the public and service sectors, especially AFSCME and SEIU, the two fastest-growing organizations, for leadership.

AFSCME and SEIU were growing into huge organizations but were still flexible enough to encourage women and racial minorities to run for top offices and to seek responsible posts throughout their systems of regional governance. Their recruitment drives were consistently successful, and the leadership included many former activists from the Civil Rights Movement and the women's movement. And so they became the first national unions to establish committees charged with concerns of sexual minorities.

AFSCME's queer activists had been meeting informally at conventions ever since the resolution of 1982. They would convene workshops on LGBT labor themes and socialize in the lesbian and gay hospitality suites. In 1989, Gerald McEntee, president of AFSCME, appointed a union-wide advisory board of prominent queer activists from twelve regions. The advisers worked through their District Councils to educate the rest of the union about upcoming LGBT political and bargaining issues. They also promoted the formation of gay-labor caucuses within the councils, and they supported internal LGBT organizing in other unions.

SEIU had adopted its gay rights resolution in 1984, at its national convention in Dearborn, Michigan. However, it was the union's extensive internal program of conferences on civil rights and women's issues that gave rise to a system of regional queer caucuses. Anne Montague, a clerical worker at Oregon State University and an activist in SEIU Local 503, the Oregon Public Employees Union, called a meeting for lesbians during a women's conference in Chicago in 1989 and discovered a core of like-minded delegates and staff. For the next three years, the network expanded. Special "Lavender" sessions were on the program whenever the union convened civil rights meetings or regional women's conferences. In October 1993, one thousand Lavender Labor activists met at the Local 250 union hall in Oakland to found SEIU's Western Conference Lavender Caucus.

The union's Eastern Region Lavender Caucus convened in Baltimore the next year during a union-sponsored civil rights conference that featured workplace and bargaining issues for gay and lesbian members. John Sweeney, president of SEIU, addressed an assembly of four hundred. "Every time he spoke about racial discrimination, he emphasized lesbian and gay workers fighting, too," recalled Tom Barbera, who was elected co-chair of the caucus.[81] For Shirley Clarke, a Boston-based delegate from Local 509 and a supervisor in a community residence for the mentally handicapped, the event was a wonderful welcome. "There's a lot of prejudice out there," she said. "It was the first time in any union when you knew you belonged."[82]

The Lavender Caucus of SEIU and other unions' queer networks drew ideas and activists from labor's strong infrastructures of community coalitions, ad hoc organizing projects, citywide organizations, and standing national committees. A new plan emerged: to organize a national lesbian- and gay-labor coalition. But in the early 1990s, union power and queer energy were inadequate to the task. Activists would have to extend their political influence beyond their reliable allies in service and public sector unions. And if they really wanted to spread labor's message beyond the few cities in America where it was almost OK to be union and queer, they would have to explore the possibilities with a wider range of communities.

No Toil nor Labor Fear: Utah and the Nation

Salt Lake City in the early 1990s was one of those difficult places, a city that was neither union-minded nor gay-friendly. Cal Noyce, a technician at the telephone company and a vice-president of Local 7704 of the CWA, served as a regular delegate to his union's annual conventions. He would attend meetings of the minority caucus, which turned out to be a good place to meet other LGBT activists. Noyce learned what queer organizers in more liberal cities and college towns were doing to make LGBT issues a priority in their union work. By supporting the programs of black delegates, queer CWA activists got backing for their own goals—for example, resolutions on sexual orientation discrimination.[83] Noyce joined a push to put queer issues on the CWA's agenda.

Back home, LGBT projects would be hard to develop. Utah's dominant Mormon Church held distinctly negative views on homosexuality. The region's antiunion political culture would present a second challenge. Utah's right-to-work labor laws had always slowed down union growth; the participation rate in 1995 was approximately 9 percent. But Salt Lake City was where Noyce lived and where he wanted to make his mark. He knew his way around the queer community, as small and quiet as it was. He was friendly with gay and lesbian co-workers at the telephone company, and he knew musicians and city employees who were out at work and in their unions. He began to think "it would be really neat if there was some sort of group in Salt Lake," he said, and in 1993 he put his connections to work.[84]

In a profoundly conservative community, Noyce served the labor movement as an out gay man. He was the AFL-CIO representative on the board of Utah's United Way and a hands-on volunteer. He distributed Thanksgiving fruit baskets to ailing union members and threw holiday parties for Salt Lake City's YWCA Retarded Youth Program. In 1993, he was elected secretary-treasurer of the Salt Lake Area Labor Council, and in 1994, he became the president.

Ed Mayne, a miner by trade and a member of United Steelworkers Local 485, was the president of Utah's AFL-CIO and Noyce's staunchest supporter. As Mayne saw it, the labor movement and the gay movement represented threatened minorities, so any opportunity to develop an alliance should not be missed. He and his wife, Karen, a teacher and an AFT member, advised Noyce as he started out. An ad in Salt Lake City's gay newspaper, *The Pillar*, got responses from many curious workers who complained of discrimination. "A lot of them were not union people. There are no unionized hotels or restaurants here, and gay people work in those professions," said Noyce. "So that was an opportunity to talk about organizing. If we can show them the benefits of joining a union, then we will have increased our potential."[85]

Mayne gave Noyce $1,000 in start-up funding and paid for an evening of drinks at Brick's, a gay tavern. Twelve people showed up for the first meeting of the Utah Coalition of Gay, Lesbian, and Bi Union Activists and Supporters. For Mayne, it was a first:

> So there I was at this bar. There were people who would wonder, what's he doing, but maybe it was a lesson that, hey, if Ed can do it, anybody can. We wanted to activate these folks as union members. So we just adopted a policy of embracing and working with our gay and lesbian union brothers and sisters.
>
> We've been trying all along to form coalitions with community-based organizations. If you want to change the laws to allow union organization, you've got to elect the people. It's just good politics.[86]

Noyce led the Salt Lake City group with Julie LeRoy, vice-president of Utah's AFL-CIO and the business manager of Local 354 of the International Brotherhood of Electrical Workers. With Noyce's pickup truck draped in "Union Yes" banners, they would drive the parade route of Salt Lake City's annual gay pride fair, distributing union flyers to the crowd.

Just before the coalition's founding meeting at Brick's, Noyce came upon a story in a gay newsletter about queer union networks and plans for a gathering at the March on Washington for Lesbian and Gay Rights on April 25, 1993. Once again, the labor movement was inviting activists to a reception, this time at SEIU headquarters. Noyce was astonished: "I thought, Jesus, this is neat. Here I am trying to form a group, and I had no idea that there were already groups in existence."[87]

Noyce could not make it to Washington for the march but was soon participating in conference calls to plan the next steps for a national gay-labor coalition. His base in Utah and his affiliation with the CWA's minority caucus brought geographical and organizational diversity to the project, but the first time he actually met any of the people he was talking with was when he traveled to Oakland, California, in October 1993 to observe the launch of SEIU's Western Conference Lavender Caucus.

The coalition assembled a founding convention at AFSCME District Council 37's headquarters in New York City in June 1994, to coincide with a week of citywide celebrations of the twenty-fifth anniversary of the Stonewall Rebellion. The assembly resolved to name the national organization Pride at Work and quickly set the next goal: to secure recognition for the organization as a constituency group of the AFL-CIO.[88]

This the coalition achieved at the AFL-CIO's national meeting in September 1997, when President John Sweeney announced the Executive Council's approval of Pride at Work—the national organization of lesbian, gay, bisexual, and transgender trade unionists—and its entry into the federation. Pride at Work took its place among five other constituency organizations: the Asian Pacific American Labor Alliance, the Labor Council for Latin American Advancement, CLUW, the A. Philip Randolph Institute, and the Coalition of Black Trade Unionists. Each of these groups has a staff and central bureau at AFL-CIO headquarters to coordinate activities in local chapters with issues important to the broad labor movement and to allied organizations.

Pride at Work convenes gay-labor workshops at national and regional union conventions, at meetings of LGBT advocacy groups, and at religious and civil rights conferences. For local unions preparing to negotiate LGBT rights in their collective bargaining agreements, Pride at Work offers training and model contract language on family policy, health insurance, and principles of nondiscrimination. Pride at Work also functions as an organizing center for ongoing initiatives, such as the campaign for a federal employment nondiscrimination act.

In February and March 2012, Pride at Work representatives rallied with

Wisconsin's LGBT civil rights groups at the State Capitol in Madison to mobilize protest against proposed legislation that would curtail public employees' collective bargaining rights. The laws against unions passed, but only in the face of rallies and demonstrations that went on for six weeks. These protests were organized by local affiliates of AFSCME, AFT, SEIU, and other unions that represent 200,000 public workers in Wisconsin.[89] Later, in Washington, DC, Pride at Work's national office solicited pledges of continued solidarity and support from sixty-seven LGBT national organizations.

Pride at Work's regional conferences and biennial conventions have put LGBT rights on the agendas of national unions and fit in with the AFL-CIO's centralized model of organization and action. But Pride at Work's national projects have come to realization only because rank-and-file organizers have developed strong local chapters. Those organizers are activists from the many local unions that form the basic units of the labor movement. In the toughest of times, it is the work of the locals that steadily maintains the life of the movement.

4

The Heart of the Matter

Union Politics, Queer Issues, and the Life of the Local

"Pretty damn good" was how Sally Otos described contractual protections for sexual orientation that her union had negotiated with Columbia University in 1985. Otos was a secretary in the university's Center for the Social Sciences and one of three co-chairs of the local that represented Columbia's office workers, a chapter of District 65–United Auto Workers (UAW), a union renowned in New York City's labor movement for brave organizing and innovative contracts. The local was a harbinger of an aggressive new wave of unionization at elite universities. To recruit 1,100 clerical and technical employees, Columbia's activists had campaigned for five years; to settle the first contract, members had walked out in the middle of the fall 1985 semester for five days.[1]

The hot issues were economics, especially wages. The union proposed a 10.5 percent increase; the university countered with 4.5 percent. The final settlement raised pay by 6 percent. By contrast, sexual orientation protection in the contract's nondiscrimination articles would cost nothing, unless the university discriminated. The inclusion became the first of many steps toward making queer existence central to the union's ethos.

In that first contract, and in every subsequent contract for the next ten years, Columbia union negotiators put LGBT issues high on the collective bargaining agenda. They bargained with a queer eye to local union politics, as had other unions before them in other industries. Otos recalled the excitement at the 1985 ratification meeting: "This guy stood up and asked why we hadn't gotten benefits for domestic partners. I answered for the negotiating committee that I would love to get them, but you need to have some organized body within the unit pressing for it. You don't get anything in the abstract. There has to be a need and a desire, so for our next contract, let's try to do that. And nobody got up and said, 'What a terrible idea.'"[2]

Otos was certain that many other members wanted benefits for their partners. The need was vital for her and Robin Lutsky, the lover with whom she lived. Lutsky, who had no health care coverage, had been hit by a bus while carrying union signs to the picket line during the strike; severe neurological injuries had rendered her unable to work. Even though Lutsky received long-term disability payments from her own unionized job, Otos was shouldering most of their household expenses. However, in 1988, when the negotiating committee was preparing for the next round of collective bargaining, a membership survey showed fewer than a dozen affirmative replies to its query on "spousal equivalent benefits." The committee dropped the issue from its list of demands. But Otos and others were set on broadening gay rights for this contract.

The union proposed extending several provisions available to spouses, children, and parents to "all family" and "all household members." Management countered by taking paid sick leave for child care off the table, a move that angered the union's work and family committee. As talks continued, the union team proposed an addition to the standing language on bereavement. "We zeroed in on 'spousal equivalent' and added 'spousal equivalent or close family member living in the household' to the bereavement clause," Otos said.

> These were the worst days of the AIDS crisis. People were dying very fast and very horribly. It was the year that my youngest brother found out he had AIDS. We were starting to lose people on the staff. We didn't use the word "AIDS" in bargaining, but we did say, "Some people are dying young. They are not married, but they have committed partners."
>
> Management had belittled every other demand we made, but they knew better than to make light of AIDS. They didn't say a thing. They just gave it to us.[3]

The members were much more interested in benefits for domestic partners during the next round of contract talks in 1992. Several other prestigious universities had already instituted health coverage for domestic partners, and professors and administrators at Columbia were adding their own pressure to the union's agitation. Columbia granted the benefits for all same-sex partners in July 1994. Columbia's plan, similar to those of other employers, was not especially expensive. Nonetheless, it was different from previous gay rights reforms: it involved money, and it came out of the university's budget for wages. Spousal equivalent bereavement leave was so rarely used that the cost was negligible, and the sexual orientation clause cost nothing if there were no violations. With the next contract in 1997, more economic reforms were added: same-sex domestic partners of union members received the special and precious benefit of half-time tuition.

The local union's contract is its living heart, the record of negotiations, and an essential first step to any expansion of workers' rights on the job. When managers and union leaders talk terms, they face each other, literally across a table. At work, one partner to the negotiation may be the supervisor of another. But at the bargaining table, the dialogue is spoken between two equally power-ful voices: each side represents a constituency necessary to the enterprise. And no matter what their agreement may be, until a majority of the union member-ship ratifies its terms, it is not binding.

This is how the clerical workers' first contract with Columbia came to be and how it evolved. For more than twenty years, the union organized thought-fully and negotiated strategically, and it achieved substantial improvements in each accord. The local's excellent bargaining record both strengthened and smartened the union's overall position within the university. And each new agreement affirmed the lives of queer workers in the ranks.

Local unions are the basic organizing units of the labor movement. They connect individual workers from different production units, service offices, or work shifts and govern themselves by electing officers, formulating and adopt-ing bylaws, holding regular membership meetings, keeping records, collect-ing dues, and maintaining the treasury. A local can be a small unit of thirty or forty people in one workplace; a sizable organization like the Columbia chapter of District 65–UAW; or a huge state- or citywide formation of thousands of employees covered by the same contract and governed by one executive board and president. Such very large local unions are usually configured into smaller subsidiary units, or shops, for day-to-day administration of the contract.

The Columbia clerical local was born strong out of the five-day strike of 1985. The union then maintained a firm record of improved wages and ben-efits. Within that secure economic context, the LGBT life of the local evolved consistently and pragmatically, from inexpensive rights (nondiscrimination protection, spousal equivalent bereavement leave) to financially substantial benefits (health coverage, tuition benefits for domestic partners), all achieved through collective bargaining.

Domestic partner benefits were invented during collective bargaining talks in 1982 in New York City, when the famously liberal management of the *Village Voice* and its small union of gay and straight workers, a local affiliated to District 65, negotiated a settlement that included "spouse equivalent benefits." The prospect of replicating the innovation excited lesbian and gay unionists around the country who were just beginning to form citywide and regional networks. They founded queer caucuses in their locals to advance contract demands for bereavement rights and nondiscrimination safeguards, and by the early 1990s the benefits had become winnable.

A local union's vitality depends on the soundness of its contract, but rati-fication is only the beginning, for no contract can be static. The dialogue con-tinues in encounters between workers and managers over the contract's limits or options, and formal processes of grievance and arbitration define the con-tract's boundaries. At unionized workplaces where workers perceived to be infected with AIDS were treated unfairly, queer advocates advised local officers or served as stewards themselves to make sure that the contract's grievance process would be applied justly.

The livelihoods of queer workers were threatened during the 1990s in Colorado and Oregon. Right-wing initiatives to place antigay referenda before statewide electorates reawakened fears dormant since 1978, when multiunion coalitions contributed to the defeat of the Briggs Initiative in California. SEIU Local 503, which represented public employees in Oregon, participated in a mighty coalition that defeated Measure 9 in 1992. That same year, antigay Amendment 2 to the state constitution of Colorado won at the polls. The coalition that attempted to halt its passage was weak; labor was not involved. In the State of Washington, gay and labor activists compared the loss in Colorado with the sustained resistance in Oregon and in 1993 prevented two antigay initiatives from reaching the ballot.

Although local unions govern themselves, they are not independent operations. They are formed by the collaboration of workers and organizing representatives of regional or national unions who conduct a petition drive among the workers toward an election to be supervised by the National Labor Relations Board (NLRB) to certify the union as the agent in collective bargaining. If the vote results in a majority voting "Union Yes," the unit receives its charter and claims standing within the national organization. Local affiliates' rights and responsibilities are defined by the national union's constitution and bylaws, and the national union provides administrative services and convenes regularly with local delegates to set the union's course.

Local union members who want to rid themselves of a national union can petition the NLRB to supervise an election of decertification. If a majority approves, the disaffiliation is set. There may be strong reasons for members to choose autonomy: unfairness, corruption, poor governance. Some locals decertify and continue to negotiate healthy contracts, but many others collapse completely.

For one remarkable gay local, a new direction began with the impetus toward autonomy. Over the course of four contractual cycles, bus drivers employed by the city of Ann Arbor and represented by the American Federation of State, County, and Municipal Employees (AFSCME) twice transformed their union. First, they renounced their status as a subsidiary unit within the larger, citywide local and received an independent charter from AFSCME; two years later, they withdrew from AFSCME altogether. The local functioned successfully and independently from 1974 until 1981, until a strike broke its treasury. The union survived by joining another national union.

Taking It to the Streets: The Ann Arbor Bus Drivers

The Ann Arbor bus drivers were no ordinary dissidents. They fused gay affirmation with labor insurgency during the city's counterculture heyday. The drivers' rebellion was consistent with the radicalism of everyday life in that community.

Their split from the sponsoring union expressed their own wild style of queer militancy and labor solidarity.[4]

Ann Arbor, home to the University of Michigan, was a thriving center of alternative politics, and in the early 1970s, its chapter of the Human Rights Party, a statewide organization, supported gay liberation, tenants' rights, the antiwar movement, and unions. Two of the party's candidates won seats on the City Council in 1972, and for the next two years, they served as swing votes to the council's five Republicans and four Democrats. The council voted in favor of the Human Rights Party's proposal to add "sexual preference" to the city's antidiscrimination ordinance, a first in Michigan.[5]

Few female bus drivers were on the payroll when the Ann Arbor Transportation Authority began hiring in 1973. Carol Ernst, a leader in the Human Rights Party, came in as a trainee. She was on the verge of breaking up with her husband and thrilled with the wages. She told her radical friends about the job openings, among them Susan Schurman, a former organizer for the Hotel Employees and Restaurant Employees Union (HERE). "Carol told me to lie about my union background. She said that the boss wanted to break the union by hiring docile women," said Schurman. "She said, 'After probation, after you get this job, I expect you to help us in the union.'" The two trained together and faced down the prejudices of their male colleagues. That first year on the job, they became a couple and soon turned their attention to union politics.[6]

The transit authority was an independent agency of the city, and its one hundred or so employees constituted one chapter in AFSCME Local 369, the union for all municipal workers in the city of Ann Arbor. Labor relations were placid, and this frustrated the new drivers. In 1974, Schurman successfully ran for president of the chapter. "Our unit behaved like a traditional mass transit local," Schurman said. "There would be an occasional grievance, but management could pretty much do what they wanted to do. We could never get any attention from Local 369."

Ernst, Schurman, and the other new drivers thought that the transit chapter would be better off without Local 369 and petitioned the national union and regional Council 51 for a separation. AFSCME promptly chartered the transit authority unit as Local 693. The next local election was a contest for the entire Executive Board, and votes were split between veterans of the old chapter and a slate of younger workers. Schurman won the presidency and Ernst became chief steward.

For the next contract, to be negotiated later that year, "We wanted something completely different," Schurman said. At the first bargaining session, the committee presented a thick ring binder loaded with provocative proposals. Committee members had been reading about systems of co-determination—the sharing of labor and management power—as it was being practiced in the Federal Republic of Germany and Sweden. "We all thought we should be making joint decisions with them and running the company together," Schurman said. "Management went crazy, and so did the staff of AFSCME's Council 51.

They said, 'You can't do this. Take those demands off the table. It's their job to manage and it's our job to grieve.' AFSCME was so adamant that we had to withdraw the proposals. They threatened to put us into trusteeship."

By contrast, Ernst and Schurman's proposal to write "sexual preference" into the contract's nondiscrimination section was not at all controversial. Workers who were not queer accepted it as a reasonable reinforcement of the Municipal Code, and management agreed. But it was historic: with the contract signed, Local 693 was one of the first unions ever to have collectively bargained a gay rights provision in its union contract.[7]

Ernst, Schurman, and the other insurgents now turned their minds to the trouble with AFSCME. Ernst pressed for independence; Schurman wanted to move more cautiously. A petition to decertify collected enough signatures to set an election to be supervised by the NLRB in October. Agents from the International Brotherhood of Teamsters and the Transportation Workers Union were offering to take the bus drivers into their organizations, but the rebels wanted complete autonomy.

Walter Oliver, head of AFSCME Council 51, did not want to lose Local 693, so shortly before the election, he invited the bus drivers' Executive Board to dinner with council officials and staff. Schurman remembered the evening as an attempt at reconciliation at which everything went wrong: "They had an open bar and steaks for everyone. And then there were grapes on the table. Three-quarters of our board people were vegetarians, and nobody drank, and we were into the grape boycott. These big guys were eating red meat and drinking and smoking. There was nothing to talk about. I knew when we left the meeting where this was headed, and I was terrified." Decertification won, 55–50. AFSCME moved quickly to confiscate the treasury. "Our naïveté was a real benefit. We were too young to know what you weren't supposed to do, that unions controlled their members," Schurman reflected. "We kept the office furniture, and we became the Ann Arbor Transit Employees Union [AATEU]." The rebels also kept their seat on the Huron Valley Labor Council.

The contract came up for renewal in the fall of 1975. "This time, we wouldn't take the co-determination stuff off the table," Schurman said. As tensions mounted, a committee of academics intervened. The university's Institute for Social Research had been studying quality-of-work-life issues in American workplaces. The transit employees' proposals seemed an appropriate topic for a new grant the institute had received from the U.S. Department of Labor to encourage labor-management cooperation. "The institute people talked with the transit authority," Schurman said. "We compromised. We agreed to drop the co-determination demands if management would consent to a single joint committee for the quality of work life."[8]

The contract of 1975 was the last that Ernst and Schurman negotiated as a couple; they broke up the next year. Ernst continued to drive, and she was involved in later contract talks, but her political focus was shifting. She ran (and came in third) for mayor on the Human Rights Party ticket; she also increasingly devoted her organizing energy to the rights of prostitutes. Schurman stayed with the bus company, but well before the 1975 contract expired, she accepted a promotion to management as director of training. Through her involvement with the quality-of-work-life committee, she had become fascinated with organizational behavior.

The city bought new Ford vans and extended its door-to-door Dial-a-Ride services; soon the transit workforce had doubled to two hundred. "Susan hired who was going to work there, and she picked a lot of union-minded people, gay men, gay women," said Harry Kevorkian, who started driving on Dial-a-Ride in 1977.[9] "Our older guys liked uniforms and rules. But the newer employees were different, musicians and activists," Schurman said. "One city official called us a 'bunch of hippies, niggers and queers,' and we proclaimed that epithet, proudly."[10] She meant drivers like Kevorkian, whose work outfits were casual. Off-duty he wore a dress and was known about town by his drag name, Kitty.[11]

The union walked out for eight days in July 1977 before settling its next contract. The State of Michigan prohibits strikes by public employees, but a judge ruled that management had committed significant infringements during the run-up to the strike deadline. The workers therefore were not in violation.[12]

The stoppage was a major public inconvenience that nevertheless garnered much civic sympathy. The local co-op discounted strikers' grocery bills by 20 percent and supplied a food wagon. Affiliates of the Huron Valley Labor Council donated to the strike fund, and delegates joined the lines. The settlement gave the union substantial monetary gains. Wages were boosted by 11.2 per cent, with a quarterly cost-of-living allowance tied to the Consumer Price Index. Further economic features were in the feminist vein: up to two years of paid maternity or paternity leave and clerical wages brought to parity with the pay of drivers, dispatchers, and other employees.[13] And once again, queer lives were written into the contract. The union won days off for the illnesses or deaths of "mates," which meant unmarried partners of either sex.

Ann Arbor's generous contract of 1977 proved to be a turning point in the political culture of both the town and its bus company. A new Republican mayor was elected, along with a Republican majority on the City Council. The mayor hired the former head of Cleveland's bus company to head the transit authority and cast his mission: to scrap the reforms and return the system to the basics of mass transportation. The Dial-a-Ride program was canceled; Schurman was fired; and quality-of-work committees ceased. Kevorkian, now president of the AATEU, called the new boss "the guy who made us all wear ties again."[14]

The new dress code was only one issue in the 1980 negotiations, but the younger drivers made it their sticking point. This time, the strike really was illegal. "If you're a twenty-something gay man or gay woman, uniforms are an awful idea," said Kevorkian. "But other people were hurt economically. The strike lasted six weeks. It was bitter and nasty."[15] Once he signed the accord, Kevorkian quit, as did other leaders. Drivers from the ranks returned to their jobs. They did what they could to save their union, which was still independent but insolvent. In 1981, the AATEU approved affiliation with the national Transportation Workers Union and received its charter as Local 171.

Gay rights won by the AATEU served as a model for unions in other locales. One of the first to be influenced was Local 1564 of the Amalgamated Transit Union, which represented bus workers at the South East Michigan Transportation Authority and in the mid-1970s added "sexual predilection" to the nondiscrimination article of its contract.[16]

The rights of gay workers came to the bargaining agendas of several newly organized white-collar unions in higher education during the late 1970s and early 1980s. Professional and technical workers at Temple University were chartered by AFSCME as Local 1723 in 1976. They made sexual orientation protection a leading strike issue in the settlement of their second contract in 1979. New York University's United Staff Association received its charter as Local 3882 of the American Federation of Teachers (AFT) in 1978 and negotiated sexual orientation as a protected class with its second contract in 1981. And the Columbia University local of District 65 wrote the protection into its first contract in 1985.

Cover Your Lover: The Invention of Domestic Partner Benefits

Employment contracts that forbade discrimination on the basis of sexual orientation or that included same-sex relationships in bereavement or sick leave policies morally affirmed queer existence. As contractual statements, the rules defined basic equity among human beings on the job and yet did not touch the essential and traditional bargain between labor and management, the fair balance of a full day's work for a full day's pay.

Could gay dignity in the workplace be realized in the economic bargain of wages and hours? Employees of the *Village Voice* took up that issue during contract negotiations in 1982 as they successfully modified their health insurance plan to include spousal equivalents. The innovation, later renamed "domestic partner benefits," though not immediately popular, sparked wider interest in the late 1980s. For the next two decades, contract campaigns for benefit equity succeeded in both the private and public sectors, from municipal employees in California to banquet waiters and chambermaids in Boston.

The typical beneficiaries in union negotiations were, at first, all unmarried couples, gay and straight. By the early 1990s, when the idea had proved viable, progressive corporations began appropriating and revising the concept, fitting the idea to their own purposes. By the turn of the twenty-first century, such benefits had become a routine perquisite in compensation packages of many of the country's largest private employers. But the range of beneficiaries had been reduced, and unions were involved only marginally.

The *Village Voice*, a weekly newspaper in New York City famous for its coverage of radical politics and culture, had a staff union; it formed in 1977 and was affiliated with District 65. The membership was young and unorthodox, a "workplace of ex-hippies, war refuseniks, feminists and queers," wrote Kitty Krupat, the union's organizer. "It was a polymorphous workplace. . . . A nine-to-five ad-taker one day could be a reporter the next."[17] The contract allowed bereavement leave for the death of any person "with whom the employee has family-type relations." And in a practice that was not contractually codified, unmarried heterosexual partners of union members did have access to health insurance. The *Voice*'s medical plan was self-insured, and the benefits were administered by District 65 itself. Thus, the union could bypass many of the bureaucratic barriers that a conventional insurer might have set up.[18]

As the negotiating committee prepared its contract demands in 1981, Jeff Weinstein, the paper's restaurant critic, proposed explicit language to make health benefits equitable for gay couples. Mainstream insurers were bent on refusing such schemes. In 1981, before AIDS had even been named, the industry knew that a devastating disease was infecting gay men. Fearing the costs, insurers refused policies for individual single men and for employer groups in queer workplaces, such as theater companies, florist shops, and restaurants.

When the union put its proposal on the *Village Voice* bargaining table, managers balked on their own. They insisted on not extending benefits "beyond what the law requires." They speculated that employees would add friends or roommates to the plan, rather than life partners, and then they worried that fickle queers would create extra hassles as they dropped or added partners. But the union stood firm and won a compromise: a plan to register spouse equivalents with a waiting period of one year before benefits would apply. The experiment succeeded. In 1989, out of 170 union members, 19 had extended their insurance to their spouse equivalents—half of them gay, and half of them straight. As it turned out, straight employees dropped and added partners far more frequently than their queer co-workers.[19]

The contract at the *Village Voice* was not easy to replicate. In the 1980s, only a handful of private sector, nonunion employers instituted partner benefits, none of them large companies.[20] Instead, the momentum shifted to unionized municipal workers in California. In 1984, SEIU Local 790, representing the city of Berkeley's 1,500 workers, negotiated coverage for domestic partners, both gay and straight. At first, Kaiser-Permanente, the city's primary insurance carrier, stymied the plan. Anticipating an increase in AIDS cases, the insurer attempted to hedge risks with a steep increase in premiums. The final deal required another year of negotiations and Local 790's concession to a surcharge. However, once the union demonstrated that the average health costs of domestic partners, including those with AIDS, were the same as the health costs of married couples, the surcharges were refunded.[21]

A few cities in California circumvented conventional insurers altogether. Santa Cruz's municipal contracts with SEIU Local 415 were already self-insured, so those 650 municipal workers easily won domestic partner coverage in 1987.

West Hollywood was incorporated as a city in 1985 and straightaway inaugurated America's first registry for domestic partners. Bereavement leave and other noneconomic benefits were made available to the city's entire workforce of two hundred, who were represented by AFSCME Local 3339. But an affordable insurer willing to deal with health benefits for domestic partners could not be found; three years went by before West Hollywood's program of self-insurance took shape. Premiums in the plan were lower than those the commercial companies had offered, so costs actually fell by $65,000 in the first year.[22]

By the early 1990s, a series of big-city municipal contracts in Seattle, San Francisco, Los Angeles, and New York City, as well as in the State of New York, were negotiated with the coverage. The need by then had sharpened. Costs were rising, and the overall quality and availability of health coverage was less and less dependable. Millions of workers were being laid off and were losing health insurance, and the new jobs that some of them found often lacked adequate benefits. More than ever, a partner's insurance was the sustaining factor in both the physical and the economic health of a household.[23]

In the private sector, the AIDS epidemic convinced many union leaders that broader coverage had to be a contractual priority. Managers reacted to the rise in costs differently: by resisting the addition of a new class of beneficiaries. Boston's HERE Local 26 was self-insured through a Taft-Hartley fund, a trust administered by a joint board of three union officers and three corporate managers. Like the unions that represented employees of the *Village Voice* and the city of Santa Cruz, Local 26 had the leeway to follow its own rules for its own plan. But with health care costs rising, some Taft-Hartley funds were failing.

In 1992, Local 26 leaders knew that their fund was heading for trouble, and they examined ways to contain the costs. "We introduced managed care and preventative health care models," said Janice Loux, the benefits director. Local 26 prepared for contract talks with a survey of the membership. A majority supported partner benefits. But at the table, hotel managers turned the proposal down. According to Loux:

> They said it was going to cost too much, but we knew this wasn't about money. Their positions were more about moral views. Sheraton and Hilton did not want to set precedents in the hotel industry. They did not want gay and lesbian workers to have these rights. So we hammered away, meeting after meeting.
> We said, "You're either going to restructure this medical program to save money, and include domestic partners, or we won't do it, and the fund will go under." It was take it or leave it. So they had to accept the proposal.[24]

The contract in 1993 between Local 26 and the Boston hotels was one of America's first and largest multiemployer contracts to cover domestic partners. Included with health insurance were other benefits administered by Taft-

Hartley trusts: legal services, subsidies for education, and financial assistance with down payments and mortgages. Thirteen same-sex and seventeen opposite-sex couples (constituting 1 percent of the 3,144 eligible couples) tested the new plan. "We didn't do it through the hotel personnel office," Loux explained. "We set up a confidential sign-up process. It became an important organizing point for heterosexual members that you don't have to be married to get the benefits."[25]

Hotel owners in Boston were resisting any talk of partner benefits during the same period when corporate managers in other industries were taking interest. High-tech companies (Lotus and Microsoft) and media conglomerates (Viacom and Paramount) were trying to recruit a diverse workforce. They noticed what liberal unions were achieving and developed their own variations. These schemes were initiated from the top and were devised as exclusive privileges for same-sex couples. Corporate systems were not as expansive as union plans. They were not secured through collective bargaining, and the pool of eligible recipients would be restricted to a much smaller group. But managers reasoned that only gay employees deserved the benefits, because heterosexual couples could marry. Gay activists in corporate employee groups, eager to privilege their status as a minority, supported that argument. And when major universities, both private (Stanford, University of Chicago) and public (University of Iowa) instituted same-sex coverage, they made the benefits even more exclusive by granting them to only faculty members and administrators.[26]

Unionized and nonunion employees at New York University formed the Association of Lesbian and Gay Faculty, Administrators, and Staff (ALGFAS) in 1992 and then lobbied the administration for partner benefits. In the spring of 1993, same-sex partners of faculty and administrators were granted eligibility, while partners of clerical and technical workers, who were members of AFT Local 3882, were left out. They negotiated their inclusion later that year, at the bargaining table.

"We were founders of ALGFAS. We were at all the meetings, we did the research," said Trudy Rudnick, the local president. "But when we negotiated our contract, management said that we would have to fight for everything that we wanted." Local 3882 invited representatives of ALGFAS to speak at a bargaining session. A gay man from central administration and a lesbian from the law school urged that union members be included, and when the contract was ratified in the fall of 1993, the benefits were part of the package. "Actually, we have it better," said Rudnick. "For us, domestic partners isn't just a piece of policy from Human Resources. It's in our contract, so they can't just take it away."[27]

Nonunion plans of the 1990s at Citicorp, Walt Disney, Wells Fargo, and other *Fortune* 500 companies defined domestic partner benefits narrowly, for active employees in same-sex relationships only. Companies with unionized workforces, such as AT&T, American Airlines, and Boeing, acted similarly, and unions that represented their employees did not push for involvement when the benefit packages were designed.

In the auto industry, corporate needs met union demands. Chrysler had come under fire in 1997 for its clumsy response to an antigay campaign against its sponsorship of the television sitcom *Ellen*, starring the lesbian comedian Ellen DeGeneres. The company dropped advertising for the historic episode in which the title character came out, a move that instigated a counter-boycott by civil libertarian and consumer groups. At Chrysler's headquarters, salaried employees formed People of Diversity, a gay and lesbian advocacy association. The group made domestic partner benefits its top priority.

The process would have to begin with Chrysler's failure to institute contractual protections against discrimination for sexual orientation. The UAW had ratified sexual orientation in its own constitutional antidiscrimination articles in 1992, but Chrysler flatly rejected such a proposal in 1996, and the union let the issue go, believing it would not be winnable in a national strike.[28] But pressure was mounting on Chrysler, and benefit reform was looking more and more feasible, especially with the Canadian Auto Workers union working steadily and successfully to achieve same-sex domestic partner benefits at all "Big Three" factories in Canada.[29]

By the time negotiations for the 1999 contract came around, Chrysler was under new management. DaimlerChrysler, eager to develop a progressive image and new policies, welcomed the UAW's proposal for sexual orientation protection. The union then introduced domestic partner benefits, and the company formally accepted. The two sides quickly agreed to start the program with a feasibility study; Ford and General Motors followed. The coverage finally adopted by the UAW and the Big Three was absorbed into the overall package of wages and benefits in the 1999 agreement, to be instituted mid-contract. The plan excluded heterosexual couples and retirees; only current workers who would sign up in 2000 or after could keep their partners covered when they retired.

The benefits may have been lean, and therefore confined to a small fraction of the industry, but the workforce itself was huge: 466,000 employees, unionized and salaried.[30] At the start of the twenty-first century, the Big Three, along with 3,400 other corporations, nonprofit organizations, and state and municipal governments, constituted 18 percent of American workplaces that were offering equity in benefits to households of gay and lesbian employees.[31] This was a turning point. What had begun as a brave little experiment in one local union was now a normal feature of U.S. industrial relations.

Enforcing the Contract, Defending the Workers

Ratification of a contract seals the deal of collective bargaining, even as it initiates a new cycle of conflict and resolution between management and labor. Each side has its own priorities as it uses the contract to interpret everyday frictions of life on the job. The dynamic of push and pull creates a practical record of rights and precedents that workers depend on when they lodge grievances. Although contested areas typically involve the most recent revisions to the contract's historical development, anything that happens at a workplace is open to contention: from production quotas and styles of service to supervisory behavior, attendance rules, health and safety protections, patterns of job promotion, and infringements of privacy.

For managers new to an assignment, the contract functions as a measure of competency: how efficiently can a fresh supervisor mark the territory, how far will the managerial hierarchy support a supervisor's moves, and how forcefully will workers react? The union side is buttressed by the processes of grievance and arbitration, which typically place rank-and-file guardians of the contract— shop stewards—at the center of disputes between employees and managers. Stewards are both advocates and co-workers who, at their best, encourage workmates to stand up for themselves and for one another. It is their watchfulness that gives the contract a life and authority of its own.

The union's bylaws determine how shop stewards obtain their positions. Some are appointed by local leaders or regional directors; others are elected from the ranks. If no one is available, delegates to the local's Executive Board or staff professionals can step into the breach. In principle, those who take on the responsibilities of stewardship must be skillful readers of the contract and wise advocates among the workers. Whether they are elected or appointed, their essential charge is to enforce the contract: to represent fairly every worker who is covered by that contract, regardless of whether the worker is a nice person or even, in the case of an open shop, regardless of whether the worker is paying dues.[32] Without consistent and vigilant enforcement, the consequences to the union are quick and serious. Unchecked, management can capture power piecemeal, eventually ruling workers' lives unilaterally. That would destroy the democratic balance laid out in the contract and weaken the life of the local.

However, the creative and satisfactory resolution of a grievance can anticipate a new direction in labor relations, even before labor and management explicitly discuss terms at the table. This happened in San Francisco, long before national unions acknowledged sexual orientation as a protected class or local unions wrote that class into their antidiscrimination contract provisions. In 1957, Walter Johnson of Retail Clerks International Association Local 1100 began representing department store workers at Macy's, Gump's, and other fine stores. Article 5B of the general contract, first negotiated in the 1930s, classified as a violation "any act by the employer or the union which interferes with their harmonious relationship." Johnson liked that clause. "It had a wide range, so you could take it to arbitration," he said. He would cite it whenever he detected prejudice. "I would drive employers nuts with it."

Johnson applied Article 5B to the complaint of a man who requested a transfer from general stock work to the counter of the Macy's men's sports clothing shop. This was the late 1960s, and the personnel manager was against the transfer, because the worker, she said, "is a queer." Johnson claimed discrimination and then followed the grievance up the chain of Macy's command and negotiated a compromise. The employee did not achieve the high-end position he desired, but he did land a decent promotion, from stock into sales.

In the mid-1970s, Johnson worked with an employee at a Macy's warehouse whose gender transition from male to female—Jerry to Becky—began with wearing makeup and then skirts. Johnson was able to keep management at bay but not the female co-workers who wanted to grieve the situation. "They were not exactly happy about Becky using the restroom," he said. But Johnson refused. His primary mission, to defend the contract, required fairness to all the workers. "I told them, 'We take care of everybody. We're the defense attorney. As long as someone isn't caught stealing or something like that, we're going to represent them, because next time, it may be you.'"[33]

A much nastier fight erupted at Chrysler's engine plant in Trenton, Michigan, in 1991, when electricians of UAW Local 372 learned that a co-worker, Ron Woods, was gay. "There was graffiti—it was vulgar—and written death threats," Woods recalled. "I am told that there was a bull's eye with my picture or my name in the middle and that someone was offering money as a reward for the death or assassination of Ron Woods." For the next several months, he withstood ostracism and took no action. But then a quarrel with an especially hostile co-worker (rumored to be a member of Michigan's Ku Klux Klan) escalated into physical assault. "He grabbed me by the neck, almost choked me, and threatened to kick my butt."[34] Woods filed a grievance three days later. Although the contract did not protect sexual orientation as a class, worker-to-worker harassment at that level would be clear grounds for discipline by the union. Mike Harrald, the plant's chairman, took charge. First he counseled Woods; then he confronted Woods's co-workers:

> [Woods] was more in fear that because of him being a homosexual, I wouldn't represent him. ... I told him about some of my experiences, the things that really happened to me. I told him that him being discriminated against was just the tip of the iceberg. I was the first black at the Hamtramck foundry in the skilled trades. . . . I went through a heck of a lot. . . . People in general can be very vicious.
>
> And I told the guys to cut the bullcrap. I know who's doing it. I already have been told about some of the incidents, and I want it stopped. If you don't stop, cease what you're doing, you will be brought up [on charges], and you will be discharged.[35]

Harrald then had Don Lingar, president of Local 372, summon Chrysler's plant manager to deal with supervisors who had harassed Woods. "They read them the riot act," Harrald said. "When they left out of there [Woods] didn't have no more problems. But he still wanted to get out of that tough situation."[36]

In August 1992, eight months after he first filed the grievance, Woods got a transfer. "It saved my life," he said.[37]

The Worst of Times: Local Unions and the AIDS Crisis

Unionized hospital workers in San Francisco and New York City in the late 1970s were among the first to care for male patients suffering with and dying from the deadly and mysterious "gay pneumonia" or "gay cancer" or "gay related immune deficiency (GRID)," as it was first known.[38] Strategies for prevention and treatment were developed without clear analysis or secure protocols.

Knowledge was scarce, and prejudice was widespread. Unions' capacities to serve members by mediating friction at work required the education of a wider public. Instead, straight workers' hostility toward LGBT co-workers, coupled with ignorance about infection and prevention, sharpened with public alarm. In 1984, Suzanne Hanen, a lesbian, worked in the cataloguing department at New York University's Bobst Library and was a steward for AFT Local 3882. "One guy wouldn't touch the photocopy machine after I had been on it," she recalled. "He told the supervisor and everybody else that he was afraid he might 'catch AIDS' from me."[39] Staff at the health center of one New York City union grew anxious after the visit of a member who they believed was infected. As soon as he left the clinic, they thoroughly sprayed waiting room furniture and telephones with disinfectant.[40]

Some unions tried to educate by example. In 1984, when fears of infection were exacerbating shortages at blood banks in New York City, AFSCME's District Council 37 urged members to contribute to a union blood drive. The council's executive director donated and then assured readers of the *Public Employee Press* that he and anyone else who joined the drive would be safe.[41] Other union officials, no better informed and no less fearful than the workers in their shops, often reinforced members' apprehensions that any human being could be a hazard.

By 1985, research was clarifying the facts about HIV transmission: the most likely routes were unprotected sexual intercourse and the sharing of needles in intravenous drug use. The information was useful and specific but also explicitly linked contagion, disability, and death to drugs and sex, thereby intensifying the stigma of being gay.

The epidemic widened, and workplace education lagged behind what public health experts knew: that casual contact was an unlikely path for infectious transmission of the virus. Workers feared that their jobs would expose them to infection, and they balked at perceived hazards. Plumbers at hospitals feared contaminated wastes in the pipes; elementary school teachers, anxious about children's nosebleeds, insisted on knowing pupils' HIV status. Managers who breached the confidentiality of employees' health records aggravated the panic, and poorly prepared shop stewards were useless when workers became targets.

In 1987, the AIDS status of a New York City sanitation worker was disclosed by his immediate supervisor; when the crew reacted with anger and fear, the boss removed the worker from his route and assigned him to isolated tasks. The worker asked Vivienne Freund of the Lesbian and Gay Labor Network to intervene. "He didn't feel that he could go to his union, and he wanted the crew to understand that working with him was not a risk," she said. "We called the supervisor and questioned the wisdom of giving in to the co-workers' fears, and we got him back to his regular job."[42]

The movement to fight AIDS developed militancy in the late 1980s, and stewards stood firmer when workers who had AIDS or were perceived to have AIDS were outed or harassed. In 1989, Susan Moir defended a fellow worker in USWA Local 8751, the Boston school bus drivers' union. "One of our members was driving a van and got into a tussle with a cop and was arrested. A boss from the company who had seen his disability records told the police that he had AIDS. At the station, the cops gay-baited him, and they taunted him about AIDS. Then they cuffed him to a radiator."[43]

The union rallied at the bus yard in support of the grievance. The settlement came quickly: $7,000 in cash and permanent health insurance, no matter what the driver's future employment status might be. The company also agreed to sponsor AIDS training for the entire workforce. "Susan said she didn't go high enough in her demands for the settlement," said Tess Ewing, the local's president. "But it was a big victory."[44]

The volatility of co-workers' fears led many LGBT union people to urge AIDS education, if only to prevent discrimination and abuse. The Centers for Disease Control issued guidelines for safe practices at work and advisories on "universal precautions," but employers failed to purchase basic gear or to implement training. Queer unionists who worked in health fields witnessed dangerous situations every day and were hardly surprised when straight co-workers panicked.

In 1986, an X-ray technician at Temple University's dental school refused to prepare the mouth of a patient with AIDS. When she was charged with insubordination, she called her union, AFSCME Local 1723. Gary Kapanowski, a gay man and the president of the local, took the call. He was familiar with the disease and with the realities of prevention, and he sympathized with both the patient and the technician. "I asked her how she thought the patient feels. I said, 'You're supposed to be wearing surgical gloves, so if you put them on, why are you afraid of getting AIDS?'" Kapanowski resolved the immediate complaint but knew that trouble might recur; AIDS education was not part of the dental school's training agenda. "At the time we thought that HIV was transmitted by saliva as well as blood, and dental assistants were concerned because they were washing equipment that had been in people's mouths."

Kapanowski contacted a new organization in town, Blacks Educating Blacks about Sexual Health Issues (BEBASHI). "We provided lunch, and BEBASHI led the training," he said. Local 1723's unit of forty dental assistants came, as did graduate students, doctors, and dentists. "I thought the school should have done this education, but when it was all over, people thanked the union."[45]

Levels of AIDS awareness in American workplaces were terribly uneven. John Ware, an autoworker in Detroit who died in 1999, began working for Chrysler at the Mack Avenue stamping plant in the early 1970s, where he was a leader in the United National Caucus and served UAW Local 212 as an elected committeeman (steward). In 1981, he transferred to Chrysler's Sterling stamping plant and to UAW Local 1264. Married and the father of two children, he also had a male lover. In 1988, he learned that his lover had AIDS. Ware assumed that he, too, was infected and kept his silence. He knew how quickly rumors could fly at an auto plant and trusted neither the company's Employee Assistance Program nor the union.[46] "He believed that because it was a stamping plant where people sustain cuts, he would face severe hostility," wrote his attorney, Ellis Boal.[47]

Ware was depressed. He took a six-week leave from work, was hospitalized, and drank heavily. A two-year record of unexcused absences led to his discharge, followed by a conditional reinstatement. In April 1990, he violated his "last chance agreement" and was fired, just two months short of twenty years' seniority, when he could have cashed out his pension and retired on disability.[48] Ware lodged a grievance, but in January 1991, the Local 1264 representative withdrew the claim before it could be argued in arbitration. Throughout this period, Ware did not reveal his bisexuality or the positive results of the HIV test he had taken in October 1990. In February 1992, Ware appealed his grievance to the UAW's Convention Appeals Committee, the union-wide internal review board. This time, he disclosed his HIV status. The committee expressed sympathy but six months later turned him down. It wrote that a long-term insured sick leave could have been arranged, to be followed by permanent and total disability support, "had Ware been forthright with those at the plant directly charged with addressing the sensitive employee problems. . . . Once beaten it's too late for Ware to remember that he had a 'secret' weapon in reserve." The opinion concluded with a ringing recommendation: "This committee, like the UAW generally, is acutely and soberly aware of the need for education in this area. It is not enough to understand the nature of this epidemic. We need to take effective action to help its victims."[49]

All members of the Convention Appeals Committee were delegates to the UAW's next bargaining convention, but their recommendations on AIDS were not included on the agenda. Neither the committee nor the delegates moved that the UAW "take effective action" by making AIDS awareness programs a demand of the upcoming contract.[50] The committee's charge had always been the oversight of grievances and contract enforcement. Changing collective bargaining and grievance systems so that local unions could better represent queer members was a different mission altogether.

National unions like the UAW adopted resolutions to affirm the rights and needs of sexual minorities in the workforce, but good intentions were not enough. The UAW stumbled because its advocacy for AIDS cases was neither consistent nor focused. Another path to power, away from the national arena, would be necessary to transform goodwill into viable action. Rank-and-file activists found that path by organizing queer caucuses in their local unions.

The AIDS Crisis: A Union Committed and Divided

SEIU Local 250 represented thirty thousand hospital workers at voluntary and public facilities in the Bay Area, and in the 1980s it was confronting two enormous challenges: the pressures of AIDS in health workplaces (San Francisco's hospitals were at the epicenter of the crisis) and an entrenched union leadership unready for rapid economic consolidation in the health industry and unwilling to work with activists in the ranks. Gay union members developed an influential brochure on AIDS in the workplace and used it to shape an effective program of worker education. Some of the activists who participated in the AIDS project were also involved in an insurgency within the local.[51]

John Mehring migrated to San Francisco from Oklahoma in 1979, got a job at Presbyterian Hospital as a psychiatric technician, and dove directly into gay community politics. He joined the Harvey Milk Gay Democratic Club and in 1982 helped produce and distribute "Can We Talk," a frank and witty brochure about AIDS, risky behavior, and safe-sex practices. The pamphlet was well received and widely distributed, and Mehring turned his attention to his union. "I knew AIDS was going to mean big problems for health care workers. We had to do something. If workers knew more about AIDS, they would be less fearful of people with AIDS and there would be less discrimination."[52]

Mehring sought fellow workers who shared his sense of urgency and found them in the Committee for a Democratic Union (CDU), an opposition caucus. "A gay man recruited me," Mehring said. "There was heavy gay involvement in CDU. They were supportive of gay people in general."[53] Bob Lewis, another gay psychiatric technician and a shop steward at St. Mary's Hospital, was friendly with many of CDU's gay regulars. "The leadership wasn't doing what they were supposed to," he said. "So after the union meeting, we would go to a bar and talk about overthrowing them."[54]

In the fall of 1983, Mehring called for the formation of a Local 250 AIDS committee. His CDU colleagues connected him with other union members who would be interested, and members of the local's staff were assigned to help. In collaboration with Bay Area Physicians for Human Rights, the group produced "AIDS and the Health Care Worker," a fact sheet that explained what was known about the epidemic, with emphasis on sexual contact and the sharing of needles as probable routes of infection—thus, the low likelihood of transmission through casual contact at work. The committee quickly put the brochure to use in training workshops for stewards and staff.

SEIU adapted "AIDS and the Health Care Worker" to include material on occupational safety and best clinical practices and then distributed it nationally.

Between 1984 and 1987, the brochure went through five editions, including a Spanish-language version, each time absorbing new research about AIDS and HIV; later updates by the national union maintained the standard. For union leaders and labor educators just beginning to struggle with constituents' fears, the work of Local 250's AIDS committee was a model of good sense.[55]

In 1984, CDU captured a substantial minority of seats on the Executive Board, and the local's internal politics grew increasingly fractious. Rising health care costs were roiling some of the union's biggest bargaining units as they prepared for negotiations. Hospital administrators wanted to tighten budgets, make double shifts mandatory, set low priority on the safety of workers, and cut wages. Union members wanted improvements in pay and no speed-ups.

Productive collective bargaining was stymied by divided leadership. The union sustained several important strikes in 1986, including one that lasted for seven weeks at Kaiser-Permanente, a major employer. With Local 250's treasury bankrupt, SEIU imposed a trusteeship early in 1987. The move suspended elections in which CDU activists hoped to win a majority.[56]

Many members of the AIDS committee wanted those elections, but other queer leaders disagreed sharply with CDU's methods and proposals and wanted the trusteeship to continue. "It was a struggle for power, not an issue of gayness," said Mehring. "It was one against another and angry and hurtful."[57] Members rewrote the constitution and ratified it early in 1988, but the trusteeship was not lifted, and a newly elected Executive Board was not seated until December. The new president, Sal Roselli, an openly gay man and an activist during the turmoil, concentrated on stabilizing the local and expanding membership.[58]

Through the troubles, Local 250's AIDS committee maintained its mission. In 1989, the group piloted a "Train the Trainer" program for the AIDS Labor Education Project at the University of California's Labor Institute with eighty workers from hospital departments not involved in direct care. The workers took educational leave to participate in the program and then led training sessions for their co-workers at lunchtime and after work.[59] During the 1990s, Local 250 settled and came to the fore of SEIU's new regional LGBT network, the Lavender Caucuses.

Inside the Public Sector: Queer Union Caucuses Rising

The first queer union caucus was New York City's Gay Teachers Association (GTA), which after 1990 became the Lesbian and Gay Teachers Association. It began as a support group in 1974, when coming out in the profession was still taboo. For many years, the pledge of "Closet Rights Respected" was printed on the newsletter's front page. The group concentrated on making schools safe for themselves and their gay and lesbian colleagues as well as for gay youth in their classrooms. At monthly forums, topics could be professional (gay-appropriate high school reading lists) or political (the difficult progress of the gay civil rights bill in the City Council).

The GTA's members valued independence as much as discretion. They held meetings in members' homes or at churches or at the gay community center rather than at the headquarters of AFT Local 2, the United Federation of Teachers (UFT), the union to which they (and sixty-five thousand other classroom teachers) paid dues. The national union's official record on gay rights was outstanding (a denunciation of antigay bias by the AFT's Executive Council in 1970, followed by convention resolutions in 1973 and 1974), but at the local level, politics took a different tack.

Relations between the gay activists and the UFT leadership were usually strained. For four years, GTA organizers lobbied UFT officials to list their meetings on the calendar of the *New York Teacher*, the monthly newsletter of the statewide federation. Those appeals were consistently ignored. The *New York Teacher* would not even accept the GTA's checks when the caucus tried to pay for ad space for its speakers' bureau. Leaders of the UFT stalled at other important requests, too. For years they would not discuss a pending municipal civil rights bill, testify in its favor before the City Council, or recommend the inclusion of sexual orientation protection in the union contract.[60]

The Gay Teachers Coalition (GTC) formed in San Francisco in 1975 and recruited classroom teachers and other school workers in public and private education. GTC had an aggressive agenda and allied itself with community groups: neighborhood campaigns for better schools, as well as Bay Area Gay Liberation. Politically, GTC kept its distance from the major teachers' unions, although many members paid dues to San Francisco's AFT Local 61 or other regional teachers' unions.

In the spring of 1975, GTC petitioned San Francisco's School Board to include sexual orientation in its revised antidiscrimination policy. Local 61 refused to endorse the proposal, and the School Board voted it down in June. But the coalition campaigned hard to keep the cause alive. Directly after the rejection, GTC posted leaflets throughout the Castro, worked the press, gathered endorsements from politicians and community leaders, and lobbied board members. July's meeting was packed with more than two hundred noisy gay rights advocates who demanded a reversal of the previous vote. That night, GTC secured the inclusion of sexual orientation in the School Board's policy.[61]

The antigay Briggs Initiative of 1978 in California changed how teachers' unions worked with their queer constituents.[62] Lesbian and gay teachers' groups active in New York City, San Francisco, Boston, and Los Angeles pushed their unions to pay attention to the trouble. In a report on Briggs, "California's Proposition 6 Aims at Homosexual Teachers but Is Threat to All," the *New York Teacher* featured interviews with five leaders of the GTA.[63] The groups in San Francisco and Los Angeles functioned as caucuses in their local unions and as coalition partners with community-based activists. Teachers' unions joined the labor section of the Bay Area Committee against the Briggs Initiative. That summer at the convention of the California Federation of Teachers, queer delegates and their allies from San Francisco, Los Angeles, and San Diego urged unity against the menace that was Briggs.[64]

New York's GTA began as an outsider group, almost by mutual consent with the UFT, but that relationship changed during the 1980s. Gay and lesbian issues were playing a more meaningful role in the city's political life, and the GTA was offering activities that appealed to diverse interests: monthly forums, an essay contest for high school students, collaborations with parent groups. The GTA formed new alliances with labor, educators', and gay rights organizations, and in 1987 the group joined a lawsuit against the Board of Education brought by two lesbians and a gay man who wanted their benefits plan to include their partners. The case took five years to settle.[65] Central to its eventual success was the GTA's coalition with the Lesbian and Gay Issues Committee (LAGIC), an officially sanctioned caucus of the city's largest, most powerful municipal union, District Council 37 of AFSCME.

With a membership of 135,000 city workers in 1988, District Council 37 was larger than many national unions. It governed fifty-six local unions, each with its own Executive Board and occupational jurisdictions. LAGIC was based in the council rather than in local subsidiaries because its founders were setting their sights on central headquarters and its bargaining apparatus, cultural resources, and political machinery.[66] Several of LAGIC's founders came from white-collar locals that already sponsored their own gay projects or gay committees—for example, Public Library Guild Local 1930, Clerical Workers Local 1549, and Public Health Local 768. They figured that a council-wide organizing strategy supported by the council's full power would give them access to lesbian and gay union members who were represented by locals that were less supportive of LGBT issues—for example, Off-Track Betting Employees Local 2021 or Construction Laborers Local 376.

More than a decade after the GTA began meeting, LAGIC's arrival was warmly received by its parent union. District Council 37's leaders had been giving prominent testimony, year after year, in favor of passage for New York City's gay civil rights bill, which finally became law in 1986. In 1990, LAGIC received official sanction from District Council 37, but well before the go-ahead, the subcommittees had begun recruiting.

Official status in District Council 37 meant a regular spot on the agenda at the council's monthly meetings and access to crucial resources—for example, the services of AFSCME's lobbyists in Albany. When issues vital to gay union members came up before the State Legislature, LAGIC could call on the union and its professionals in Albany to work the political connections. Generous material support included an office at headquarters, a budget, a telephone, and rooms for meetings and social events. At the city's annual Lesbian and Gay Pride celebration of 1992 and for several years thereafter, LAGIC members decorated the District Council 37 flatbed float and danced their way down Fifth Avenue to loud thumping disco music, equal to the sounds of any float in the parade.[67]

For all their differences in structures and jurisdictions, GTA and LAGIC were well suited for successful collaboration. Benefit equity was a common and vital issue, and both groups pressed their parent unions to move the reform as expeditiously as possible. While GTA kept its lawsuit alive, LAGIC was at the table, pushing its proposal for District Council 37's contract talks in 1990. The contract that the union and the city signed included the significant first step toward full partner benefits: paid bereavement leave.

In the next contract cycle, LAGIC proposed comprehensive domestic partner benefits for gay and straight workers, active and retired. The committee argued that queer workers' rights would be best protected by extending the coverage to as many union members as possible. The council's committee on disabilities and its retirees association supported the proposal. Many of their heterosexual constituents were living in domestic partnerships and could not marry without losing income—for example, workers whose partners received disability insurance from the State of New York or widowed members who received survivors' payments from Social Security.

A citywide coalition formed to build momentum for the domestic partner proposal. LAGIC joined gay political groups and unions representing municipal administrators, police, and firefighters. The teachers' slow-moving lawsuit woke up. A week before the mayoral election of November 1993, a tight race between David Dinkins and Rudolph Giuliani, Dinkins settled the teachers' lawsuit and District Council 37's contractual negotiations in one stroke with an executive order that granted full domestic partner benefits to all city employees—a workforce of 350,000—and retirees.[68]

Other public sector unions supported similarly effective caucuses. Social service workers in Massachusetts were represented by SEIU Local 509, a statewide organization. Ginny Cutting, who worked as a claims examiner on AIDS cases and served as delegate to the union's Executive Board, wanted to see LGBT issues on Local 509's agenda and in 1987 placed a notice in the union newsletter to see whether there was interest. Some who replied were looking for fellowship; others were looking for political action. They met regularly for a year, before receiving official standing as the Gay and Lesbian Concerns Committee (GLCC), with a budget, a meeting space, and access to the union's legislative apparatus. Michael Dias was one of many GLCC members drawn to the group simply for queer community. "At first I was not even aware of the grievance process," he said. "But the committee pulled me into union concerns."

Dias set about learning his way around the union, and in 1993 his unit of eighty social service caseworkers elected him steward. He represented two lesbians who were fired in what he suspected was a case of bias. They lost their grievance, but in the process Dias came out at his workplace and in the union, "because those who aren't out should know where to go if they need the support." The state's Department of Social Services was a liberal workplace, Dias thought, but once he was out, he found day-to-day office culture much less friendly. "Other stewards were uncomfortable," he said. "Some people don't talk to me. But now I see myself as getting stronger in the union and stronger about gay rights."[69]

Queer caucuses in public sector locals influenced the development of national union strategies in AFSCME and SEIU during the 1990s. The caucuses supported LGBT issues in collective bargaining and strengthened local organizing. Both unions developed national plans to link the local LGBT groups to larger union purposes. AFSCME connected LGBT caucuses and committees in district councils and large locals to its national advisory board on gay and lesbian policies. Educational and political conferences sponsored by SEIU's regional Lavender Labor networks influenced the union's national policies.[70]

An Injury to All

The Oklahoma State Legislature enacted the nation's first statewide antigay law—the Helm Act—in April 1978, by a majority of 88–2. The law required the dismissal of school employees who engaged in "public homosexual activity" and proscribed the employment of any teacher, gay or straight, who advocated "public or private homosexual activity."[71] Later that year, California's more notorious Proposition 6, the Briggs Initiative, which would have mandated similar sanctions, was defeated by public referendum. The absence of organized resistance to Oklahoma's measure meant that seven years of civil rights litigation were needed to reverse the law. The Briggs Initiative was stopped at the ballot box, with a coalition of labor, gay, and civil rights groups playing a crucial role in the campaign.[72]

For the next fourteen years, there were no more attempts to codify antigay discrimination as state law. But when a new wave of voter initiatives put both Colorado and Oregon on the firing line, a pattern reemerged. Voters in Colorado, a state with weak gay, labor, and civil rights defenses, approved an antigay amendment to the state constitution; in Oregon, however, gay, labor, and civil rights groups mounted resistance vigorous enough to persuade the majority of voters that the measure should be rejected.

Colorado for Family Values (CFV), a small Christian group based in Colorado Springs, successfully petitioned to have its amendment to the state constitution placed on the November 1992 ballot. Behind CFV's homegrown efforts stood two formidable national organizations deeply rooted in Colorado's right-wing political culture: Focus on the Family and the Christian Coalition. All agreed that the time was ripe for a new message that would replace the lurid rhetoric of the "Save Our Children" movement with more sober-sounding political principles. Campaign resources would be focused on motivating voters who were already sympathetic to the Christian Right.

The ballot measure asked voters whether they would have Article II of Colorado's constitution prohibit the enforcement of any "statute, regulation, ordinance or policy whereby homosexual, lesbian, or bisexual orientation, conduct, practices or relationships shall constitute or otherwise be the basis of, or entitle any person or class of persons to have or claim any minority status, quota preferences, protected status or claim of discrimination."[73]

The agenda was specific: the curtailment of standing gay civil rights ordinances in Aspen, a resort town (1977); in Boulder, a university center (1987); and in Denver, the state's capital and largest city (1990), as well as the suppression of any future efforts. The initiative further threatened two recent executive orders of Governor Roy Romer: to protect people with AIDS from all discrimination (1989) and to protect state employees from employment discrimination (1990).[74]

On its surface, the amendment seemed to be neutral. The campaign's statements to the general public made no mention of "saving" children. Its watchwords, "equal rights, not special rights," seemed solid and reasonable and suggested the unfairness of "privileges" bestowed on queer citizens by equal protection laws. But according to the sociologist Didi Herman, CFV's essential purpose was "to construct lesbians and gay men as a minority undeserving of rights."[75]

CFV concentrated on this goal at the grassroots level. In rural districts and suburban neighborhoods, church-based activists worked intensely with individual voters. There the talk was all about homosexual pedophilia and eternal damnation, the standard fundamentalist rhetoric of fear and loathing that had won municipal antigay referenda in the late 1970s in Miami, Wichita, St. Paul, and Eugene, Oregon.[76] Meanwhile, CFV maintained a low profile in Colorado's cities and holiday resorts by keeping advertising to a minimum, avoiding the news media and refusing debates with liberal opponents.

Equal Protection Colorado (EPOC) ran a countercampaign that raised and spent twice as much money as its opponents, received endorsements from civil rights and liberal religious groups, and maintained open relations with the press. Polling in the early months indicated that Amendment 2 was likely to be defeated. But EPOC squandered the lead by failing to activate supportive citizens beyond the usual liberal enclaves in Denver and the mountain towns, where skiing and tourism were the mainstays of local economies. Their overconfidence lasted into the final weeks of the campaign. Meanwhile, CFV was reserving the last of its resources. On election eve, volunteers were deployed to the likeliest strongholds throughout the state. They moved door to door, distributing 800,000 brilliantly inflammatory brochures. The next day, Amendment 2 garnered 814,000 votes, a majority of 53.4 percent.[77]

EPOC's failure to make a preelection push and its incapacity to organize beyond the liberal base were huge strategic mistakes, but its detachment from organized labor was another remarkable weakness. LGBT activists in Seattle and California had pushed their unions for financial support, phone banks, member lists, and political expertise. Union-conscious campaigners in Colorado would have understood the necessity of grassroots organizing to get out the vote. They probably would have urged EPOC to canvass working-class black and Latino neighborhoods, and they would have reminded white union members in the blue-collar suburbs that an injury to one is an injury to all.

But Colorado is a right-to-work state, and its labor movement was not inclined to undertake such a task. In 1987, unions and the gay rights movement did collaborate when brewery workers struck Coors's main plant. Gay communities far from Colorado sustained the boycott of Coors products; the cause faltered only when the AFL-CIO withdrew. But in 1992 there was no gay-labor connection in the run-up to Amendment 2.[78]

The majority of Colorado's local unions represented blue-collar workers: the construction brotherhoods, the Machinists, the Teamsters. Gay organizing did not exist in any of these locals in 1992, and antidiscrimination resolutions on sexual orientation that the AFL-CIO had approved a decade earlier were absent from their agendas. As for Colorado-based affiliates of AFSCME, SEIU, and other progressively inclined unions in the public and service sectors, their regional caucuses for gay rights were just starting up. Local units were not yet connected to those networks and were not involved in EPOC's efforts.

For this election, Colorado's labor movement was focusing its meager political clout on a different voter initiative, the Taxpayer Bill of Rights. Amendment 10 would severely curtail funds for schools and other public services.[79] The two amendments appealed to conservatives, but in different ways. The focus of Amendment 10 excited fiscal conservatives, while Amendment 2 fit in with the agenda of social conservatives. With both initiatives on the same ticket, the right had two very compelling issues with which to cross-mobilize its base. By contrast, the labor movement and the gay movement pushed their issues in political isolation.

Amendment 10 inspired taxpayers' rebellions in other states and still stands as the country's most restrictive limitation on public spending. The life of Amendment 2 was shorter. November's election results arrived just as the state was preparing for the winter tourist season. Participants in Aspen's annual gay ski festival were shocked that Colorado had wiped out their rights. The vacationers reacted with a national three-year boycott of the "hate state" that cost the convention and tourism industries $40 million and tainted Colorado's name as a hip vacation destination for many more years.[80]

Amendment 2 was never enforced. Just as its restrictions were about to take effect in January 1993, the American Civil Liberties Union and other national organizations launched the first of a battery of legal challenges (*Romer v. Evans*). The tennis champion Martina Navratilova, a resident of Aspen, was one of the plaintiffs, and eight states and the District of Columbia filed amicus briefs; only one AFL-CIO union joined the suit: AFSCME. For the next three years, state and federal appeals courts consistently ruled against Amendment 2. The U.S. Supreme Court struck it down in 1996.[81]

The defeat of gay rights at the polls in Colorado in 1992 paralleled a resoundingly successful campaign in Oregon, where an antigay ballot initiative, Measure 9, was rejected by 57 percent of the electorate. One important difference between Colorado and Oregon was the intensity of union involvement. Oregon's labor movement participated in a robust coalition to hold the line on bigotry and backlash. The campaign in 1992 was the first of a series of statewide electoral battles that continued into the twenty-first century. The courts were never involved.

Busting Bigotry in Oregon

The antigay referendum known as Measure 9 was defeated in 1992 by a coalition that drew strength from several of Oregon's political cultures. Gay organizers were the first to sound the alarm, but other activists who understood the religious right as a threat to the safety of their communities quickly found their way into the fight. Civil liberties and liberal religious organizations, the usual first volunteers in such an effort, enlisted Native American, Latino and African American communities, rural organizations, Catholic prayer groups, veterans' associations, moderate Republican clubs, student groups, and advocates of rights for the elderly.[82]

Measure 9 proposed eliminating safeguards for the civil rights of sexual minorities from Oregon's Bill of Rights and banned future adoption of such protections. It proposed the prohibition of state funds or facilities "to promote, encourage, or facilitate homosexuality, pedophilia, sadism or masochism"; it required "homosexuality, pedophilia, sadism or masochism" to be recognized by all state agencies, "specifically the State Department of Higher Education and the Public Schools . . . as abnormal, wrong, unnatural, and perverse . . . to be discouraged and avoided."[83]

SEIU Local 503, the Oregon Public Employees Union, quickly became an important center of resistance. Local 503 was a huge and lively union with a big political agenda and a membership of twenty thousand. Measure 9 mandated the dismissal of any of them who were openly gay or even openly sympathetic to gay rights.

The controversy's roots lay in the backlash against feminism in the mid-1980s. In 1986, radical conservatives mounted a strong challenge in the Republican primary to the candidacy of Senator Robert Packwood, an advocate of abortion rights. With the support of feminist organizations, Packwood won, but the radical conservatives had found their political audience. They formed the Oregon Citizens Alliance (OCA) and in 1987 lobbied against funding for preschool programs (because they were "anti-family") and parental leave (because it was "antibusiness").

In 1987, the union's lesbian and gay network had just become active among subunits along the Willamette Valley, near Oregon's western coast. Local 503 was surveying the membership in preparation for contract talks, and queer activists urged all union members to request the addition of sexual orientation to Article 22, the nondiscrimination section of the contract. This would be the first mention of gay rights in the union agreement, and Ann Montague, a clerical worker at Oregon State University in Corvallis, spoke about its importance to her colleagues and to other office workers in Salem, the state capital and her hometown. She contacted Bob Ralphs, who chaired Local 503's sub-local at the Dammasch psychiatric hospital in nearby Wilsonville. "We had gay members throughout the unit, and our Executive Council was mostly queer," said Becky Capoferri, another officer at Dammasch. "As far as noneconomic terms were concerned, that Article 22 issue had more interest than any other item."[84]

Local 503's economic ambitions were formidable ones. Capoferri, Montague, and other feminists in leadership wanted to eliminate patterns of gender-based wage inequity among state workers. Many single mothers who worked for the state were being paid so poorly that they qualified for food stamps and had children in school who were eligible for free lunch. The feminists wanted to make "comparable worth" their top demand for the new contract. The union and the state would sponsor studies of work performed in all female-dominated job classes, to be followed by reevaluations of those jobs and system-wide adjustments of wages. A similar plan by the federal government of Canada had been mandated in 1977, and in 1981, employees of the city of San Jose, California, represented by AFSCME Local 101, went on strike for two weeks to win job studies followed by wage adjustments. At the state level, Minnesota and Washington implemented wage adjustments following comparable worth studies during the early 1980s.[85]

The bargaining team arranged public hearings on the campus of Oregon State University, featuring testimony by women who could barely pay their bills. Montague, whose take-home pay was $568 a month, pressed the men of Local 503 to support the campaign. "We said, 'These are your wives and your daughters.' The men understood that it meant more money for their whole families if we could win this."[86]

Local 503 walked out in September 1987, with comparable worth the leading issue. This was a "rolling strike," a weeklong series of three-day actions at sites throughout the state. Capoferri recalled the enthusiasm at Dammasch. "We were the stars of that strike. We had 97 percent compliance and maintained two picket lines over three shifts." Although the plan was to balance three days of picketing with two days of work, "We stayed out for five days. We just couldn't get our people to go back." The strike was settled quickly, and the final agreement included substantial economic adjustments for workers at the bottom. "We had a lot of women in low-paid job classes. They had been eligible for low-income housing, but after we settled the strike, [they were] not anymore."[87]

The new contract added protection of sexual orientation, an innovation that set the pace for the rest of the state's workforce. Workers represented by

AFSCME Council 75 negotiated similar safeguards in their next contract, and Governor Neil Goldschmidt issued an executive order to extend sexual orientation protection to administrators and other employees of the executive branch.

To fiscal conservatives, pay equity was a terrible idea: state taxes would underwrite the studies and the corrections of sex-based imbalances in wages. But the expansion of rights for homosexuals employed by the state was far more worrisome than wage adjustments, as far as radicals in the OCA were concerned. They counterattacked with a petition drive to place a referendum question on the ballot for November 1988. The rights that had been ratified in the contract could not be taken away, but Measure 8 would repeal the governor's executive order. The OCA distributed campaign literature that featured vivid photos of men having sex. Capoferri noted the reaction at Dammasch: "Our members looked around and realized that the officers were all queer. Some of them said, 'I'd really like to be a steward, but I'm afraid people will think I'm gay.'" The referendum passed by 53 percent. "It was our first round with the OCA, the first time they tasted queer blood."[88]

The OCA's next effort was the Abnormal Behaviors Initiative of 1991, which proposed amending Oregon's constitution to ban "the promotion of homosexuality, pedophilia, sadism, masochism, necrophilia and bestiality." It would also nullify all civil protections for sexual orientation. For some advocates, the inclusion of necrophilia and bestiality was too much, so the OCA withdrew the initiative entirely. A modified proposal for the election of 1992 retained homosexuality, pedophilia, sadism, and masochism, as well as the annulment of statewide civil protections. This version was buttressed by local initiatives aimed at primary elections for the cities of Springfield and Corvallis and in November's general election for the city of Portland: to rescind municipal human rights ordinances specific to gays and lesbians.[89]

Ann Montague and the gay and lesbian caucus of Local 503 had been developing a training program for shop stewards on discrimination at the workplace. "I knew we had to start at home, with the union," said Capoferri, now a staff organizer.[90] "Our timing on the stewards' training proved to be just right," Montague wrote. "Had the educational work not been done over the previous year, I doubt that our union would have been ready to oppose Measure 9 as aggressively as we did."[91]

The first round of local elections in spring 1992 came out a draw. In Springfield, the OCA won its bid to exclude gays and lesbians from civil rights protection by a margin of 55 percent to 45 percent, but in Corvallis, 65 percent of voters rejected the attempt. Meanwhile, the OCA was petitioning at shopping malls in Portland's suburbs.

The measure would need eighty-nine thousand signatures to be placed on the ballot. Bob Ralphs, who had been an officer of Local 503 and a picket captain at Dammasch during the 1987 strike, was now volunteering full-time for Portland's No on Hate Political Action Committee. He devised a system of rapid responses to squelch the OCA's petitioners: Bigot Busting. Capoferri and other union people assisted on weekends:

> The OCA was everywhere and desperate, so we mobilized, too. Some of the mall managers would call us when the OCA showed up. We'd stand twelve feet away from their table and talk to people who were approaching them. We would make a ruckus, and then people would give their table wide berth.
>
> It's hard to calculate how many signatures we actually prevented, but we believe it was about the same margin that brought the OCA underneath what they needed to repeal Portland's city ordinance. That piece didn't make it to the polls.[92]

Nevertheless, with 137,000 signatures, the OCA handily won a place for Measure 9 on the next statewide ballot.

The OCA's campaign aroused wide opposition. Religious and civil rights groups rallied with community organizations. "It's a danger to us all," declared the chairs of the state's Republican and Democratic parties, appearing together for a bipartisan "No on 9" television spot. The state AFL-CIO warned that "passage of Measure 9 would create a climate of intolerance, and could result in chilling business trade with other states, reducing the number of out-of-state visitors and tourists. Jobs would be lost. Oregon doesn't need such negative publicity and we can't afford it."[93]

The list of "abnormal behaviors" was colorful but far less alarming to trade unionists than the OCA's plan to annul rights that had been established through collective bargaining. Alice Dale, Local 503's executive director, called together a "No on 9" labor coalition to oppose the measure and assigned Capoferri to the campaign full time. Union endorsements meant money and volunteers and the possibility of educating a broader electorate than the gay community's usual liberal allies. The AFT, AFSCME, and NEA were obvious partners; like Local 503, their constituents stood in the direct line of Measure 9's fire. Other unions came in: affiliates of the Communication Workers, the Postal Workers, the United Food and Commercial Workers, and, in the last weeks, the Teamsters. Local unions in manufacturing, construction, and the maritime industries stayed neutral; no unions endorsed.

Some Local 503 members in Oregon's eastern counties objected to the "No on 9" campaign and resigned their membership. But Salem, the state capital, is in the West, and that is where fifteen members employed at Oregon State Hospital joined their chief officer at a press conference—on hospital grounds—to denounce Local 503's advocacy. "He was threatening to lead the entire unit out of the local, and some of the people who wanted to withdraw were in the OCA," said Capoferri. She found out that the officer had worked part time as a bouncer at a topless bar, "and we let that be known. Once these ultra-Christian conservatives realized that they were taking moral directions from a bouncer in a titty bar, they came back to the union pretty quickly."[94]

One morning, a disgruntled young waiter visited Capoferri in her office. He was a member of HERE Local 9, and he wanted his union to endorse the labor coalition. She said:

> He didn't think the leadership was representing the membership. So we told him what to request of the union's Executive Council. At first they wouldn't listen to him because there was no quorum at the meeting, so we showed him how to stack the next meeting. He got thirty members to show up, gay guys and Latina women. He got the Executive Council to donate to our campaign and to recommend "No" in their newsletter.
>
> It was the beginning of new leadership for that local. The members got together with the staff and took over. Now they're a union that's organizing.[95]

Measure 9 was defeated, 56.5 percent to 43.5 percent. At the victory rally, Alice Dale pledged training on combating homophobia for all stewards in Local 503.[96]

The OCA soon announced a new campaign for 1993. This version would tamp down the fiery rhetoric and apply the line of "no special rights" that had worked so well for the Christian Coalition in Colorado. But what worked in Colorado fell flat in Oregon. For the next eight years, whenever the OCA attempted a referendum against gay rights, the proposal would lose—thanks to a continuing alliance of Oregon's citizens in all of their racial, political, religious, economic, and sexual diversity.

Labor's role in defending the civil rights of all LGBT workers was disproportionate to the number of Oregonians who were actual union members. But the labor movement's influence among working families in Oregon's socially conservative interior regions was substantial. There, unions were essential to the economy of communities, and their advocacy of an issue was more likely to be trusted than messages from less familiar political sources.

Throughout the late twentieth century, union membership fell off, in Oregon and in the nation. Bucking that trend would have required huge recruitment efforts, and in the manufacturing sector, campaigns to organize the unorganized fared poorly. Queer issues had better chances of being taken up by local unions in the public sector and in service industries, where membership was flourishing and recruitment campaigns were more likely to succeed. These unions formed effective alliances with popular movements and ran strong political campaigns. These were the unions that fostered LGBT caucuses, explored gay-labor political collaborations, and won innovative benefits. But during the 1980s, unions were not yet ready to target queer workplaces for recruitment drives or see queer workplace issues as valuable items for the organizing agenda.

LGBT people were employed in shops where unions were recruiting, but their queerness either went unnoticed by organizers who were cultivating the workforce or was disregarded as a useful factor in the development of a drive. As gay people heightened their visibility in the politics and culture of their own expanding communities, union organizers began to pay attention. They considered how queer people might be enlisted in the basic and vital mission of the labor movement: to organize the unorganized.

III

Conflict and Transformation

5

Organizing the Gay Unorganized

Talking Union, Talking Queer

The election was imminent; its outcome, uncertain. Bill Olwell's union, the United Food and Commercial Workers (UFCW), was campaigning at a new meat-packing plant in a small town in the southern Midwest, one of several in the profitable company the union had targeted. The company was eager to consolidate operations in expanding markets, and this shop was key to its strategy. Olwell, the UFCW's executive vice-president, had flown out from headquarters in Washington, DC, for a cookout in the backyard of a union supporter. The other guests would be employees from the Quality Control Department, all twenty of them gay men.

Having had no luck organizing the men, the union's field organizer had turned to Olwell. "We can't crack 'em," he reported. The men of quality control constituted less than 10 percent of the workforce. But because their jobs were central to every other operation in the plant, they were vital to the larger campaign. Would they listen to Olwell's message? He planned to talk union with them, using gayness as his gambit. Before his rise to national prominence, he had tried to hide his own homosexuality, and he recognized in this tight-knit group gay habits of self-protection. "There are lots and lots of pockets of gays out there in rural America," he said. "They're segregated and they don't talk about it, but it's known and accepted as long as you don't flaunt it in public."

The company had been spreading fear for weeks, and Olwell knew that the men in quality control were afraid for their jobs. Supervisors had told them that union dues had underwritten violence and corruption in the modern labor movement. These were "captive audience" sessions, scripted and directed by union busters, consultants retained by management to keep the unions out. Documentary movies enhanced the message with sinister images of the AFL-

CIO's elderly chiefs, cloaked in clouds of cigar smoke. Should the union prevail, the bosses warned, layoffs were possible, and a shutdown of the entire plant was not out of the question. For any worker who seemed resistant, there were confrontational one-on-one sessions to threaten that individual's job.

"I can hire one half of the working class to kill the other half" is how the railroad financier Jay Gould put it in the 1870s, when strikebreakers from the Pinkerton National Detective Agency disrupted union organizing by provoking bloody brawls. Latter-day union busters of the 1970s and 1980s were not so vulgar as to break heads. Instead, they skirted labor laws the best they could. For example, they ran training sessions for line supervisors on how to run compulsory meetings, strictly rehearsing them in the delivery of dire news, but refraining from direct contact with their real targets, the workers. "Union avoidance was the hot topic and hot business of the decade," wrote one veteran union buster.[1]

"Those guys had the typical stereotypes of trade unionists, big burly white males running roughshod, wasting money," Olwell recalled. His very presence contradicted the propaganda. Here he was, a top union guy, trim, confident, openly gay. He was enjoying the cookout, pleased to soak up the hospitality, sympathetic and at ease. The evening continued with stories and songs, barbecue and beer. Eventually the holdouts dropped their guard. "A few days later, they had their election." The union was in.[2]

For the UFCW's national program of industrial organizing, Olwell's visit to the gay crew played out as a turning point: a key plant was unionized. The UFCW was a new union, chartered by the AFL-CIO in 1978 from the merger of several smaller unions, with jurisdictions in retail and food production industries. By 1985, it had become the AFL-CIO's largest affiliate, with a membership of 1.3 million. But after the win at the meat-packing plant, there were no follow-ups, no efforts to locate clusters of queer workers at other shops with ongoing campaigns and appeal to them directly. Could Olwell's intervention have set a useful pattern? Or would it be just another randomly helpful incident along the way?

Union Recruitment and LGBT Workers

The UFCW was one of several unions to change strategies and structures in the 1980s. Other unions, such as the United Auto Workers, the Amalgamated Clothing and Textile Workers Union, and the International Brotherhood of Teamsters, were streamlining internal operations, merging with compatible unions and extending their jurisdictions into related industries and services. Their ambitious programs of restructuring emphasized the launch of aggressive drives into new industries and new territories, including right-to-work states, to counter long-term trends that would be difficult to reverse. Could a renewal of labor's historical mission—to organize the unorganized—offer corrections to the downward drift?[3]

Considerations of workers from sexual minorities were not part of this program. This was as true in the manufacturing sector, where businesses were failing and membership was diminishing, as in the public and service sectors, where organizing was still robust. Nevertheless, queer activists from Ann Arbor to Seattle had been busy since the early 1970s developing union campaigns that would integrate gay and lesbian politics. In California, the Coors beer boycott and the campaign to defeat the Briggs Initiative demonstrated a community's willingness to collaborate in disciplined coalitions. At national union conventions, gay and lesbian delegates formed caucuses that succeeded in adding protection for sexual orientation to their union constitutions. And in New York City in 1982, employees of the *Village Voice* made a winning case for economic equity in their pioneering negotiations for partner benefits.

These were internal union projects. Founding new union shops would mean waging external campaigns on the far tougher turf of nonunion workplaces. Organizing drives in the private sector are overseen by the National Labor Relations Board (NLRB). A union drive can start out with agents contacting workers who seem ready to organize or with employees agreeing to make the initial contact. A committee of workers forms and meets with union staff to assess risks and estimate interest. Only when the prospect seems viable does the committee take the next measure: a public announcement that names the members of the organizing committee and invites other workers to join. The declaration, sanctioned by the NLRB to protect activists from retaliatory dismissals, signals the next stage of open organizing: now the union can strengthen its advantage among core constituents while developing its plan for the wider workforce.

The organizing committee talks union with co-workers and develops priorities for wages, work rules, safety practices, and other aspects of life on the job subject to collective bargaining. These conversations drive the collection of authorization cards that will validate a petition to be filed with the NLRB; no election is permitted until 30 percent of qualified workers have signed. Bosses can agree to the union's petition by simply checking the cards. If more than 50 percent have signed, direct recognition is granted, and negotiations commence.

Employers who prefer a contest ask the NLRB to conduct stipulation hearings that will rule on the validity of the petition, the structure of the bargaining unit, and the voting eligibility of all signers. The employer can make counterclaims that the union can rebut. The board's final determination either rejects the petition or defines the bargaining unit and sets the date for election. The period between the first declaration of the union's presence and the election day may last a few weeks or many months, depending on the weight of arguments between pro- and antiunion forces and the efficiency of the board as it hears stipulations. Meanwhile, the campaign and its goals are publicized: at the shop, in the community, and in the local media. On election day, if a majority of unit members vote "yes," the NLRB can certify the shop and negotiations can proceed.

During the 1960s and 1970s, union organizing campaigns were linked to movements for civil rights. In 1968, Dr. Martin Luther King Jr. took his campaign for economic justice to Memphis to stand with 1,300 municipal sanitation workers who were striking for a contract and recognition of their union, AFSCME Local 1733. He was shot down; the union still stands. Beginning in 1965 and continuing for fifteen years, the United Farm Workers and Cesar Chavez led Mexican American migrants' battles against poverty wages and racial discrimination. Picket lines in the vineyards and lettuce fields were bolstered by public fasting, mass marches, and consumer boycotts.

During the mid-1980s, the public and service sectors of the labor movement maintained their strong sense of workers' rights as civil rights. Although their recruitment programs were effective, other alliances had worn thin, and the will to organize had weakened. Many unions in construction and manufacturing lost membership as their shops closed, but even in fields where business was booming—for example, financial services, information technology, and the hospitality trades—private sector unions were not keeping adequate pace.

The old ways of political radicalism were at a low point during the same period that a new lesbian and gay liberation movement was finding its first political potency. Starting in the early 1970s, pioneers of the movement challenged more and more lesbian, gay, bisexual, and transgender people to come out and live and love openly. Many activists were veterans of the civil rights and women's movements; their agendas reflected those traditions, as well as the unique needs of emerging queer communities. Understanding that their greatest source of power would be communities where they would be welcomed, they settled into neighborhoods that historically had been havens for artists and intellectuals, older gay people, and other outsiders.

Queer pioneers set up clinics and social service centers to take care of their own. They created fresh styles of art, food, politics, and spirituality. An exuberant and sophisticated night scene arose, with sly phallic puns to designate disco bars and bathhouses, as well as a humbler sort of daytime culture with little shops—bakeries, bookstores—named for matriarchal deities. Entrepreneurs started small businesses and ambitiously envisioned economic autonomy in a gay environment.[4] As enlightened managers, they would hire their gay neighbors for jobs that would be humane and more fun than conventional businesses. Work itself would be different, employment a form of community privilege.

These dreams of economic autonomy often excluded the realities of the people who were actually doing the work. Businesses were small, rarely employing more than fifty workers, and managers were almost always other LGBT people. But the presence of a gay boss was no guarantee of justice on the job. Queer employers demonstrated again and again that they would move as surely and swiftly as straight bosses if their power and profits were threatened.

Workers who complained of mistreatment often so feared the trouble a union might bring that they coped with the trouble they knew. Those who did initiate contact with organizers offered complaints common to many nonunion jobs—underpayment for overtime, harassment, abuse, arbitrary discipline—but then failed to follow up. What they wanted was relief, but they were halted by fears of the difficult and deliberate processes that would be necessary if they were ever to get decent pay and fair treatment. Managers recognized the ambivalence and cultivated resistance. They posited the queer workplace, no matter how bad the jobs were, as a rare refuge. The ploy would often work.

First attempts at gay unionization in the 1970s and early 1980s in California roiled queer communities with spontaneous strikes. Organizers call such workplaces "hot shops" and keep tabs on the action with hopes of converting frustration to coherent campaigning. These shops popped with petitions and picket lines but did not move past initial protests.

Focused union organizing arose in the San Francisco Bay Area right after the successful campaign to defeat Proposition 6 (the Briggs Initiative) in 1978. Queer migrants were taking jobs in the expanding and volatile health, hospitality, and clerical service sectors, where upheavals in union politics were stirring a racially and sexually diverse workforce. Rank-and-file activists from leading unions challenged incumbents and agitated for a new agenda. They rooted their unorthodox strategies in successful labor-community alliances.

In two unions, the Hotel Employees and Restaurant Employees (HERE) Local 2 and the Office and Professional Employees Local 3, reformers recognized the predicaments of LGBT workers in queer workplaces and initiated drives directed at their interests. They approached queer communities with an open attitude and found a base. Gay employers put up a hard resistance. They told clients, customers, and the general LGBT public that unionization threatened queer progress. Many shops that attempted unionization failed, and those that did elect unions were not major units. But each success at a gay-staffed workplace marked a wider territory beyond the small unit it represented.

The onset of the AIDS epidemic transformed gay communities throughout the country politically, ethically, and economically. Independent clinics started up on very low budgets, operating as crisis centers staffed by volunteers and financed mainly by private charity. With the epidemic quickening, more public money became available for centers to expand their services and to hire professional clinicians, counselors, and administrative staff. An AIDS clinic in Los Angeles was unionized by direct recognition shortly after it opened in 1985. At other major centers, workers were dismayed by growing discrepancies between their wages and the salaries of directors, their sacrifices and the privileges of management. Organizing efforts in Seattle, New York City, San Francisco, and Washington, DC, were not simply received; intense community politics accompanied harshly contested drives.

Gay Hot Shops: Spontaneous Frustration

Gay businesses prospered in the lively counterculture scenes of large cities and college towns starting in the late 1960s. Throngs of young people were living adventurously and forming their own communities, and LGBT migrants were in the mix. Gay workplaces offered enticing alternatives to straight jobs in a straight world. Language was more casual, and dress codes were more permissive. When Criss Romero quit his corporate job in 1993 to join the San Francisco AIDS Foundation (SFAF), he was pleased that "the place was mellow, and I [c]ould wear my hair very, very long, down to my waist."⁵ Although he and other gay people employed in community businesses appreciated laid-back work rules, they still wanted the basics: good pay, safe working conditions, respect.

Workers would grumble among themselves. A few filed formal complaints with the NLRB or their state's Department of Wages and Hours. Many quit individually; a few walked off the job in groups. Union agents noticed from time to time and attempted to sign protesters to their locals. They understood the jobs and the unfairness, but what puzzled them was the guarded sense of community at these unconventional workplaces. Why were their interventions generating such intense friction? What was so important about those intricate loyalties that bound customers, clients, business owners, and workers? And what was it that made the obvious next step of unionization not quite right?

Queer bosses understood that a union contract would require them to negotiate for power and profits they had thus far held for themselves. Their plans for a self-sustaining queer economy did not include collective bargaining. Scandalous quarrels and vivid job actions ignited strikes at two hot shops: the Gay Community Service Center of Los Angeles (1975) and Labyris Auto Repair in San Francisco (1982).

The Gay Community Service Center of Los Angeles, founded in 1972, supported its busy clinics and peer counseling programs with donations and grants. In 1975, the center relocated to Highland Avenue, with a paid staff of thirty and a strong corps of volunteers. That April, nine staff members and two volunteers confronted the Board of Trustees about financial malfeasance. They were ousted immediately. Other staff made accusations of sex, race, and class discrimination. When management forbade staff from using the center's equipment, funds, or their own salaries to publicize grievances, more staff and volunteers walked out, and a strike was on. Throughout the summer, supporters picketed daily. Some services continued, and a few donors kept writing checks, but as long as the pickets were up, the center's regular clientele stayed away.⁶

Agents from AFSCME Local 1108 visited the lines. The union would have been an appropriate organizer; its jurisdiction was the city's nonprofit service sector. But a proper campaign never materialized. Factions could not agree on their reasons for striking, or even on whether formal collective bargaining would be a solution worth the trouble. Lesbian feminists saw themselves struggling against the "male-dominated hierarchy," while socialists wanted to establish "worker control." Picketing petered out by summer's end, but bad feelings and the boycott lingered for three more years. The dispute concluded with a settlement but still "left a deep scar in the collective memory of the L.A. community," according to the historian Yolanda Retter.⁷

A failed strike at Labyris Auto Repair in downtown San Francisco seven years later agitated the Bay Area's lesbian community.[8] Lynn MacLeod and Nancy Rupprecht, the business owners, had dropped out of their careers as social workers to seek on-the-job training at local auto shops. Once they learned the basics, they took their capital—$1,400 and a collection of second-hand tools—and in 1978 opened a garage.[9] By 1981, Labyris had eight employees, all lesbians. A few came to their jobs with years of training. Others had picked up skills at independent garages, and still others apprenticed. Pay was based on commissions: for each specific job, the shop and the mechanics split the fee for labor.[10]

Labyris was going to be the ultimate dyke workplace: auto mechanics in an all-lesbian milieu serving a primarily lesbian clientele. The sound system played women's music; friends and lovers could drop by and visit; a phone line was available for personal calls; social connections flowed. "Working for and with other women eliminates much of the controversy, the competitiveness and the compulsion of male society," wrote one observer. "You have to deal with less superficiality, which makes it heavier," said a worker.[11]

But with the idealism came economic discontent. Without base salaries, commissions meant fat checks some weeks, thin ones at other times. Work was distributed unevenly. Less experienced employees who performed routine repairs would frequently out-earn expert mechanics whose projects were more complicated and time-consuming. Further friction arose because the owners had no training plans for women who had come to Labyris expecting to acquire basic skills. Experienced mechanics did not want to coach novices if it meant sacrificing earnings from fee-based services. MacLeod was baffled. "We had always tried to be very loose around here in terms of being basic disciplinarians," she said.[12]

During Christmas of 1981, without warning, MacLeod and Rupprecht shut the shop for a week—no paychecks, no bonuses, just a few modest presents. Now the mechanics were really mad. When work resumed, they presented demands: base weekly pay of $200, paid sick days and vacation, a shop supervisor, better ventilation. The bosses countered with "non-negotiable" job descriptions and a schedule of hourly wages. On February 8, the mechanics demanded negotiations. Once refused, they filed unfair labor practice charges with the NLRB and declared their intent to organize. They returned to work the next day as the Labyris Employees Association and found themselves locked out. Picket lines went up directly.[13]

An organizer from Local 1305 of the International Association of Machinists came to the line to collect authorization cards. Local 1305 represented service mechanics at small repair shops; in terms of the trade, this union was a good fit. It was a gay-friendly local, too. Just five years earlier, Local 1305 had been one of the first unions to endorse Harvey Milk's successful run for the city's Board of Supervisors.[14] But then the organizer returned from meeting MacLeod and Rupprecht with the dismaying comment that the bosses "seem like nice girls."

The NLRB was no help either. Having investigated Labyris's finances and commission system, the board ruled the dispute out of its jurisdiction.[15]

Without official sanction, the Labyris Employees Association withered away. Picketing had lasted only a week, time enough to damage business. The skilled mechanics found jobs at conventional garages. MacLeod and Rupprecht were able to maintain the shop for two more years, staffed with temporary "apprentices." Most of the customers never returned.[16]

San Francisco's Gay Workers Enter Labor's Mainstream

HERE Local 2 of San Francisco, one of the largest unions in the city, with seventeen thousand members, was also one of its gayest and most contentious. In 1978, insurgents from the Alliance of Rank and File (ARF), a caucus within the local, ran a robust campaign against a well-entrenched old-line administration and captured three top offices and a close majority of the Executive Board.

ARF's platform focused on the union's most poorly paid jobs and on the immigrants and racial minorities who held those positions. The top priority was to expand external recruitment while restructuring internal governance. Redistribution of power would loosen the conservative faction's grip, support new leadership, and energize community-based recruitment drives. The national administration of HERE sided with the old guard and imposed a trusteeship. A federal judge ruled the intervention invalid and ordered a new election. Most of the insurgents recaptured their previous positions and moved ahead with ARF's program of militant reform, beginning with a contract campaign to raise the pay of hotel workers, whose wages were at the bottom of the union's scale.[17]

In the summer of 1980, at the height of the tourist season, six thousand workers struck forty-six major hotels. Ethnic groups—Mexicans, Chinese, and Filipinos—were the economic base of the hotel workforce, and Local 2 rallied members with their neighbors and families to picket lines and demonstrations that empowered the struggle. After twenty-six days, a settlement was reached. Now the union was on the move, with community action taking a central place in its revitalized organizing strategy.[18]

Gay workers were widely employed in the city's hospitality industry, but gay issues were not on the agenda of the strike. A caucus of lesbian and gay waiters, bartenders, and cooks was part of the reform coalition and wanted to unionize bars and restaurants in the Castro and in other queer enclaves. Newer taverns and cafés, popular with the city's gay male migrants, were underrepresented within the union's vast jurisdiction. These places were typically small affairs and structured differently from the corporate restaurants and hotels in which an immigrant workforce had driven ARF's great wave of union reform.

The Tavern Guild, an association of bartenders and bar owners, had supported the Coors beer boycott, and Local 2 had a good name in the community as an early endorser of the coalition to defeat the Briggs Initiative. But when it came to staff in their own kitchens and front rooms, business owners wanted loyal service and no union cards. Proprietors kept their scenes hot and their businesses successful by hiring cute newcomers for front-of-the-house jobs. "They took it as a privilege to work for these gay establishments," recalled Vince Quackenbush of the Lesbian/Gay Labor Alliance (LGLA).[19] Many employees agreed: tips were good, and a sexy sense of high life could make a night of bar or table service much more fun than tedious talk about health plans, job security, and overtime pay.

Peter Tenney, a cook who often worked as a waiter, would try to talk union with waiters he met at catering gigs. "They were gay-waiter-artist-dancer types" who took no interest in unionization, he said, because "art was the passion. They were not really a waiter but an artist or a dancer." Tenney, a poet and a performance artist, would think, "So, what are those two plates in your hand?"[20] What was being touted as liberation was closer to exploitation. "I'm finding that the gays screw the gays faster than anyone else does," remarked Phil Mathis, a housekeeper at the gay-owned York Hotel. "Being gay and working for a gay person is not what it's cracked up to be."[21]

Local 2's first few attempts in the Castro failed. At the Patio/Bakery, café workers who had been negotiating on their own for many months walked out in December 1979. Local 2 assigned an organizer, a picket line went up, and neighborhood activists rallied. The protest was undermined by local merchants who urged their friends and customers to cross the lines. "If the Patio went union, all the other bars and restaurants would have followed" said Tenney.[22] The strike continued for six months; then new owners took over with new staff. Strikers suspected a sham sale, which would have been a violation of labor law, but had no proof. With prospects for recognition poor, workers halted their protest.[23]

At Church Street Station, a thriving bar and restaurant, Local 2 narrowly lost an election in the fall of 1980. The NLRB sustained the union's charges of unfair labor practices and ordered a second election in the spring of 1981. A gay organizer, Richard Koblentz, took over the campaign, but the margin of loss was even wider: 25–16.[24] Koblentz was also helping eleven gay male housekeepers as they picketed the York Hotel to protest underpayment for overtime. The boss laid them off and then hired replacements through Jobpower, an employment agency with a federal contract to find jobs for queer refugees from Cuba who had come over on the Mariel boatlift. Koblentz informed Jobpower that its federally sponsored clients were being resettled in scab jobs. The agency dropped the York and withdrew the Cubans, but the original eleven housekeepers never got their jobs back.[25]

Many worthy fights, no new members: the Castro needed a sharper strategy, and the union had thus far offered only reactive help. Agents would respond to calls about trouble, a campaign would materialize, and straightaway the boss would offer a tolerable fix, all the while attacking the union as the straight interloper and disturber of gay peace. Whether the organizer himself was gay did not seem to matter.

Gary Guthman had led Local 2's community and labor mobilization during the hotel strike. He and his colleagues in the Organizing Department discussed taking on the Castro. With the hotel contract now secure, the time was right for another community-based campaign, this time on queer turf. Guthman, a straight white man, trusted the militant panache of Local 2's gay rank and file. "We were trying to get an NLRB election at a main-line restaurant downtown, the Lafayette," he said. "The maître d'hotel was an older gay man, very proper and professional, and the customers all knew him. We struck that place for almost a month, and every day he'd be out there on the picket line in his tuxedo."

The organizers decided to sidestep gay-owned businesses. If the goal was to develop a pro-union wedge by appealing to customers and workers, then Local 2's most winnable targets would be medium-size cafés and restaurants staffed or patronized by gays but not owned by gay people. The neighborhood's flourishing restaurant economy offered several opportunities. The scope could be widened once a few shops were won.[26]

This new direction was a creative response to a changed organizing environment. Unions preferred moving to election as quickly as possible, but in a climate that was increasingly hostile to labor, they had to scramble just to hold the line. During President Ronald Reagan's administration, the NLRB and its regional offices were giving managers and their consultants wide latitude. The board would stall on validations for a petition for election, and the extended deadlines would weaken the drive.

Local 2 was going to have to come up with new tactics. Organizers were talking about direct recognition, or the card check, a nimbler process that had worked well in the past and was especially suitable for small bargaining units. When direct recognition is the goal, organizers exceed the 30 percent minimum for an NLRB election by collecting authorization cards from 50 percent or more of workers; they then press management for a review of signatures. The sides either check the cards informally or agree to the count of an independent arbitrator. With a valid majority, the NLRB certifies the count, and collective bargaining commences. An employer can always turn down the union's request for a card check and insist on a formal election, complete with preliminary hearings at the NLRB to contest the voting eligibility of individual employees and to define the jobs eligible for the bargaining unit.

Guthman's first call for a card check turned out well. Little Italy was a midsize restaurant in the Castro and just the kind of shop that he was seeking: a bustling business with an owner who was not part of the gay merchant scene. Lisa Jaicks, a waitress with a family background in liberal politics, had been talking union. The boss was clueless, but only for a while; then he fired everyone. Staff was already on the street when Guthman arrived, so he recommended a push for recognition directly from the line. After four days of noisy picketing and very little income, the boss permitted a card check. Strikers were rehired; Local 2 was certified; and negotiations commenced. "But that guy was tough," Guthman recalled. "To get people to that point, you have to be pretty bad."[27]

Union wins were rarely so rapid. To sustain campaigns, Local 2 would need backup. Guthman relied on LGLA, whose contacts with a citywide network of queer Democratic clubs and other political groups could be activated at short notice. For broader outreach, the union embraced the culture of the Castro. Local 2 rallied LGBT union members and straight allies for a contingent at the Gay Freedom Day parades in June 1981 and 1982. They carried "Local 2 Works for You" signs and chanted union slogans along the route. They were greeted with rousing cheers: Local 2 was on the map.

The next target was Luisa's. "That place was always packed, it was a gold mine in the Castro," said Guthman. The entire staff of twenty-five signed cards; then, when the owner refused negotiations, they walked out. Local 2 and its community supporters spread the word: the restaurant was off-limits, except for the street, where all were welcome to join the line. "We visited Alice B. Toklas and Stonewall [the gay Democratic clubs]. Every night, we had pickets. We could see Luisa through the big glass window just sitting there, all by herself," said Guthman. "I've never seen such effective picket lines. Even if we had only two people, that's all we needed. She held out two months; then we negotiated."[28]

Local 2's battle at the New York City Deli, at Sixteenth Street and Market, ended in a stalemate. James Yu had bought the business in 1982 and dismissed six waiters during his first week of ownership. For the next eight months, he refused to pay overtime, fired several more workers, and harassed those who stayed. Early in 1983, Guthman and the organizing committee presented Yu with authorization cards signed by 80 percent of the staff, more than enough for a card check. Yu would not budge.

Although the staff did not strike, they did demonstrate, intermittently, choosing times when the café was at its busiest. They called the picketing "walk and work." Staffers would serve their shifts, clock out, and then walk the line. Community activists joined them. "Those people were really dedicated. Most of them were gay, and the straight ones had nose rings and tattoos, and they were ready for a fight," said Guthman, who predicted that one weekend of coordinated loudness would be enough to push a settlement. Instead, as soon as the line went up, Yu would close down.[29] "Nobody is going to make any money at that restaurant so long as we picket," boasted one worker. After the seventh walk-and-work demonstration, Yu shuttered the store, posted signs that claimed a change of ownership, and left the Castro for good.[30] The lockout was no victory, and the site at Sixteenth and Market remained empty for years to come. But the action at the New York City Deli was nothing like the standoff three years earlier at the Patio/Bakery. This time it was the boss who was isolated.

Local 2 never broke through to gay-owned businesses, but the campaigns at Little Italy and Luisa's did prove that queer workers could be mobilized when a union reformed itself to become more aggressive in its organizing and more inclusive in its outreach. It was not long before the challenge of confronting gay bosses at gay workplaces was taken up by another union in San Francisco's service sector: Local 3 of the Office and Professional Employees International Union. With a membership of 3,500, Local 3 was one-fifth the size of the hotel and restaurant union. But like Local 2, Local 3 was being goaded by an opposition caucus determined to reform internal governance and eager to make organizing of the queer unorganized a major priority.

Queer Organizing Ripens

A lengthy strike at Blue Shield, a private medical insurer, gave rise to the reform of Office and Professional Employees Local 3. The strike itself failed, but in its aftermath, activists who had walked the picket line and coordinated community support pushed the union to develop an aggressive organizing program that would include among its targets gay-managed businesses and nonprofits. Insurgents ran for union offices, won significant leadership spots, and then launched new campaigns that challenged gay bosses' claims to gay workers' loyalties. Local 3 came to be known as a hotbed for gay-labor solidarity and in the process found its heart for organizing.

Local 3 represented clerical workers in a wide range of workplaces, many in the nonprofit service sector: charities and social service agencies, colleges, unions. Lesbians—some open, others not—had always been part of the city's clerical workforce and Local 3's membership. The union's elections were rarely contested, and contracts ran placidly.

However, in the late 1970s, Local 3 became a union of innovation: clerical jobs changed, and so did the values of the workers. A fresh generation of sexual migrants was settling in the city. The new arrivals were seeking a more tolerant milieu, as well as jobs that could support their quests. The jobs they took required clerical skills but involved very different tasks from those they had known in offices back home.

San Francisco was emerging as a center for the kind of microchip-based modernization that eventually would dominate clerical workplaces throughout the country. The old model of secretaries at typewriters serving individual bosses was giving way to production-driven work environments organized around pools of workers trained in data processing and other rapid technologies. Reductions of the clerical workforce would be one eventual outcome, but ahead of that, the boom was on. Skilled workers could switch jobs frequently, but the flexibility of their assignments at high-volume service centers presented their own pressures. Meanwhile, the basics—fair treatment, workplace safety, raises, and promotions—were as hard to come by as ever.[31]

Union-minded feminists observed the pressures. Could micromanagement by the keystroke and other detached modes of supervision be the beginning of new organizing opportunities that might revitalize the labor movement?[32] Experts in corporate management seemed to agree. "Your Clerical Workers Are

Ripe for Unionism," they warned.[33] But chiefs of the AFL-CIO were lukewarm. They still thought that women in white-collar service jobs were "marginal" and that blue-collar construction and manufacturing jobs performed by men would continue as the core of organized labor.

Blue Shield was Local 3's flagship: 1,100 workers, 80 percent of them female, 60 percent of them Filipino. By the late 1970s, data processing had transformed Blue Shield's claims center into an electronic sweatshop. Fifty-two thousand claims were turned over daily, thirty-seven thousand of them from Medicare and the remainder from insurance programs sponsored by unions in the Bay Area. When the contract came up for renewal in the fall of 1980, the union proposed that production demands be reduced. Blue Shield, pressed by competition from nonunion firms, countered with proposals to cut costs. The workers walked out.[34]

The strike lasted nineteen weeks. Initial participation of 70 percent in the first months lagged seriously toward the end. Blue Shield ignored pressure from client unions and from the wider community, refused negotiations, and eventually quit the city. "They went out to the boonies, Marysville, Placerville," said Nancy Wohlforth, a pension analyst at the Carpenters Trust Fund and a volunteer with the strike committee. "The union tried to organize there, but Blue Shield was the biggest thing ever to come to that town. They were offering benefits and paying five bucks, and that was more than three bucks at McDonald's."[35]

Feminists who had been avid strike supporters continued to meet and eventually formed a caucus, which they called "A Growing Concern" because, said Wohlforth, "our growing concern was that Local 3 wasn't organizing." The caucus members wanted the union's organizing program to prioritize women's issues and gay rights. They put up a booth for the Gay Freedom Day rally in June 1981. "We made it look like a video display terminal, and we talked about repetitive stress and eyestrain," Wohlforth recalled. "Some members made themselves up with papier-mâché eyeballs popping out of their heads. Our leaflets said right up front that gay people need unions."

The caucus ran its first slate in 1983, and Wohlforth was elected to the Executive Board. Three years later, the caucus took more seats, and Wohlforth won the local's top paid position, senior business representative. The old guard did not like Wohlforth's tough politics or her frank queerness and spread a rumor that she was sexually involved with two of her close allies, both straight women. In truth, her love life was not that racy. However, new organizing opportunities were coming up, and Wohlforth's reputation as an openly lesbian union official became an advantage.

The union's first queer campaigns ran at nonprofit service organizations. A committee from the Episcopal Community Service selected Local 3 for its organizing drive because the committee's members "wanted to talk about gay issues in their shop, and my activism made a difference," said Wohlforth. The union won the election; contract negotiations moved swiftly; and Local 3 served the shop attentively. A lesbian who was one of the shop leaders at Episcopal got a new job a year later at the St. Vincent de Paul Society, a Catholic charity. She spoke up for Local 3 when the union approached its eighty employees, and her endorsement clinched the drive.

Local 3 did not go after gay bosses until the late 1980s. Organizers had been talking with employees at the Information Store, a group of fifty young gay men who researched, brokered, and distributed information to link databases with corporate clients. This was a small firm that could not afford first-rate union busters, so when management ordered workers to attend a captive audience meeting, Wohlforth heard about it the next day: "They showed one of those old union-busting films from the 1970s, with the brass of the AFL-CIO, the old bureaucracy. Our guys just laughed. They said to the bosses, 'Do you know that there's a lesbian in charge of Local 3? Have you even heard of the Office and Professional Employees?' We won that shop."

A few years later, Local 3 ran another gay drive at Hospitality House, a self-help program for street youth in the Tenderloin district. Again, there was a captive meeting, this time at a gay bar. "The bosses told the staff that they didn't need a union, that unions are all straight white males." Local 3 retaliated with dinner at a Chinese restaurant and set a much lighter tone. "Our leaflet had information about the Lesbian/Gay Labor Alliance and a picture of me, a co-chair of the group. The workers asked about the gay-labor connection, and we just talked about what unions do," said Wohlforth. "And then they voted yes."[36]

AIDS Clinics Organize

During the early years of AIDS, surviving friends, lovers, and kin joined with the struggling sick to create community-based services specific to a crisis that conventional health systems could barely address. Lay people formed basic systems of care—buddy teams—and took on daily needs of patients too weak to look after themselves. Community health centers started up to integrate medical referrals with social, legal, and financial assistance. Proceeds from charity events financed the few professional salaries an organization could afford, as well as its most necessary services: for the sick, housing, meals, and medical supplies; for the dead, burials; for the worried well, education about safer sex.[37]

By the mid-1980s, clinic populations were diversifying. Slowly the epidemic was coming to be regarded less as a disaster that afflicted a few minorities (hemophiliacs, gay men, intravenous drug users) than as a substantial public health battle to be waged and won by all. The base was still gay, white, and male, but many more than had been counted in the epidemic's early census were people of color. Clients could be mothers, babies, street youth, transgender people, lesbians, or bisexuals. Federal grants and donations from private foundations supported social services, medical care, and new directions in scientific research. By 1990, AIDS clinics had become the best-funded and leading employers of gay people in the nonprofit service sector.

Unions at first did not regard these workplaces as likely organizing projects, but the field was feasible. Workers were exhausted and frustrated. They knew that organizing a union would spark a whole new world of trouble, but they were desperate. "The salary was not great, we were putting in fifty, seventy hours a week, and we had friends and colleagues dying left and right," said Joe Izzo, a counselor at the Whitman-Walker Clinic in Washington, DC. "No matter how we were feeling, we were still expected to continue working."[38] At the Gay Men's Health Crisis (GMHC) in New York City, work sometimes seemed to be taking place in a war zone. Bomb threats were not unusual and required building-wide evacuations. Even on ordinary days "anyone could walk in and have free access. Computers and telephones were being stolen; women's purses were being taken from their desks. The supervisors would be, 'Oh, whatever,'" said Scott Melvin, a case manager. "Nobody was thinking about how work would be structured so that managers and subordinates would get along. We didn't even have a policies and procedures manual."[39]

Staff at most agencies never unionized. But at five leading AIDS centers, during the heaviest years of the epidemic, unions did reach certification. Unions affiliated with the Service Employees International Union (SEIU) sponsored winning drives at the Ed D. Edelman Clinic of Los Angeles (1986), the Northwest AIDS Foundation of Seattle (1989), the San Francisco AIDS Foundation (1994), and the Whitman-Walker Clinic (1993). The drive at GMHC in 1993–1994 was led by District 1199, an independent health care union in New York City, which merged with SEIU in 1998.

The Ed D. Edelman Health Clinic opened in 1985 as an expansion of medical services provided by the L.A. Gay and Lesbian Center's Southern California AIDS hotline. In the clinic's first year, SEIU Local 399 signed up enough nurses and other clinicians to qualify for direct recognition. The new nursing specialty of AIDS care was much in demand in the city's health labor market, and Local 399 was trusted by many staff who knew the organization from previous hospital jobs. Edelman needed skilled people ready to go and did not contest.[40] The first contract, ratified in 1987, included the pledge that the employer would "continue to explore the feasibility of group insurance for significant others."[41]

SEIU, a leading union in the movement for gay rights and AIDS advocacy, by then had negotiated domestic partner coverage for employees of several California municipalities but had not yet bargained for the benefit with private employers. Edelman's contract came up in 1990, and management was now willing to implement its pledge. The terms were spare: Edelman would continue full coverage of workers' policies, with participation in the group plan for domestic partners and heterosexual spouses as an option to be paid separately by union members.[42]

Edelman's example was not repeated at any other major AIDS agency. Four subsequent drives did attain certification, but at three agencies, bruising counter-campaigns effectively left the security of the union deeply compromised. Local 6 at the Northwest AIDS Foundation maintained collective bargaining through four contractual cycles, but union participation dwindled even as staffing expanded. Local 790 at the SFAF held on through only two contract cycles—five years—and the GMHC decertified its union, District 1199, without ever negotiating a first contract. The union at Whitman-Walker, Division 1199-E, was the only one to secure its position well enough to endure with strong agreements into the twenty-first century.

Seattle Story

The openly gay work culture at the Northwest AIDS Foundation (NWAF) was rare for Seattle in the 1980s. The foundation was founded in 1983 as a center for advocacy and counseling. It emphasized social needs rather than direct medical care and offered referrals to doctors and clinics, advocacy for health insurance and subsidized housing, and counseling for mental health problems. Staff came to the jobs with professional credentials in counseling and social work and political backgrounds in gay activism. By 1988, the agency employed forty people.[43]

The epidemic intensified, services and programs expanded, and work rules tightened. Early in 1989, the Board of Directors affirmed management's right to fire at will. A few workers grew concerned enough about their rights to contact organizers from SEIU Local 6, a health care workers' union for the greater Seattle region.

Union representatives made little headway. They were familiar with work cultures of self-sacrifice, but the intensity of NWAF was a much more extreme version of nonprofit zeal than anything they had seen in conventional health workplaces.[44] Most of the staff were inexperienced with unions, and many perceived the drive as an antigay distraction from the profound mission that kept them going: the fight against AIDS. In spite of long hours, modest pay, high stress, and low morale, it was the outside agitators—the union—who took the blame for any trouble that arose.[45]

A consulting attorney guided management's antiunion course with a direct focus on the structure of the bargaining unit. There were no captive audience meetings or tacky movies. The style was low-key; the advice, effective. Key union supporters were promoted to supervisory or professional positions, reclassifications that would compromise their eligibility to vote.[46] Local 6 filed its petition and, after two weeks of hearings, received the ruling that six of those recently promoted would be disqualified from the unit. Only seventeen of the original twenty-three eligible remained.[47]

The union won the election in mid-November by a thin majority, and conflict shifted to the bargaining table. Delegates to the negotiating committee included a faction of those who had voted no, and they insisted on excluding a provision, standard in many contracts, that would affirm workers' rights to walk out. The contract of July 1990 was ratified without the clause as were all contracts that followed.[48]

NWAF received funding increases in the early 1990s to develop more sophisticated services and hire more workers. But increased staffing did not mean new members. In 1996, NWAF had one hundred employees, thirty-one of them eligible for union membership, with only seven paying dues. The rest took advantage of an agency shop rule, ratified with the first contract, that permitted voluntary membership with the payment of fees in lieu of dues. Some made payments to Local 6, but several others claimed "conscientious objections" to turning money over to the union and instead made equivalent donations to the American Cancer Society, People for the Ethical Treatment of Animals, and other charities. "They were political radicals, but they didn't see how the union was helping them, except during contract negotiations or when there was a crisis about layoffs," said Christa Orth, a steward. "With the constant turnover of staff, it was difficult to keep the shop steady."

In 1998, the antiunion faction petitioned the NLRB for an election to eliminate the requirement of dues or fees, to create an open shop. That bid was voted down, "but we still had those charitable donations," said Orth. A few years later, with Seattle's economy booming, "Those same folks quit us and got themselves the good jobs—Amazon, Microsoft, Starbucks."[49]

NWAF merged with the Chicken Soup Brigade, another local AIDS group, to become the Lifelong AIDS Association in 2000. Local 6 held its place in the merger, and the new arrangement eased tensions. "Their managers were less manipulative of those 'nice' service workers," said Marc Earls, president of Local 6.[50] The union itself merged later with 1199 Healthcare Northwest, an SEIU regional affiliate that continues to represent employees of the Lifelong AIDS Association.

Unionization at AIDS Centers in the 1990s

Ardent politics marked the trajectories of three hard-fought union drives during the mid-1990s. The agencies—GMHC, SFAF, and Whitman-Walker—were leaders in community-based AIDS care and renowned for huge outreach, innovative programs, and compassionate service. When unions made their bids, Boards of Directors and administrators responded with hostility. Some bosses blundered; some provoked. Almost all were players in antiunion schemes.

President Ronald Reagan made union-busting respectable in September 1981 when he fired 11,376 members of the Professional Air Traffic Controllers Organization (PATCO) for defying a ban on strikes by federal employees. The decertification of PATCO in late October dismantled an entire union at the center of a critical industry and signaled labor's increasingly endangered status and diminishing influence. Antiunion campaigns flourished and labor relations deteriorated, with few instances of abatement.[51]

The post-PATCO period of diminishing union power coincided with the onset of the AIDS epidemic. While the federal government's antagonism toward organized labor was widely known, its policies on AIDS simply did not exist. Even as the epidemic spread rapidly, Reagan and then George H. W. Bush adamantly stayed their course of neglect. Pilot projects in medical research, health education, and patient services were supported by state grants or private philanthropy, but these thinly distributed resources were inadequate. The AIDS Coalition to Unleash Power (ACT-UP) formed in New York City in 1987 to confront the crisis of deliberate neglect and practiced vigorous acts of civil disobedience. Proclaiming the slogan "Silence = Death," ACT-UP disrupted traffic, television shows, and the functioning of government bureaus.[52]

The first federal AIDS agency, the National Office for AIDS Policy, began under the administration of President Bill Clinton in 1993. Substantial grants enabled independent AIDS centers to upgrade services and expand programs. The rise of increasingly capable treatments, from combination protocols in the early 1990s to protease inhibitor therapy in 1996, improved the chances of many AIDS patients. Educational initiatives emphasized prevention and articulated more clearly and widely than ever how the fight to end AIDS was essential for the safety of all.

AIDS centers had started out poor and were still nonprofit operations. Now the movement to stop AIDS was being taken seriously by a broader public. The money was a profound shift as far as clinics' capabilities were concerned, but the increased funding did little to change the everyday work culture of burnout and self-sacrifice. Wealthy gay business leaders prominent in philanthropy were recruited for leadership boards, and corporate influences grew more persistent. Top administrators were being compensated with six-figure salaries, and a rich range of funding streams emerged to feed multimillion-dollar budgets.

It was then that AIDS service workers began talking union, although few of them foresaw how hard the struggle would become. "It felt disloyal to organize," said Joe Izzo, a staff member at the Whitman-Walker Clinic, echoing sentiments that had hobbled the drive at NWAF in Seattle. In the mid-1990s, Whitman-Walker had become such a troubled workplace that Izzo and his colleagues—like their counterparts in New York City and San Francisco—were ready to take the risk.[53]

Directors did not take the onset of union activity as good news and did what many business leaders would have done. Tough countercampaigns reflected changes in the economics of the epidemic, as well as cold new realities for labor relations in queer communities overall. Managers discriminated with subtlety, harassed with regularity, and sometimes just blatantly broke the law.

Unionization at AIDS clinics meant trouble and liberation all at once. The AIDS workforce was made up of educated people—white-collar workers—who had plenty of gripes but were dubious about fighting hard for themselves. Some wanted, more than anything, to avoid controversy and so resisted unionization. Others expected a fast remedy and were unprepared when the complexity of a campaign presented its own frictions. And there were the clients, many of them eager to help, though vulnerable. At GMHC, they wrote pro-union letters to the board, while a group of volunteers distributed booster buttons that read "Collectively Fabulous" to be worn at the 1994 AIDS walk.

For all the enthusiasm, the organizing drives were loaded with mistakes. Organizing committee members were supposed to push the union message past their own departments but wavered and missed potential allies. Union staff expected widespread suspicions but did not always know how best to encourage activists to overcome their co-workers' mistrust and spread the word. Some union agents were sophisticated enough about queer life to engage community activists to support the campaign, but others served their campaigns poorly by being unprepared for the particularly queer tones natural to the work cultures of major AIDS agencies.

Because the community and the workforce were so deeply driven to keep on with "the fight," union activists were at their best when they were able to expose managerial incompetence. Frequently they found opportunities to do so, because everyday clinical affairs, from fund-raising and financial policies to employee relations and basic supervision, were not always overseen at appropriate professional or ethical levels. Yet the agencies often seemed much safer as workplaces than what was available in the straight world. Managers learned to play those fears. They wielded the familiar principle of queer loyalty against what the unions were offering: labor solidarity.

First in the Fight

The Gay Men's Health Crisis was founded in 1982. Its medical, social, legal, and financial systems, geared to everyday AIDS care in New York City, quickly became models for the rest of the country, and as services expanded, checks from local donors and out-of-state benefactors poured in.[54] GMHC's growth in its first decade reflects the rising status of the fight against AIDS. The group's first office was a free rental in the basement of a hotel in the up-and-coming gay neighborhood of Chelsea. To meet the accelerating epidemic, GMHC purchased its own building in 1988, and by 1993 operations had spread to five nearby sites, where a paid staff of 275—medical specialists, social service workers, fundraisers, counselors, health educators—served more than 3,500 clients on a budget of $25 million.[55]

Scott Melvin arrived in New York City in 1990 at twenty-two and quickly landed a job as a coordinator in GMHC's case management department. His starting salary of $25,000, with health insurance and paid vacation, was on par with compensation standards throughout the city's nonprofit service sector.

Melvin soon began attending lunchtime discussions sponsored by the staff caucus, a group that had been meeting for a year. "We were asking, 'Is this a black disease? A white disease? Is it a poor man's disease? A rich man's disease?'" he said. Before long "we were bitching about what was going on in the office." Complaints, though various and serious, went unresolved "because the issue was always what was happening to people with AIDS."[56]

In the early months of 1992, a multi-drug-resistant tuberculosis broke out in city hospitals among HIV-positive patients, some of them clients of GMHC.

The caucus wanted immediate protection for staff, an estimated 30 percent of whom were thought to be HIV-positive, and pressed for a program of TB tests to be sponsored by the agency. The caucus also demanded high-efficiency particulate air filters, standard protective equipment for TB environments, to be installed right away in any rooms where clients and staff met face-to-face. The need was urgent, but the response was slow. Only after several months of complaints did on-site TB testing and education commence; purchase and installation of room filters took even longer.

Tension tightened with the summary firing of a client advocate in financial services. He had been a stalwart in the caucus, and co-workers decorated his emptied desk with a mock obituary and a cardboard tombstone. "This was a busy area, and the installation was up for a week. We circulated a petition and we said, 'Look how this person was fired without any procedure,'" said Melvin. "Right after that, we called a meeting, and about forty staff showed up." So did the executive director and the head of operations, neither of whom had been invited. Melvin argued with the bosses and then led thirty-five workers out of the building. Before an hour was up, they were back at their desks. But now the direction was clear: five days later, Melvin and a few others formed an organizing committee and began talking to representatives from the city's most powerful health service union, District 1199.

The union organizer instructed the committee about the basic tasks: how to canvass, how to chart responses, how to recruit for the union and remain safe. A target for contacts was set: all non-managerial staff members would be offered authorization cards. A week later, the committee made its move. While managers huddled in the boardroom for a lengthy conference, "We just went to people in their offices and talked. There was so much anger about unfair treatment, they just wanted to know where to sign," said Melvin, who monitored the blitz at his desk. "I had my e-mail going, my phone going, I was marking sign-ups and where they worked. That first day we signed up eighty or ninety." By June 1993, the committee had collected enough cards to qualify for direct recognition and certification.[57]

But neither the Board of Directors nor the clinic's administrators wanted to accept the bid. The executive director's temperamental reactions to challenges from the staff had embarrassed everyone, and the board knew that more disciplined resistance was needed. A consulting attorney was retained, a partner from Proskauer Rose, the city's premiere management law firm. The standard fee of $300 per hour would be underwritten by a leading donor, a board member who was particularly intent on keeping GMHC union-free.[58] Directors turned down the petition and demanded hearings at the NLRB, to be followed by an election. GMHC then issued its first personnel manual, which included the statement that "employment at GMHC is an 'at will' relationship, which means the agency can terminate employment at any time, at its discretion."[59]

A pro-management caucus, Concerned Employees against Union, arose. The concerns it publicized had to do with the "bureaucratic force of 1199" and its membership of 117,000. "Can 1199 Be Trusted Not to Mislead Us?" the caucus's leaflet asked.[60] The union committee countered with a comparison of salaries. Tim Sweeney, the executive director, had earned $125,000 the previous year; no GMHC staff members made more than $40,000. Comparing this disparity with the $50,000 salary of Dennis Rivera, the president of District 1199, the committee argued that "Dennis could represent us better because he was closer to our interests."[61] The pro-management caucus and the propaganda about big-union bureaucracy were standard union-busting ploys. But in Rivera's presidency of District 1199, the countercampaign found a special opportunity.

Rivera's leadership of the hospital union had earned him a special relationship with John Cardinal O'Connor, the Roman Catholic archbishop of New York and chief pastor to many of Rivera's Latino constituents. O'Connor's reputation as a pro-labor priest went back to his bishopric in Scranton, Pennsylvania, and he maintained this stance in New York City. As leaders of management and labor for the city's Catholic hospitals, O'Connor and Rivera had famously conducted efficient and cordial negotiations of pace-setting contracts.

To the AIDS community, these manifestations of the cardinal's goodness were irrelevant. O'Connor was a prime enforcer of the church's doctrine on homosexuality. He opposed anything but abstinence as protection against HIV infection and condemned the use of condoms and the distribution of clean needles. He became the focus of queer fury, most notoriously during the "Stop the Church" demonstration by ACT-UP on the morning of December 10, 1989, when more than four thousand protesters entered St. Patrick's Cathedral during Sunday's high mass. They tossed condom packets in the air, lay down in the aisles, and shouted down the cardinal's homily. Police arrested forty-three people in the church and sixty-eight more on the streets.[62]

O'Connor and Rivera did not agree about AIDS. Contingents from District 1199 participated in the annual AIDS walks, and Rivera had been a featured speaker at "United for AIDS Action," a huge union rally co-sponsored by GMHC and other AIDS groups during the Democratic National Convention in New York City in the summer of 1992.[63] But GMHC officials negated the gestures of solidarity and insisted that for gay workers in a gay workplace, District 1199 would be a terrible mistake. Gay workers who needed protection should rely on their gay bosses; society at large was far too homophobic. A queer slur made the rounds: "Rivera is in bed with the cardinal."[64]

Organizers found themselves hard-pressed to cite examples of how District 1199 would stand up for gay people. The union's history in civil rights was a proud one (Martin Luther King Jr. had called it "my favorite union"), but District 1199 had yet to declare its advocacy for the rights of sexual minorities. There was no gay and lesbian caucus, and there were no discussions of gay rights in the newsletter; nor did the constitutional antidiscrimination statement mention sexual orientation, disability, or HIV/AIDS status. An affirmative action statement encouraged leadership roles for "Blacks, Latinos, Asians and women, among others," but did not articulate who those "others" might be.[65]

Organizers pinned their hopes on a "get to know the union" dinner and expected Rivera to make a fiery speech, but he kept his remarks general. "He never said the word 'AIDS' in the open discussion," wrote Yadira Bonilla in a "Vote No" letter to her co-workers.[66] Union staff tried to make up for Rivera's detachment by introducing the organizing committee to a union elder, a gay man on the Executive Board. He was one of the union's founders, a legendary street organizer and a consummate negotiator. "But the guy wasn't out," said Melvin. "He was high up, but he was closeted."[67]

The NLRB began its review of the petition in August 1993 and continued for five months, with management attorneys challenging eligibility for the bargaining unit for almost every position, worker by worker. Precise allocations were important, and District 1199's lawyers could bicker with the best of them, but the slow stipulations were doing double damage. While attorneys picked at the unit in NLRB hearing rooms downtown, managers kept the pressure going in Chelsea. They claimed that the union would prevent workers in the Ombudsman Department from supporting complaints on behalf of their HIV-positive clients if those patients' rights were being endangered by hospital workers who were also members of District 1199.

In early November, management's legal team arrived at the hearing room with two hundred client files to be introduced as evidence to exempt the Ombudsman's Department from the bargaining unit. Managers wanted to show that ombudsman staff routinely filed complaints against health care providers, including District 1199 members. However, the legal team not only neglected to edit the documents, which bore the names of clients, both dead and alive, but sent the files to the home of the union's lawyer.[68]

Article 27F of the State of New York Public Health Law, adopted in 1989, articulated strict guidelines for confidentiality of HIV status, with provisions for recourse and penalties. GMHC had vigorously advocated its passage, and the agency's standard practice was to permit no one but workers assigned to particular clients to touch their records. "You could be working right next to somebody at the agency and have no idea that this person was a client," said Melvin. "It was just none of your business. These were hearings at a federal agency, and the files would become part of the public record." GMHC was now violating state law as well as its own code of ethics. The union filed a complaint with the State Department of Health, but it was not until after the election that the charges were substantiated and corrective measures were ordered.[69]

Activists were so preoccupied with the constant flak that they could barely push their own way forward. "We should have gone after management aggressively, and we should have been educating employees about what was going to happen," said Melvin. The committee did maintain its lead in departments where first responses had been robust but failed to move past its base.

"People who interacted with clients every day, they were our meat and potatoes. Development and finance didn't work that much with clients and they never did sign a lot of cards."[70]

Management was gauging support throughout the hearings and was pushing for a definition of the bargaining unit that would split the professional staff who provided direct services—educators, nutritionists, lawyers, case managers—from the majority of workers who had minimal contact with clients. The NLRB determined two divisions: a large unit in back-office operations and a smaller professional group. The Organizing Committee made its own assessment that the union could win among the professionals but not among the other staff.[71]

The election results on February 4, 1994, gave a 78–28 "no" vote for the larger unit. The professional section came in with a narrow 10–8 "yes" vote, a very weak standing within the larger, nonunion workforce. Management never got serious about bargaining, and many of the organizers quit within the next few months. Professionals still on the job petitioned for a second election, and early the next year decertified their unit.

The organizing committee had chosen District 1199 because of its excellent record in health services, but the union's squeamishness with gay people and their workplace issues turned out to be a serious liability, and management's willingness to rely on Proskauer Rose's expert hostile counsel surely sealed the deal. The defeat did serve as a useful example. Whitman-Walker's organizing team was starting its drive during the same season that the GMHC campaign was languishing in stipulations, and the first flurry of sign-ups in San Francisco overlapped with the disappointing results of GMHC's election. Key activists maintained a loose but alert three-city network to share tactics and provide mutual encouragement. "We didn't want what had happened to us to happen to them," said Melvin.[72]

Struggle in San Francisco

The San Francisco AIDS Foundation, one of the earliest organizations to respond to the epidemic, never claimed a purview as broad as that of GMHC. SFAF's services intersected with those of several other local agencies in AIDS services. During SFAF's period of unionization in 1994, staff numbered approximately 130. Pay was decent, and there were no major complaints about overwork. "People dressed casually and spoke openly. They really wanted you to get away from your desk for lunch hour," said Florence Cepeda, a part-time coordinator of SFAF's services with those of other agencies.[73]

Nevertheless, social workers were organizing—behind closed doors. Criss Romero, the new administrative assistant in client services, had no idea that anything was up until the day he spoke up on his colleagues' behalf. The director of policy had just laid down new rules for reduced services, and everyone was upset. Clients were still to receive basic medical treatments, but access to food, clothing, and shelter had been cut back: clothing vouchers were down to $10 per month from $15, and production and distribution of the department's English-Spanish guide to food banks, cheap housing, and other resources had been halted altogether. "The director told them if they didn't like it, they could go get a job someplace else." Romero jumped in and scolded the boss. "He was blocking their work and threatening their jobs." That day, Romero was recruited to the organizing committee.[74]

Three unions active in the city's queer labor scene courted the campaign: Local 3 of the Office and Professional Employees, Local 10 of the International Longshore and Warehouse Union, and Local 790 of SEIU, a large public sector outfit that was just then starting up its 790A division for nonprofits. The nod went to SEIU 790A. Just a few months earlier, Local 790 had participated in SEIU's "Coming Out, Coming Together" Lavender Caucus leadership conference in Oakland. Moreover, two municipal agencies with compatible missions and represented by Local 790 had headquarters in the same building as SFAF, the Human Rights Commission on the eighth floor and the San Francisco AIDS office on the fifth. Members from both agencies helped the new campaign with meeting space and sponsorship of a "meet the union" reception.

Petitioning started in January 1994 with excellent results: one hundred employees signed cards within a two-week period, "including some managers who sympathized."[75] But top managers did not, especially Pat Christen, a straight woman who had risen from volunteering with the AIDS hotline to executive director. The board appreciated her cool head and did not much care whether people were offended by her abrasive style. She became a magnet for resentment, especially among the agency's founding constituents, who were angered by her big salary. By 1993, she was making $118,000, and generous raises continued throughout her tenure.[76]

GMHC was now on the verge of its election, and its management team was trading information with Christen. Greg Pullman, an organizer with Local 790, set Romero up with Scott Melvin, who explained the importance of resisting elaborate stipulations at the NLRB. "We told them to just come out hard and fast and don't wait," said Melvin.[77] According to Romero, "They wanted to kick out as many people as they could, and they wanted to divide the unit between social workers and everyone else. They did get us down to sixty-four. But they couldn't split the unit."[78]

Expert advice was provided pro bono to Christen and her team, thanks to a board member who was a partner with Morrison and Foerster, a major San Francisco firm with a strong practice in management law. "Their campaign was subtle," said Pullman. "They called it 'informed choice,' and the antiunion meetings were voluntary rather than captive."[79] Romero nevertheless felt the heat. "They had one-on-one sessions. They offered to send me to school if I would drop out of the drive," he said.[80] Inevitably, an antiunion committee emerged. "They spurred on these hostile workers who were in-your-face types," said Pullman. "So we asked our supporters to make a public statement, 'I'm voting yes because . . . ,' and then we put those statements on a flyer. When it came to the vote, our people stuck to it."[81]

On April 21, 1994, the unit voted 36–21 to elect Local 790A. "The day we won, some of our management actually cried," Romero wrote to Melvin. "Our victory has really impacted the city in that we are being approached by other AIDS organizations on how to go about this process. I'm sure many an [executive director] is wondering if they're next."[82]

Only when negotiations commenced did real rancor materialize. The first fight, over the structure of the unit, brought the rhetoric of choice back into play. Management's proposal for an open shop was presented by a board member who was an official of Planned Parenthood. She argued that "since gay people didn't have a choice about being gay, they shouldn't be forced to join a union," said Romero.[83] The compromise was an agency shop. Membership would be available but not required; the alternative would be a fee to be paid in lieu of dues.

The union made health coverage for domestic partners its most important economic demand. The benefit was guaranteed to municipal employees but not yet available from any private firms in the Bay Area. Christen was adamant that the coverage would be impossible to implement. But she was overruled because of pressure from the wider community. "We were running a field campaign while we were negotiating," said Stephanie Batey, the chief negotiator from Local 790.[84] Unions, gay political organizations, and employees of neighboring agencies represented by Local 790 rallied on the corner in front of SFAF's headquarters to support the demand for partner benefits. The director of policy asked politicians to stay away, and the city's entire Board of Supervisors cooperated but one, the newly elected Tom Ammiano, who spoke for the union. At the next bargaining session, the sides agreed on "heterosexual equivalency." Upon receiving an affidavit of domestic partnership, SFAF would add the equivalency of what heterosexual staff members received in benefits to the member's paycheck. "Our partners needed help immediately. The money could be applied to insurance or to any other costs we were incurring in their care," said Romero.[85]

The settlement brought no peace. "Christen never forgave the employees for organizing," said Batey. "Usually at nonprofits, the managers and the union develop a decent relationship to resolve disputes, but that wasn't her intention. She never settled down."[86] African American and Latino workers had participated prominently in the organizing drive and at the bargaining table. During the year that followed ratification, eight disciplinary procedures were filed, all against minority and immigrant employees. Romero and two Latino colleagues countered with complaints to the Equal Employment Opportunity Commission (EEOC) for unfair treatment and promotions denied.[87]

The union's hold was weakening. Jobs turned over frequently, and membership dwindled. Some workers took the agency option and then abstained from paying fees to the union by donating equivalents to charity. New employees were put through lengthy probationary periods, when they could be fired at will. "They would show an interest during probation and come to steward training and then, boom, they'd be on the hit list," said Batey. Afraid for their jobs, they would avoid the union long after their status had become permanent.[88]

Florence Cepeda, who had been hired in 1994 as a temporary part-timer, became permanent in 1995 and joined the union, but the meetings upset her. "It was an us-against-them atmosphere with a lot of grousing," she said. "Some of them were angry all the time. I didn't feel that way about my supervisor, so I stopped going. My hiring anniversary was coming up. That was when you could drop your membership, so I did."[89]

Romero and several others in leadership quit their jobs in 1996. "We didn't feel things were going to change. I was always being disciplined. Some of us resigned. Some were fired. In the end, only twenty people were still paying dues."[90] Complaints of discrimination and unfair labor practices continued to mount—at the EEOC, at the NLRB, at the state's Department of Fair Employment, and at the city's Human Rights Commission. The union pushed a second contract to ratification but could not adequately enforce it, and workers were less and less protected.[91] Collective bargaining ceased. In 2001, a petition to decertify was filed with the NLRB, but no election ever took place.[92]

Whitman-Walker: Union Yes

Joe Izzo started at the Whitman-Walker Clinic in Washington, DC, in 1986 as an educator in HIV prevention. In 1991, he became a mental health counselor. He was proud of the clinic and its no-fee policy, but he was also chronically exhausted. He was not alone. Among the 120 non-administrative employees, morale was low and turnover high. "All the managers were gay and lesbian, but they were like bosses everywhere, always trying to see how much they could get out of us and how little they had to give back," Izzo said. "There was nothing available to support or care for staff. Jim Graham, our executive director, was great at raising money, and he had wonderful political connections, but he was a major micro-manager."[93]

Izzo had a best friend at work. Bill Taylor was an addictions counselor, a recovering alcoholic and a great troublemaker. Before coming to Whitman-Walker, Taylor had been employed by the Federal Aviation Authority for fifteen years as an air traffic controller. He had been the president of PATCO Local 572 at the Tucson airfield and a leader in the strike of 1981. Taylor was among five union officers who were jailed on August 5, the day PATCO defied President Reagan's return-to-work order. Taylor was convicted of felonious striking against the federal government and received a sentence of probation in lieu of a year in prison. In 1983, he made his way back to PATCO's post-strike headquarters in Washington, where he served as a counselor on the hotline and coordinated appeals to reinstate his fired colleagues. In 1985, he began writing and publishing *PATCO Lives: The Lifeline*, a newsletter for veterans of the strike and their supporters. His marriage ended. He continued his education toward a career in counseling. He came out as a gay man.[94]

Taylor and Izzo made an odd pair. Before his career at Whitman-Walker, Izzo had taken vows as a teaching brother in the Xaverian order and had trained to be a clinical pastoral educator. In his studies, he learned from liberation theology; in therapy, he acknowledged his homosexuality. He joined the Gay Men's Counseling Collective; the Washington chapter of Dignity, an organization for gay Catholics; and other local gay groups. In 1982, after Izzo had spent seventeen years in the brotherhood, his superior demanded that he halt all advocacy of gay rights and withdraw from the gay community. Izzo prayed hard and quit the order.[95]

Taylor urged Izzo to face his workaholic compulsions and invited him to come along to twelve-step meetings. "On our way over, we would commiserate." Whitman-Walker was having trouble with the costs of employees' health insurance. In the previous six months, premiums had almost doubled from the original $149 per month per person, and in mid-1993, the clinic's bill was close to $1 million. "Many of our workers were themselves sick. Management was saying, 'Maybe we'll drop insurance altogether. Maybe we'll self-insure.' They weren't looking out for us. We were providing free services to people with HIV—but were close to losing our own coverage." Taylor sensed in his buddy the makings of a good organizer. "I said, 'We need to stop bitching and either shut up or do something,' Bill said 'We can unionize.' That had never occurred to me."

That summer, Taylor took a call from the clinic's property manager, Steve Fesler, who had just quarreled with Graham and been summarily fired. Fesler was planning legal action but also wanted revenge. He urged Taylor to have a union talk with his friend Larry Ginsburg, an organizer with Division 1199-E, SEIU's regional health care affiliate. Taylor went to the meeting at Fesler's home with Izzo and four other staff members. They got busy right away. "Larry explained that while we were organizing, we would be protected. Then he gave us a game plan."[96]

Whitman-Walker was on the verge of its twentieth anniversary, and the coming season would be crucial financially and spectacular socially. The AIDS walk and the United Way and Combined Federal drives were expected to bring in millions of dollars, and a gala evening was being planned for November 19 to inaugurate the Elizabeth Taylor Medical Center, with the movie star an honored guest. Strategic timing would be essential. "We knew that this would be the best time to get things going, because management was going to be extremely distracted," said Izzo.

The organizing committee members surveyed their co-workers and reported results in a leaflet in early October: "High turnover in your ranks. Not enough resources. Cramped, noisy work stations and far too much stress." The message was well received. A meeting was set for two weeks later, at a nearby Universalist church.[97] During the next month, one hundred of the staff signed up.

Graham had been talking with managers at GMHC and had been briefed about the tactics of slow stipulations as they were being played out in NLRB hearings. "They thought maybe they could weaken our thing like they were doing in New York," said Izzo. "But we had been talking with our counterparts, so we knew that we had to avoid that split between professional and nonprofessional units. We told our co-workers that we were all in this together."

Less than two weeks before Elizabeth Taylor's arrival to dedicate the new medical center, Graham called a staff meeting. "He wanted to discuss the union drive," Izzo said, "and he was just beside himself, not understanding why his people were against him, unionizing."[98] Before the meeting took place, Izzo and Taylor wrote to Graham, urging him to cancel. Such a meeting, they warned, could trigger unfair labor practice charges. "As much as you may not like it, Jim," they wrote, "many of our members see your actions as constituting . . . interference."[99] Graham confronted Taylor directly. There was shouting, a threat of dismissal. "But Bill had gotten into Graham's face before. He had been fired by Ronald Reagan. He had gone to jail," said Izzo. "He wasn't afraid, and neither was I."[100]

A cooler, wiser man stepped in. Bill Olwell of the United Food and Commercial Workers had already served for several years on Whitman-Walker's board and at the time was a vice-president. He was well known in Washington's gay political world and important to the clinic for his fund-raising appeals among union colleagues. Just that year he had raised $75,000 for Whitman-Walker, and now he was slated to assume the presidency of the clinic's board. His term would begin the day after Elizabeth Taylor's visit—which would be the same day that Division 1199-E was planning to file for an election at the NLRB.

"We were seeing how New York was tearing themselves apart," said Olwell, who sat down with Graham to warn that he would resign if they ran "an anti-union campaign. I said, 'Jim, this is crazy. I'm raising all this money from labor to support the clinic.'" Enough staff had signed authorization cards to make a card check a feasible next step. In December 1993, the count was overseen by the American Arbitration Association. By a margin of 87 to 21, Division 1199-E achieved direct recognition.[101]

For the next half-year, the union prioritized contract demands in preparation for collective bargaining. Then, in July 1994, Bill Taylor died suddenly from lung cancer. "It was a shock. We still kept on meeting and proposing, but for six months I walked around the clinic like something was missing from my own body," said Izzo. Bargaining brought no economic breakthroughs. "There just wasn't any money," said Olwell. "But now the employees had their vehicle to protest, and that gave them dignity." The contract's three-year term ensured the union's continuity, as did its requirement of membership for all workers at three of Whitman-Walker's four sites. By state law, the facility in Arlington, Virginia, would remain an open shop.[102]

With the union secure, negotiators could press for improved wages and innovations favorable to LGBT staff. The five-year contract of 1997 achieved full domestic partner benefits and protection of gender expression. "Our dress code was pretty relaxed, and a couple of transgender guys wanted to wear skirts at work without supervisors threatening them," explained Izzo. "This wasn't about doing drag on a whim. This was to protect the person who is making the transition from male to female and can verify it." A renewal in 2002 added "alternate family favorable provisions" to bereavement, parental, and family medical leaves and strengthened support to workers in transition. The contract of 2005–2006 and every other agreement since then has included "treatments and procedures relating to sex reassignment surgery . . . or any other health condition relating to an employee's gender identity and expression."[103]

Talking Union, Talking Queer

The three union drives of 1993–1994 took place in cities where labor was well represented in the overall workforce, especially among service workers. Although immediate conditions seemed favorable for union wins at all three agencies, the results were mixed. Some initiators of the campaigns could rely on previous labor or community organizing experiences to guide their practice, but many others learned their fundamentals in the immediacy of campaigning. Their opponents in organizing were, in the fight against AIDS, their everyday allies: supervisors and donors who were making sure that the AIDS centers stayed open and solvent.

The GMHC's organizing committee chose District 1199 to lead the campaign. The union was famous for its advocacy of minority workers' rights but failed to catch on to what the unit was all about, even though its very name, Gay Men's Health Crisis, told its compelling story. Never in the lengthy drive did District 1199 display any sophistication about the clinic's constituencies or its mission. The situation started out as a winnable opportunity for gay-labor solidarity, but management easily took advantage of important gaps permitted by District 1199's indifference.

During a brief organizing season at SFAF, organizers from SEIU Local 790 practiced politics of gay-labor solidarity as a matter of course. But a fatal compromise at the bargaining table, to adopt an agency shop arrangement, weakened the structure of the unit. Persistent harassment of leading activists during the next contract cycle combined with diminishing enrollment (because of the agency shop) left the unit too weak to survive.

Whitman-Walker's union has endured. The unit's staying power was set by its founding organizers, two fervent and focused gay men who persisted with their vision of meaningful service appropriately rewarded. A well-placed mentor intervened at a critical point, but it was Izzo and Taylor's disciplined collaborations with co-workers and staff organizers, their steady strategies, and their dogged campaigning that won the day for both the agency and the union.

Epilogue

When Connie Married Phyllis

July 24, 2011: a steamy Sunday in New York City, thirty days after Governor Andrew Cuomo signed the Marriage Equality Act into law and the first day that gay and lesbian couples in the State of New York could legally marry. The Marriage Bureau in downtown Manhattan, typically a Monday-to-Friday operation, was open for business, as were City Clerks' offices throughout the five boroughs. Connie Kopelov and Phyllis Siegel were first in line.

The state mandates a twenty-four-hour waiting period from the time an application for a marriage license is filed until it is issued, a rule that can be waived only by court order. Kopelov and Siegel had already filed their application and requested the dispensation, as had hundreds of couples throughout the state. In New York City, eighty-two justices of the State Supreme Court were on hand to sign orders and officiate, along with other dignitaries. Kopelov and Siegel said their vows before Michael McSweeney, the city clerk, and were pronounced married at 9:05 A.M. The ceremony flashed to the top of the news.

By day's end there had been 484 ceremonies: 293 in the three chapels of the Marriage Bureau in Manhattan and 191 more in the municipal buildings of Brooklyn, Queens, and Staten Island and at the Bronx courthouse. Tasks of dispatching so many extraordinary procedures were accomplished by clerical-administrative city employees, members of AFSCME Local 1549. The union, District Council (DC) 37's largest affiliate, was known for its advocacy of gay rights. Local 1549 sponsored the Lesbian and Gay Issues Committee in 1991 when it bid for official standing with the council, and the local continued its support when the committee pressed for benefit equity for domestic partners. In 1993, the benefits were made available to all municipal workers.

Fourteen years later, DC 37 endorsed the introduction of the state's first bill for marriage equality in the legislature and lobbied steadily for passage. The State Assembly approved the bill in 2007 and 2009, but the Senate delayed voting on the proposal until a special session in December 2009, when the bill was defeated by a wide 38–24 majority. On June 15, 2011, the bill was reintroduced and passed by the Assembly, and then it was voted up by the Senate the evening of June 24 and signed into law before midnight.

Now members of Local 1549 were clocking in on a Sunday morning to make marriage equality a civil reality. They checked waivers, collected fees, and processed certificates. Throngs of same-sex couples gathered at their counters. Ajah Griffin took the overtime assignment "because I have a parent and a couple of friends who are gay," and Chue Keung Mock was there because "I wanted to witness history."[1]

Siegel, a retired bookkeeper, and Kopelov, a retired labor educator, had been together for more than twenty years. Kopelov was closeted when she began working at the Amalgamated Clothing Workers of America in 1958, and she maintained her private shell throughout her union career. She served on the boards of the Coalition of Labor Union Women (New York City chapter), the Workers Defense League, and the New York Labor History Association into retirement. But not until the late 1980s, when she and Siegel became lovers, did she make her lesbian identity a public fact. "I remember how it used to be and still is for many gays and lesbians," she told the labor historians Debra Bernhardt and Rachel Bernstein. "Evasions, silences, fears of disclosure, hiding relationships. . . . May the future bring openness and acceptance to all."[2]

One silent place was District 1199's Education Department, where Kopelov led political training programs in the late 1970s. The union was at the forefront of civil rights activism but fell short when it came to the rights of sexual minorities. Other unions in New York City's public and service sectors advocated for LGBT rights as early as the 1980s; by the mid-1990s, the movement was widely supported, but not at District 1199. That absence became a telling weakness when District 1199 attempted to unionize the Gay Men's Health Crisis between 1992 and 1994. The agency contested the union's bid at the labor board, and the bargaining unit was split in two for the election. A small unit of professional employees voted for the union; the larger unit of clerical and technical workers found District 1199's message unsympathetic to their concerns and voted "no." Only after the election did District 1199 revise its constitutional nondiscrimination statement to include sexual orientation as a protected class.

Costs for health care soared during the late 1990s, and major hospitals responded to the crisis by consolidating resources and facilities. Health care unions kept pace with these rapid changes by refocusing strategies for organizing and bargaining. In 1998, District 1199 joined the Service Employees International Union (SEIU) and its affiliated health care locals to form 1199 SEIU United Healthcare Workers East. SEIU by then was a 1.8 million-member giant with a twenty-year record of leadership on gay-labor issues. District 1199 entered the merger with no staff assigned to issues of sexual minorities and no caucus or membership committee to support gay-labor activity. But with the consolidation, a new generation of rank-and-file activists emerged. They were excited by the promise of SEIU's gay-friendly political environment and determined to focus 1199's attention toward LGBT rights.

Carmen Acosta, a staff member in the union's Education Department, traveled to Pittsburgh in 2000 for SEIU's national convention and attended sessions of the Lavender Caucus. "Up till then, I wasn't so involved in gay rights," she said. "I was one of those people who was just trying to survive economically." Discussions with queer delegates opened her eyes to the "kinds of things we were being denied." Acosta shared her insights with colleagues at home, and in 2003, a group began meeting informally as the 1199 SEIU Lesbian and Gay Committee. For the next few years and with union support they formed delegations to annual "Creating Change" conferences of the National Gay and Lesbian Task Force. There they participated in labor-gay workshops that analyzed LGBT issues in terms of union processes—for example, collective bargaining strategies for domestic partner benefits.

In 2007, George Gresham was elected president of 1199 SEIU United Healthcare Workers East. Gresham, an astute student of the union's civil rights heritage, had been a member since the mid-1970s, when he was first hired as a hospital housekeeper. The merged union was now 350,000 members strong, with 250,000 concentrated in the State of New York. Gresham and his team intended to fortify the organization with aggressive recruitment and solid coalitions. Queer union activists saw the new agenda as an opportunity to lead.

In 2008, staff and members from several districts formed the 1199 SEIU Lesbian, Gay, Bisexual, Transgender, and Queer Caucus, and in 2009, the group achieved official authorization. "We were recruiting, and we were tight," said Acosta, "and Gresham encouraged us." SEIU had recorded its support of marriage equality in 2004 at its national convention; now Gresham applied that resolution to 1199's legacy of civil rights.

In the spring of 2010, same-sex marriage was already a matter of law in Massachusetts, Connecticut, Iowa, Vermont, New Hampshire, and the District of Columbia. The question remained lively in New York; a majority of the Assembly was likely to repeat the "yes" vote; and advocates argued that the Senate's previous "no" vote in December 2009—a disappointment marked by fractious politics—could be overcome. The Empire State Pride Agenda was consolidating its growing coalition of civil rights and religious groups, businesses, and unions, and national advocates were eager to join the campaign.[3]

A victory in New York, with its 19 million inhabitants, would more than double the total population of the six places where same-sex marriage was already a matter of law. New York's example also would advance the likelihood for successful campaigns in states more densely populated and more economically, politically, and ethnically complex than some of the primarily rural states where the reform had been adopted.

New York's main political events of 2010 were senatorial and gubernatorial elections in November; no new vote would be scheduled for the legislative session. That summer, the Pride Agenda surveyed the Queens district represented by the incumbent Republican, Senator Frank Padavan, a leading opponent of same-sex marriage. Tony Avella, the Democrat and challenger, had already pledged to make marriage equality his top campaign issue if enough supporters could be identified in the electorate.

Acosta, on leave from her regular staff assignment, recruited a squad of eight seasoned union campaigners to canvass the district. The Pride Agenda and Freedom to Marry funded the project as it continued through the summer, Monday through Friday, 4:00–8:00 P.M., with help from volunteers on two Saturday afternoons. The survey used lists of registered voters who participate regularly in elections: in this district, primarily Catholic, white, retired Democrats. "Talking with people door-to-door is the most effective tool a campaign can have," Acosta said. "It's what moves people into the voting booth. We had to get into their faces; we had to say to them, 'Do we have your support?'"[4] Canvassers knocked on ten thousand doors, talked with six thousand voters, and collected two thousand two hundred pledge sheets, most of them signed by newly identified supporters.[5]

Avella won by a close margin of fewer than two thousand votes. "Flips" in a few other districts signaled that the Senate might be budged, but it would take six more senators with solid "yes" intentions to shift the balance for sure. Until then, advocates would not risk the Senate floor.

The Democrat candidate for governor, Andrew Cuomo, made marriage equality a major issue, easily beat the Tea Party–oriented Republican Carl Paladino, and then reaffirmed his commitment in his State of the State Address of January 5, 2011. In early April, Cuomo conferred with leaders from all pro-marriage organizations to demand disciplined adherence to a plan that he would direct. Two weeks later, the groups announced the formation of New Yorkers United for Marriage. The vote would have to be accomplished before the adjournment of the legislature at the end of June, and the coalition declared its readiness to follow the governor's lead. Organizations would concentrate on their primary constituencies while coordinating fieldwork for several dozen organizers.

Marriage Equality New York staged "Wedding Marches," vibrant demonstrations with activists in wedding gear, while Freedom to Marry deployed social media for direct actions. The League of Women Voters and the Log Cabin Republicans promoted the issue among moderates. And the Human Rights Campaign raised enough money to cover the salaries of twelve more organizers, as well as the costs of television spots performed by celebrity volunteers such as Sean Avery of the New York Rangers, Barbara Bush (the former president's daughter), Whoopi Goldberg, Julianne Moore, and Kevin Bacon.

The Pride Agenda gathered its "marriage ambassadors," clergy, business leaders, and labor and community activists. A fleet of fifteen buses took them to Albany for the annual Equality and Justice event on May 9, a day of lobbying, networking, and rallies. Four weeks later, the SEIU 1199 LGBTQ Caucus joined George Gresham and the entire executive council for their own lobby day in Albany. They talked with Democrats who were holding to "no" and Republicans who were considering "yes." Acosta observed Gresham as he challenged the lawmakers. "He told them, 'When you decide to vote in favor of something that helps our members, we have a long memory.'"[6]

With the deadline close, organizers agreed that a final grassroots push could make the difference. Dozens of volunteers from the National Gay and Lesbian Task Force were poised for action, "but for rural towns upstate, you can't do door-to-door," said Acosta. She asked union officials for the use of SEIU 1199's modest phone bank in suburban White Plains, but they offered a bigger idea: the union's state-of-the-art call center at midtown Manhattan headquarters "I was so proud," said Acosta. "They were making the connection that LGBT rights are civil rights."[7]

The blitz was on. Volunteers from all of the groups in New Yorkers United for Marriage reported to SEIU 1199 headquarters every weekday evening from mid-May until the hectic last days of June. Calls went out to all senatorial districts that might swing to "yes." Joan Reutershan, an artist and community activist from Brooklyn, had volunteered on phone banks before, "but always with pieces of paper and regular telephones," she said.

> This was streamlined. We had maybe eighty stations, each with a computer and a headset and a screen with the script and the range of options. We would talk with the voters. If they said the issue was important, we would ask them to call the senator or offer to patch them through directly to the district office to leave a phone message.
>
> We patched quite a few through. We had to move quickly, but we still took time to talk to people. They were in towns all over the state and that was the best part. The interest was high, and it wasn't just me; the whole room was charged.[8]

The Marriage Equality Act passed the Senate on Friday evening, June 24, by a 33–29 margin and directly the governor signed it into law. "Our caucus was having our first ever party at the union hall that night. We knew that the Senate was in session," said Acosta. "We were dancing in the Martin Luther King auditorium. I was there with Christian Abreu, my son. The DJ kept playing 'Tonight Is the Night,' and Leah Gonzalez from our Political Action Department kept checking her phone. We got the word around 10:00 P.M."[9]

Acosta, Abreu, and others from the union headed downtown to Sheridan Square, where crowds were gathering to celebrate. This was the site, forty-two years earlier, of the Stonewall Rebellion. "People were coming in from all over the city," said Acosta. "We had our friends, our lovers, our families there—and we were in heaven."[10] The euphoria continued into Sunday afternoon, in the form of the city's annual Gay Pride March to commemorate Stonewall.

The Pride March a year later was sunny and sparkling. A roaring fleet of "dykes on bikes" from the Sirens Motorcycle Club cleared the way for Connie Kopelov and Phyllis Siegel, who were being honored as grand marshals. The couple rode down Fifth Avenue in a green convertible, just a month short of their first wedding anniversary.

When It Changed

Marriage equality in New York was a legislative process, not a ballot initiative. New York permits referendum questions only for constitutional amendments, and those questions must be initiated by the legislature, not by citizen petition. At the time, most advocates for gay marriage understood this limitation as a good thing. They asked: Why should equal rights for minorities be granted by the majority? Wouldn't fairness lie in having those rights decided by judicial decree or by legislation? Following the Defense of Marriage Act (DOMA) of 1996, voters in the more than thirty states where prohibitions on gay marriage were put to referendum approved the bans. In California, 52 percent of voters approved Proposition 8 on November 4, 2008; the initiative, titled "Eliminates Rights of Same-Sex Couples to Marry," went into effect the day after it won. And in Maine, a year later, a legislated marriage equality act signed into law by the governor in May was rejected by referendum just six months later.

New York was among six states and the District of Columbia to enact same-sex marriage between 2004 and 2011—all by legislation or litigation; none by popular vote. But when marriage equality came up on Maine's ballot once again in 2012, voters reversed the referendum of 2009. That vote was taken on November 6, national Election Day, as were ballots in three other states. In three states, approval for same-sex marriage won: by 51.5 percent in Maine; by 52.4 percent in Maryland; by 53.7 percent in Washington. In Minnesota, the question before voters—a ban on same-sex marriage—was rejected by 52.5 percent. The four new states brought the count of gay marriage jurisdictions to eleven.

A leading factor in the turn to electoral victories was an overall positive American experience with gay marriage, following Massachusetts's lead eight years earlier. Although marriage equality was not yet widespread, the record was good. People who heard about weddings in other states or traveled to witness weddings of relatives or friends did not see why the reform could not come to their home states. Public perceptions of same-sex marriage were changing. It was being seen less as a threat to heterosexual marriage than as a value shared by queer and straight people alike.

The Democratic Party's national platform backed the repeal of DOMA during the election campaign of 2008, but President Barack Obama delayed his personal endorsement until his second run for the presidency in 2012. That statement of support reflected his personal observations of the benefits of marriage equality. At the same time, his words encouraged the pro-equality base then preparing for their election days in Maine, Maryland, Minnesota, and Washington. They kept campaigning for marriage equality and pushed even harder for the Democratic ticket.

The strategically successful mobilization of diverse political communities during the New York campaign in 2011 was an important model, but electoral politics in these four states reflected LGBT communities' regional cultures and histories, too. Local projects joined with Freedom to Marry's national networks and funding sources. The money supported statewide marriage equality organizations and encouraged alliances among local community groups.

Although many union members did not vote for the issue and many unions did not support the cause, labor was a significant force among political sectors allied with marriage equality electorates. This was true in Maine, with its 64,000 member labor movement (11.5 percent of the employed population); Maryland, with 280,000 members (10.6 percent of the employed); Minnesota, with 351,000 members (14.2 percent of the employed); and Washington, with 513,000 members (18.5 percent of the employed).

Maine's campaign ("Yes on 1") arose soon after the electoral loss of 2009. Mainers United for Marriage built on lists and contacts from the previous campaign to develop a grassroots canvass directed at rural communities, where support had been weak. Trained volunteers worked door to door. The conversations they initiated focused less on political rights than on the importance of marriage in people's personal lives and in society as a whole. In the run-up to the 2012 election, the campaign staffed phone banks and sponsored television ads with everyday people who supported the reform. Some of the ads featured union members—firefighters and teachers—talking about what they wanted for themselves, their family members, and their friends.[11] Unions that endorsed the campaign included the Maine Education Association and the Southern Maine Labor Council, which coordinates activities for thirty-five local union affiliates in service and public employment, construction, and heavy industry.

Maryland's same-sex marriage contest came to the ballot with a contentious twenty-year history of tough court cases and legislative battles. When Governor Martin O'Malley signed the Civil Marriage Protection Act of 2012, to take effect January 1, 2013, advocates knew that a challenge by referendum was coming. Opponents collected twice the number of signatures needed, and Question 6 was set for the ballot of November 2012.

Question 6 tested Maryland's African American electorate, nearly a third of the state's population. Influential black clergymen opposed the issue, convinced that approval would hurt their communities. Some of their younger colleagues resisted that position and were backed by testimonials from respected entertainers (Mo'nique) and politicians (President Obama and members of the

Legislative Black Caucus of Maryland). Ezekiel Jackson, a straight black organizer for SEIU 1199, led Marylanders for Marriage Equality. This was a broad
coalition of the Human Rights Campaign and unions with large numbers of
African American members, including SEIU Locals 500 and 1199, Maryland's
AFL-CIO, and AFSCME District Councils 3 and 67.[12] The coalition's well-
funded mobilization started in February and stayed active until the polls closed.
The win was strong: an approval for Question 6 by 52.4 percent.

Washington United for Marriage, centered in Seattle, led the campaign for
Referendum 74. Unions in the state had a great heritage of involvement in gay
rights issues. Several local unions had worked on the "No on Proposition 13"
referendum campaign of 1978 that successfully overcame a challenge to Seattle's
gay rights ordinance, and in 1994, SEIU Local 1199 Northwest endorsed the
Hands Off Washington coalition that was formed to squelch right-wingers'
attempts to put antigay initiatives 608 and 610 on the state ballot. These had
been defensive moves and long ago, but the history of labor-gay collaboration was still valid for marriage activists as they organized with confidence for
Referendum 74.

Washington United for Marriage worked most closely with Local 21 of the
United Food and Commercial Workers. With a membership of forty-two thousand, it was the state's largest union in the private sector. Local 21 was strong
in suburban communities of the greater Puget Bay region and represented store
workers in rural areas, too. This made a political difference in the framing of
marriage equality as a statewide cause rather than as an issue of primary benefit to queer people in Seattle. Millionaires from the city's high-tech industry
donated generously to the coalition campaign, but Local 21 made its own mark,
with one thousand shop stewards volunteering in their communities and a
sophisticated phone bank at headquarters available for blitz calling.[13] The coalition's union base of three hundred thousand union members kept the campaign
moving through the state's diverse and large labor movement of public workers,
machinists, teamsters, teachers, and construction workers. Washington's electorate approved Referendum 74 by 53.7 percent.

Minnesota's marriage equality campaign started out from a defensive position in 2011 when a Republican majority in the State Legislature approved a
ballot measure for the election of 2012 that would add a ban on same-sex marriage to the state constitution. The Minnesota AFL-CIO, regional labor councils, and most of the large public employee councils joined Minnesotans United
for Families, a powerful and popular statewide coalition.

The state's labor movement sponsored phone banks and urged direct conversations among workmates during lunch hours and shift changes so that
LGBT workers and their allies could talk about their core values and the integrity of their families. The campaign became a statewide opportunity for everyday workers to share truths about their gay lives, including their fears should
the amendment pass.[14]

A majority of 52.5 percent voted the marriage amendment down on November 6. It was a powerful outcome and a relief—but not an approval of any reforms that would enhance the security of queer Minnesotans. That would wait until May 2013, when Minnesota's House of Representatives, and then its Senate, approved legislation to legalize same-sex marriage. Governor Mark Dayton signed the bill into law on May 13, and weddings commenced on August 1.

By the time this book went to press in the spring of 2014, DOMA had been struck down by the U.S. Supreme Court, and same-sex marriage had been enacted by legislation or court order in Delaware, Hawai'i, Illinois, New Jersey, New Mexico, and Rhode Island. Lawsuits that were underway in fifteen states had received a first favorable decision in Kentucky, Nevada, Tennessee, and Utah. These four states and the other eleven with decisions pending reflect queer America's newly visible breadth and regional diversity. Same-sex marriage in 2014 became a viable political issue in regions where gay rights had been previously shunned. The exuberance has its own dynamic. It is a momentum inspired by a succession of prominent and winning court cases, legislative campaigns, and ballot initiatives that began in Massachusetts in 2004 and spread to other northeastern, far western, mid-Atlantic, and northern Midwest regions during the decade that followed. Labor-gay coalitions were substantial forces in many of these efforts and would be capable in new territories. The templates had been crafted. The primary barriers were down. Anything could happen.

What's Next?

The LGBT and labor movements developed excellent collaborations during their decades of joint organizing. Much beyond marriage still needs to be accomplished. A federal employment nondiscrimination act with strong provisions for gender expression and identity remains a priority. Unions and LGBT rights organizations will have to push hard to break through the political obstacles set by a conservative Congress.

The largest, most rapidly expanding, and nonunionized sectors of the workforce are food service workers and retail workers. New efforts at unionization would benefit from dedicated outreach to LGBT employees in those jobs. Unions could try to learn from the advances and retreats of organizing drives at queer workplaces during the 1990s.

LGBT immigrants and the unions they join have a major stake in developing a strong outcome to contemporary campaigns for comprehensive immigration reform. In addition to the usual and often serious problems that face most immigrants, queer people entering the United States often have suffered persecution in their countries of origin and are sometimes unable to access networks of support from family members in their new homeland. Unions are great advocates for immigrants' rights, and the inclusion of queer topics in regular work with members could develop routes for broader LGBT support for immigration reform.

These are just three examples of contemporary activism that could build on the five decades of collaborative organizing that *Out in the Union* has described in historical depth. I look forward to seeing this great dialectic continue to develop. I also hope that this book inspires historians and activists as they seek out, create, and document an even wider exploration of the labor history of queer America.

Notes

A BRIEF CHRONOLOGY OF LGBT LABOR HISTORY, 1965–2013

1. For a time line of queer history in the United States, see Vicki L. Eaklor, *Queer America: A People's GLBT History of the United States* (New York: New Press, 2008), xvii–xxx. For narratives of LGBT-labor connections, see Christian Arthur Bain's chronological essay "A Short History of Gay and Lesbian Labor Activism in the United States," in *Laboring for Rights: Unions and Sexual Diversity across Nations*, ed. Gerald Hunt (Philadelphia: Temple University Press, 1999), 58–86.

PROLOGUE

1. Havelock Ellis's account of Bill is in Jonathan Ned Katz, *Gay American History: Lesbians and Gay Men in the U.S.A.—A Documentary History* (New York: Avon, 1976), 383–384. The story is retold in John D'Emilio and Estelle B. Freedman, *Intimate Matters: A History of Sexuality in America*, 2d ed. (Chicago: University of Chicago Press, 1997), 125.

2. Katz, *Gay American History,* 384.

3. Ibid.

4. Lodge 27 was identified as Bill's probable union home by Tom Wands, archivist of the International Brotherhood of Boilermakers. A membership roster of the lodge has been preserved from the first decade of the twentieth century, but the union's custom was to list last names and first initials only; other records have not survived: personal communication with Tom Wands, Kansas City, KS, February 1, February 2, and February 11, 1996.

5. Allan Bérubé, "Lesbian Masquerade," in *My Desire for History: Essays in Gay, Community, and Labor History*, ed. John D'Emilio and Estelle B. Freedman (Chapel Hill: University of North Carolina Press, 2011), 41–53; D'Emilio and Freedman, *Intimate Matters*, 125–126; Lillian Faderman, *Odd Girls and Twilight Lovers: A History of Lesbian Life in Twentieth-Century America* (New York: Columbia University Press, 1991), 41–45; Katz, *Gay American History,* 317–422.

6. Desma Holcomb and Nancy Wohlforth, "The Fruits of Our Labor: Pride at Work," *New Labor Forum* 8 (Spring–Summer 2001): 18–19; "NYC Transgender Rights Are a Trade Union Issue," leaflet, Pride at Work, AFL-CIO, 2002, in my possession.

7. André Wilson, interview by the author, Ann Arbor, January 12, 2012.

8. Doug Lederman, "Deal for Michigan and Its Grad Students," *Inside Higher Ed*, April 4, 2005; Andy Guess, "Trans-ition," *Inside Higher Ed*, March 30, 2009.

9. Unions and allied organizations of the early twentieth century range from the Women's Trade Union League (WTUL), chartered by the American Federation of Labor

(AFL) in 1903, to the anarcho-syndicalist Industrial Workers of the World (IWW), founded in 1905, and the Communist Party of the USA, founded in 1919. For a study of romantic friendships and cross-class politics in the WTUL, see Anneliese Orleck, *Common Sense and a Little Fire: Women and Working-Class Politics in the United States, 1900–1965* (Chapel Hill: University of North Carolina Press, 1995); see also Lillian Faderman, *To Believe in Women: What Lesbians Have Done for America* (Boston: Houghton Mifflin, 1999), 110–113, 139–146.

Elizabeth Gurley Flynn joined the IWW in 1907 at seventeen; led the mass strike of textile workers in Lawrence, Massachusetts, in 1913–1914; and was jailed during the silk strike in Paterson, New Jersey, of 1914. She was married briefly and had a son, and she took male lovers. A nervous collapse in 1926 halted her hard-charging activism, and she lived for the next ten years in Portland, Oregon, in the care of Dr. Marie Equi, an anarchist and open lesbian. Flynn returned to New York in 1936, joined the Communist Party, and rose quickly to leadership. Papers of her Portland years are the remarkable gap in Flynn's otherwise extensive archive, now at New York University's Tamiment Library. For a discussion of Flynn's bisexuality, see Rosalyn Fraad Baxandall, *Words on Fire: The Life and Writing of Elizabeth Gurley Flynn* (New Brunswick, NJ: Rutgers University Press, 1987), 7–78.

Bettina Aptheker discusses Flynn in "Keeping the Communist Party Straight, 1940s–1980s," *New Politics* 12, no. 1 (Summer 2008): 22–27. The same article considers the forty-five-year relationship of Anna Rochester and Grace Hutchins, founders of the Labor Research Association. Rochester's studies in capitalism and Hutchins's research in applied economics influenced generations of organizers. See also Janet Lee, *Comrades and Partners: The Shared Lives of Grace Hutchins and Anna Rochester* (Lanham, MD: Rowman and Littlefield, 2000).

10. See, e.g., Nan Alamilla Boyd, *Wide-Open Town: A Queer History of San Francisco to 1965.* Berkeley: University of California Press, 2003; George Chauncey, *Gay New York: Gender, Urban Culture and the Making of the Gay Male World, 1890–1940* (New York: Basic, 1994); John D'Emilio, *Sexual Politics, Sexual Communities: The Making of a Homosexual Minority in the United States, 1940–1970* (Chicago: University of Chicago Press, 1983); Lillian Faderman and Stuart Timmons, *Gay L.A.: A History of Sexual Outlaws, Power Politics, and Lipstick Lesbians* (New York: Basic, 2006); Elizabeth Lapovsky Kennedy and Madeline D. Davis, *Boots of Leather, Slippers of Gold: The History of a Lesbian Community* (New York: Routledge, 1993); Marc Stein, *City of Sisterly and Brotherly Loves: Lesbian and Gay Philadelphia, 1945–1972* (Chicago: University of Chicago Press, 2000)

11. Allan Bérubé, *Coming Out under Fire: The History of Gay Men and Women in World War Two* (New York: Free Press, 1990), 57–66.

12. Allan Bérubé, "Queer Work and Labor History," in D'Emilio and Freedman, *My Desire for History*, 259–269.

13. Allan Bérubé, "No Race-Baiting, Red-Baiting, or Queer-Baiting! The Marine Cooks and Stewards Union from the Depression to the Cold War," in ibid., 294–320.

14. By contrast, union density during the following two decades declined to 15.5 percent in 1994 and by 2011 had dropped to 11.9 percent: Neil Sheflin, Leo Troy, Industrial Relations Data Information Service: *U.S. Union Sourcebook: Membership, Finances, Structure, Directory, 1947–1983* (West Orange, NJ.: IRDIS, 1985); Steven Greenhouse, "Union Membership in U.S. Fell to a Seventy-Year Low Last Year," *New York Times*, January 21, 2011.

15. The Mattachine Society's elaborate rules of secrecy were developed by Harry Hay, a longtime member of the Communist Party, who first proposed the idea of a homosexual rights organization to a circle of gay friends, several of them comrades or former communists. Influenced by the tight disciplinary practices of the party, they applied similar codes of concealment to the new organization. The Daughters of Bilitis masked their identities, too, and were especially cautious with mailing lists for *The Ladder*, their monthly magazine. For more on the origins of the Mattachine Society and the culture of secrecy, see D'Emilio, *Sexual Politics, Sexual Communities*, 57–74; Stuart Timmons, *The Trouble with Harry Hay: Founder*

of the Modern Gay Movement (Boston: Alyson, 1990), 127–171. For the roots of the Daughters of Bilitis and issues of pseudonyms, see Marcia M. Gallo, *Different Daughters: A History of the Daughters of Bilitis and the Rise of the Lesbian Rights Movement* (New York: Carroll and Graf, 2006), xv–xvi, 1–55; Del Martin and Phyllis Lyon, *Lesbian/Woman* (New York: Bantam, 1972).

16. D'Emilio, *Sexual Politics, Sexual Communities*, 72; Gallo, *Different Daughters*, 6; Martin and Lyon, *Lesbian/Woman*, 246–247.

17. D'Emilio, *Sexual Politics, Sexual Communities*, 109–110, 115. Photograph of Jack Nichols at Independence Hall in Philadelphia, July 4, 1995, carrying a sign that reads, "15 MILLION HOMOSEXUALS / ASK FOR / EQUALITY / OPPORTUNITY / DIGNITY": J. Louis Campbell, *Jack Nichols, Gay Pioneer: "Have You Heard My Message?"* (New York: Harrington Park Press, 2007), 115.

18. D'Emilio, *Sexual Politics, Sexual Communities*, 190–191.

19. The July 4 pickets in Philadelphia were called "the Annual Reminder": Vicki L. Eaklor, *Queer America: A People's GLBT History of the United States* (New York: New Press, 2011), 107–109. The words on the signs are from photographs of Barbara Gittings in Philadelphia, in Faderman, *Odd Girls and Twilight Lovers*, facing p. 87; Eaklor, *Queer America*, 109.

20. Jackie Harris, interview by the author, New York, March 1, 1995; Shirley Clarke, interview by the author, Boston, March 27, 1995; Ian Lekus, "Losing Our Kids: Queer Perspectives on the Chicago Seven Conspiracy Trial," in *The New Left Revisited*, ed. John McMillian and Paul Buhle (Philadelphia: Temple University Press, 2003), 199–213.

21. Estelle B. Freedman, *No Turning Back: The History of Feminism and the Future of Women* (New York: Ballantine, 2002), 86–88; Anne Koedt, "The Myth of the Vaginal Orgasm," and Kathie Sarachild, "A Program for Feminist 'Consciousness Raising,'" in *Notes from the Second Year: Women's Liberation*, ed. Shulamith Firestone and Anne Koedt (New York: Radical Feminism, 1970), 37–41, 78–80.

22. Anne Koedt, "Loving Another Woman," in *Notes from the Third Year: Women's Liberation*, ed. Shulamith Firestone and Anne Koedt (New York, 1971), 25–30; Radicalesbians, "The Woman-Identified Woman," and A Gay Male Group, "Notes on Gay Male Consciousness Raising," in *Out of the Closets: Voices from Gay Liberation*, ed. Karla Jay and Allen Young (New York: Pyramid, 1974), 172–176, 293–301.

23. For more on the Stonewall events and the movement that followed, see Martin Duberman, *Stonewall* (New York: E. P. Dutton, 1993).

24. The proposal was brought to the floor of the convention by Madeline Davis, delegate from Buffalo. Davis was an officer of her local Mattachine chapter and a member of the Librarians Association of the Buffalo and Erie County Public Library, an independent union that later affiliated with the AFT. "We have suffered from oppression—from being totally ignored or ridiculed to having our heads smashed and our blood spilled in the streets," she said. "Now we are coming out of our closets": Madeline Davis, "Address to the Democratic National Convention," in *Speaking for Our Lives: Historic Speeches and Rhetoric for Gay and Lesbian Rights (1892–2000)*, ed. Robert B. Ridinger (Binghamton, NY: Harrington Park, 2004), 179. Many denounced the party's entire platform, which included demands for immediate withdrawal of troops from Vietnam, before he directly attacked the gay delegates. "We listened to the gay-lib people—you know, the people who want to legalize marriage between boys and boys and between girls and girls. We heard from abortionists, and we heard from the people who looked like Jacks, acted like Jills, and had the odors of Johns about them": quoted in *John Herling's Labor Letter*, September 12, 1972.

25. For the AFT, see Christian Arthur Bain, "A Short History of Gay and Lesbian Labor Activism in the United States," in *Laboring for Rights: Unions and Sexual Diversity across Nations*, ed. Gerald Hunt (Philadelphia: Temple University Press, 1999), 62. For the NEA, see "Job Protection for Gays: Teachers Union Votes Rights Stand." *The Advocate*, August 28, 1974, 3.

26. Even in the sex industry, where sexual diversity is openly acknowledged as part of workplace culture, traditional trade union issues—wages, hours, health and safety—prevailed during organizing drives among seventy-two janitors, cashiers, and exotic dancers employed at the Lusty Lady Theater in San Francisco in 1996. Working with the Exotic Dancers Alliance, they signed union cards with SEIU Local 790 and ratified a first contract in April 1997. Many of the union's leaders were lesbians or bisexual: Heidi M. Kooy, "Trollop and Tribades: Queers Organizing in the Sex Business," in *Out at Work: Building a Gay-Labor Alliance*, ed. Kitty Krupat and Patrick McCreery (Minneapolis: University of Minnesota Press, 2001), 112–133; Julia Query, dir., *Live Nude Girls Unite*, First Run/Icarus, Brooklyn, NY, 2000.

27. Nobody really knows just how many Americans are lesbian, gay, bisexual, or transgender. The number remains a hotly debated question, ranging from Alfred Kinsey's challenging estimate in 1948 of 10 percent (Kinsey's definition included anyone who engaged in homosexual or bisexual behavior in his or her lifetime) to the Alan Guttmacher Institute's 1999 estimate of 2–3 percent (based, like the Kinsey survey, on questionable methods of self-reporting). The U.S. census began collecting data on same-sex households in 2000 and again in 2010, both times relying on self-reporting and providing a category for gay couple and family formations only. The demographer Gary J. Gates of the Williams Institute and Frank Newport of Gallup analyzed these data on a state-by-state basis and in February 2013 reported densities ranging from 1.7 percent of the population in North Dakota to 5.1 percent in Hawai'i and 10 percent in Washington DC. Their calculated national average was 3.5 percent. "LGBT Percentage Highest in D.C., Lowest in North Dakota," *GALLUP Politics: State of the States,* available at http://www.gallup.com/poll/160517/lgbt-percentage-highest-lowest-north-dakota.aspx (accessed January 10, 2014).

28. Inclusion of sexual orientation in civil rights and antidiscrimination articles was widely practiced after the mid-1980s; inclusion of gender identity and expression is not yet commonplace.

29. Ruth Milkman and Laura Braslow, "The State of the Unions: A Profile of Organized Labor in New York City, New York State and the United States," report, Joseph S. Murphy Institute for Worker Education and Labor Studies, Center for Urban Research, and New York City Labor Market Information Service, City University of New York, 2011, 3.

30. That Oakland conference was special. Harry Hay and John Burnside showed up at the morning plenary, and I managed to pass them a copy of *Pride at Work* before the session adjourned.

31. Two excellent recent books about queer lives in specific *unionized* work sectors are Anne Balay, *Steel Closets: Voices of Gay, Lesbian and Transgender Steelworkers* (Chapel Hill: University of North Carolina Press, 2014); Philip Tiemeyer, *Plane Queer: Labor, Sexuality and AIDS in the History of Male Flight Attendants* (Berkeley: University of California Press, 2013).

32. Debra Bell, "Unionized Women in State and Local Government," in *Women, Work and Protest: A Century of U.S. Women's Labor History*, ed. Ruth Milkman (Boston: Routledge and Kegan Paul, 1985), 280–299.

CHAPTER 1

1. Jackie Harris, interview by the author, New York City, March 1, 1995.

2. James Mitchell, interview by the author, New York City, August 11, 1995.

3. Cliff Flanders, interview by the author, New York City, January 12, 1998.

4. From www.hrc.org/laws-and-legislation/federal-legislation/employment-non-dis crimination-act (accessed January 12, 2014).

5. "Employment Non-Discrimination Laws on Sexual Orientation and Gender Identity," Human Rights Campaign, available at http://www.hrc.org/resources/entry/cities-

and-counties-with-non-discrimination-ordinances-that-include-gender (accessed January 12, 2014).

6. Robert De Santis, interview by the author, New York City, June 29, 1996.

7. Stipulation of Settlement, *Gay Law Students Association et al. v. Pacific Bell*, no. 691–750, Superior Court of the State of California, County of San Francisco, December 4, 1986; Larry D. Hatfield, "Pac Bell to Pay Gays $3 million," *San Francisco Examiner*, December 5, 1986.

8. For a thorough exploration of campaigns in Miami-Dade County, Florida, in 1977 and in California in 1978, see Chapter 3. For a discussion of campaigns in Oregon and Colorado in 1992, see Chapter 4.

9. Gay male construction workers had no supportive networks and kept themselves much more carefully hidden, knowing that workmates would tolerate their presence neither at the work site nor in the union hall. Nevertheless, men in blue-collar trades did have sex with one another, according to Ramon de la Fuente, who described after-work pleasures in the shower room during his summer sojourn as an apprentice electrician at the NASSCO shipyards in San Diego in the late 1970s: Ramon de la Fuente, interview by the author, Washington, DC, June 10, 1995.

10. Portions of this section were previously published as Miriam Frank, "Hard Hats and Homophobia: Lesbians in the Building Trades," *New Labor Forum* 8 (Spring–Summer 2001): 25–36.

11. Nancy Brown, interview by the author, Detroit, May 1, 1995.

12. For an extensive discussion of policy, see Susan Eisenberg, "Women Hard Hats Speak Out," *The Nation,* September 18, 1989, 272–276.

13. Susan Eisenberg, *We'll Call You if We Need You: Experiences of Women Working Construction* (Ithaca, NY: Cornell University Press, 1998), 87–96.

14. Connie Ashbrook, interview by the author, Portland, OR, July 16, 1995.

15. On the passing of the trade from fathers to sons and other details of the masculine mystique, see Francine A. Moccio, "Contradicting Male Power and Privilege: Class, Race and Gender Relations in the Building Trades," Ph.D. diss., New School for Social Research, New York, 1992, 280–281.

16. Elizabeth Kadetsky, "Woman's Work," *New York Newsday*, October 26, 1992.

17. Janet L. Rogers, "Lesbian Women in the Building Trades," 1990, unpublished ms. in my possession, 3.

18. Francine A. Moccio, *Live Wire: Women and Brotherhood in the Electrical Industry* (Philadelphia: Temple University Press, 2009), 168.

19. See, e.g., Jean Reith Schroedel, ed., *Alone in a Crowd: Women in the Trades Tell Their Stories* (Philadelphia: Temple University Press, 1985); Molly Martin, *Hard-Hatted Women: Life on the Job* (Seattle: Seal, 1997); Eisenberg, *We'll Call You if We Need You*; Jane LaTour, *Sisters in the Brotherhoods: Working Women Organizing for Equality in New York City* (New York: Palgrave Macmillan, 2008); Moccio, *Live Wire*.

20. Barbara Trees, interview by the author, New York City, October 29, 1987.

21. Ann Jochems, interview by the author, New York City, February 24, 1999. For more on Jochems's ordeal, see LaTour, *Sisters in the Brotherhoods*, 113–129. In an interview with LaTour, Venus Green described the presentation of a dildo to a young woman who was employed in a craft job at the telephone company: see LaTour, *Sisters in the Brotherhoods*, 175.

22. Ashbrook interview.

23. Karen Wheeler, interview by the author, Boston, March 26, 1995. Several lesbians in the trades responded to the survey question "What are some lesbian issues that heterosexual women are uncomfortable discussing?" by citing "being in the bathroom with them [lesbians]" as a specific fear: Rogers, "Lesbian Women in the Building Trades," 43.

24. Irene Soloway, interview by the author, New York City, March 4, 1999.

25. Brown interview.

26. Wheeler interview.

27. Brown interview.

28. Soloway interview. For more on Soloway's civil service job, see LaTour, *Sisters in the Brotherhoods*, 209–210.

29. Ashbrook interview.

30. For extensive coverage of these campaigns, see Chapter 4.

31. Venus Green first broke into the telephone crafts in 1973 as a black female switchman at the New York Telephone Company. Green describes the climate of constant tension and conflict in *Race on the Line: Gender, Labor and Technology in the Bell System, 1880–1980* (Durham, NC: Duke University Press, 2001), ix–xi. LaTour discusses the effects of the consent decree and Green's experience: see LaTour, *Sisters in the Brotherhoods*, 160–180.

32. Faith Robinson, interview by the author, Detroit, April 30, 1995.

33. Ibid.

34. Ibid.; Cathy Trost, "One Woman's Ordeal on Line Job," *Detroit Free Press*, March 12, 1979.

35. On CLUW and labor feminists of the CWA, see Dorothy Sue Cobble, *The Other Women's Movement: Workplace Justice and Social Rights in Modern America* (Princeton, NJ: Princeton University Press, 2004), 201–204.

36. Robinson interview.

37. Rosalie Riegel, interview by the author, New York City, February 14, 1995. For more on Local 1101 and the *Bell Wringer* caucus, see LaTour, *Sisters in the Brotherhoods*, 176–178.

38. Sandra Lara, interview by the author, New York City, March 21, 1995.

39. Madelyn Elder, interview by the author, Portland, OR, July 17, 1995.

40. Shelley Crites, interview by the author, Seattle, July 14, 1995.

41. Ashbrook interview.

42. Shelley Ettinger, interview by the author, New York City, September 11, 1998.

43. Tess Ewing, interview by the author, Boston, March 25, 1995.

44. Sue Schurman, interview by the author, Silver Spring, MD, July 18, 2001.

45. Ettinger interview.

46. Ewing interview. The International Union of Mine, Mill, and Smelter Workers was expelled from the Congress of Industrial Organizations (CIO) in 1950, and the USWA absorbed many of its local affiliates, including those in Boston that represented workers at public utilities.

47. Susan Moir, interview by the author, Boston, March 24, 1995.

48. Ewing interview.

49. Ettinger interview.

50. Moir interview.

51. Helen Vozenilek, "Changing Times, Changing Leadership: Interview with Janis Borchardt," *Tradeswomen*, Winter 1991, 21.

52. For reflections by autoworkers about work, the culture of the auto plant, and connections between their work lives and their personal hopes and dreams, see Richard Feldman and Michael Betzold, *End of the Line: Autoworkers and the American Dream* (New York: Weidenfeld and Nicholson, 1988).

53. For the UAW and its discontents during the 1960s and 1970s, see Dan Georgakas and Marvin Surkin, *Detroit, I Do Mind Dying: A Study in Urban Revolution* (New York: St. Martin's Press, 1975).

54. "Jeff Cooper," in Feldman and Betzold, *End of the Line*, 28.

55. "Liska Reports," Ed Liska Collection, box 2, file 10, Walter P. Reuther Library of Labor and Urban Affairs. I thank Jeremy Milloy of Simon Fraser University for alerting me to this material following his presentation of the paper "Killing Floor: Responses to Violence at Detroit and Windsor Auto Plants in the 1970s" at the Labor and Working Class History Association conference, New York City, June 7, 2013.

56. Jim Monk, interview by the author, Windsor, ON, April 28, 1995.

57. Ron Woods, interview by the author, Detroit, April 27, 1995.

58. Keith Truett, interview by the author, Detroit, April 27, 1995.

59. Richard Feldman, interview by the author, Detroit, July 23, 2002.

60. Bob Burrell, interview by the author, Detroit, July 24, 2002.

61. Harry Kevorkian, interview by the author, Boston, June 6, 1999. For an exploration of gay men, sex, and automobiles in Flint of the mid-twentieth century, see Tim Retzloff, "Cars and Bars: Assembling Gay Men in Postwar Flint, Michigan," in *Creating a Place for Ourselves: Lesbian, Gay and Bisexual Community Histories,*" ed. Brett Beemyn (New York: Routledge, 1997), 227–252.

62. Jim Justen, interview by the author, Oakland, CA, June 28, 1996. American Motors merged with Chrysler in 1987, and the Kenosha plant became a Chrysler operation.

63. Dennis O'Neil, interview by the author, New York City, February 9, 1999.

64. Burrell interview.

65. "Gary Bryner, President, Lordstown Local UAW," in Studs Terkel, *Working: People Talk about What They Do All Day and How They Feel about What They Do* (New York: New Press, 1972), 187–194.

66. For Cisek, music was a sustaining avocation before and during gender transition. As Joni Christian she has performed widely as a solo singer of contemporary, gay-affirming Christian music.

67. Joni Christian, interview by the author, Ravenna, OH, July 28, 2002.

68. Ibid.

69. Restroom issues persist as flashpoints in transgender work politics. James B. Stewart reports that a forklift operator at Chrysler's Trenton Engine plant had male-to-female surgery in the early 1990s, returned to work, and was challenged when she attempted to use the women's restroom closest to her station. The controversy was resolved only when she agreed to use the women's bathroom in the office workers' area: James B. Stewart, "Coming Out at Chrysler," *New Yorker*, July 21, 1997, 38.

70. Gary Bryner, interview by the author, Detroit, August 12, 2002.

71. Christian interview.

72. Ibid.

73. Bryner interview.

74. The UAW represented Canadian employees of Ford, Chrysler, and General Motors until 1985, when Canadian divisions split to form the autonomous Canadian Auto Workers.

75. Monk interview.

76. Gerald Hannon, "Gay on the Line," *Body Politic*, September 1978, 28.

77. *The Guardian*, UAW Windsor, ON, March 1978.

78. Monk interview.

79. The Canadian Charter of Rights and Freedoms, an important instrument for lesbian and gay rights law, was incorporated into the federal constitution in 1982: Cynthia Petersen, "Fighting It Out in Canadian Courts," in *Laboring for Rights: Unions and Sexual Diversity across Nations,* ed. Gerald Hunt (Philadelphia: Temple University Press, 1999), 39. On gay rights and religious conservatism in Canada, see Gerald Hunt and David Rayside, "The Geopolitics of Sexual Diversity: Measuring Progress in the U.S., Canada and the Netherlands," *New Labor Forum* 8 (Spring–Summer 2001): 44–45.

80. Monk interview.

81. For more on Woods's grievance at Trenton Engine, see Chapter 4.

82. Michael Funke, "Pride and Prejudice," *UAW Solidarity*, January–February 1993, 18–19.

83. The "Solidarity Letterbox" section published a remarkably wide-ranging correspondence of ten letters in the next three issues that debated Funke's original "Pride and Prejudice" report: *UAW Solidarity*, April 1993, 5, May–June 1993, 6, August 1993, 5.

84. Martha Grevatt, "What a Difference a Fight Makes: How We Beat Chrysler," discussion paper presented at the Creating Change Workshop, National Gay and Lesbian Task Force, November 10, 2000, available at http://www.prideatwork.org/archive/chrysler (accessed June 16, 2008); Stewart, "Coming Out at Chrysler," 46–47. For another account of the campaign for the equal application clause, see Monica Lynn Bielski, "Identity at Work: U.S. Labor Unions' Efforts to Address Sexual Diversity through Policy and Practice," Ph.D. diss., Rutgers University, New Brunswick, NJ, 2005, 118–125.

85. Bill Roberts, interview by the author, Los Angeles, May 19, 1995.

86. Allan Bérubé, "'Fitting In'—Expanding Queer Studies beyond Gay Identity, the Closet and Coming Out," 1990, unpublished ms. in my possession.

87. Allan Bérubé, "'Queer Work' and Labor History," in *My Desire for History: Essays in Gay, Community, and Labor History*, ed. John D'Emilio and Estelle B. Freedman (Chapel Hill: University of North Carolina Press, 2011), 261.

88. For gay and bisexual men working in occupations that are considered more traditionally male, there are also significant wage gaps, but they are not based on the occupational sector of the job. "Gay and bisexual male workers earned from 11% to 27% less than heterosexual male workers with the same experience, education, occupation, marital status, and region of residence," writes M. V. Lee Badgett in "The Wage Effects of Sexual Orientation Discrimination," *Industrial and Labor Relations Review* 48, no. 4 (July 1995): 729. Badgett's survey indicates that gay men "are less likely to be in managerial and blue-collar occupations but are more likely to be in professional/technical and service occupations," and she suggests that wage discrimination against gay men might mask AIDS discrimination: ibid., 734.

89. Roberts interview.

90. Peter Tenney, interview by the author, San Francisco, April 10, 1995.

91. Scott Reed, interview by the author, Seattle, July 13, 1995.

92. Sidney Sushman, interview by the author, Boston, March 22, 1995.

93. Ibid. For Sushman's own description of his life as a performer, see "My Name Is Tangerine: Sylvia Sidney," *Fag Rag*, Summer 1972, 16-17, 32. For a profile and photo of Sushman as Sylvia Sidney, see History Project, *Improper Bostonians: Lesbian and Gay History from the Puritans to Playland* (Boston: Beacon, 1988), 182–183.

94. Sushman interview. "Bitch of Boston Dies on Dec. 16," *Bay Windows*, December 17, 1998. The AFL-CIO's Solidarity Day rally in Washington, DC, on September 19, 1981, protested President Ronald Reagan's firing of 11,376 members of the Professional Air Traffic Controllers Organization who had struck the Federal Aviation Authority. The rally drew 250,000 union members and supporters and was the largest national labor demonstration in decades.

95. For a review of the fashion business, high camp, and queer union militancy at Barneys, see Andrew Ross, "Strike a Pose for Justice: The Barneys Union Campaign of 1996," in *Out at Work: Building a Gay-Labor Alliance*, ed. Kitty Krupat and Patrick McCreery (Minneapolis: University of Minnesota Press, 2001), 78–91.

96. Irving Smith, interview by the author, New York, August 9, 1999.

97. Ibid.

98. Ross, "Strike a Pose for Justice," 88–89.

99. *Barneys Runway*, videorecording, Local 340, ACTWU/UNITE, New York, 1996. "Secure Union Jobs Are in Style at Barneys," *UNITE!* July–August 1996, 10.

100. Smith interview.

101. Ibid.

102. Donna Levitt, interview by the author, San Francisco, February 17, 1999.

103. It is not unusual for a very small proportion of eligible workers to register for domestic partner coverage. Because so many workers typically do not take advantage of

the benefit, the reform is actually an inexpensive one. For more on collective bargaining of same-sex and opposite-sex domestic partner benefits, see Desma Holcomb, "Domestic Partner Health Benefits: The Corporate Model versus the Union Model," in Hunt, *Laboring for Rights*, 103–120.

104. For a survey and chart of thirteen national unions' responses to sexual diversity, see Gerald Hunt and Monica Bielski Boris, "The Lesbian, Gay, Bisexual and Transgender Challenge to American Labor," in *The Sex of Class: Women Transforming American Labor*, ed. Dorothy Sue Cobble (Ithaca, NY: Cornell University Press, 2007), 91–94.

105. Desma Holcomb, "It All Begins with Coming Out," in Krupat and McCreery, *Out at Work*, 247.

CHAPTER 2

1. Marcy Johnsen, interview by the author, Tacoma, WA, July 13, 1995.

2. The name "Hands Off Washington" referred to the hands of right-wing activists. Antigay campaigns of the Oregon Citizens Alliance (OCA) in 1992 were the inspiration for Initiative 608 and Initiative 610. For an analysis of Oregon unions' involvement in the defeat of OCA-sponsored referenda, see Chapter 4. For more on the successful Hands Off Washington campaign against the petition drive for Initiative 608 and Initiative 610 and for subsequent Hands Off Washington gay civil rights activities, see Liz Latham, dir., *We're Here to Stay: The History of Hands Off Washington*, Lizard Productions, Seattle, 1998.

3. Johnsen interview.

4. Ibid.

5. Nancy Wohlforth, secretary-treasurer of the Office and Professional Employees, joined the council in 2005, and Randi Weingarten, president of the American Federation of Teachers, was seated in 2008.

6. A notable exception was the Marine Cooks and Stewards Association of the CIO. Allan Bérubé, "No Race-Baiting, Red-Baiting, or Queer-Baiting! The Marine Cooks and Stewards Union from the Depression to the Cold War," in *My Desire for History: Essays in Gay, Community, and Labor History*, ed. John D'Emilio and Estelle B. Freedman (Chapel Hill: University of North Carolina Press, 2011), 294–320.

7. Edith Windsor began her sixteen-year career as a systems programmer at IBM in 1958. A 5–4 ruling by the Supreme Court on her suit, *Edith Windsor v. the United States of America*, rendered the Defense of Marriage Act of 1996 unconstitutional and awarded her a $363,053 tax refund on the estate of her deceased spouse, Theya Spyer. The decision was handed down on June 26, 2013, and at a press conference that evening, Windsor recalled her years in the closet at IBM. "I lied all the time," she said. "Internalized homophobia is a bitch!": quoted in Ariel Levy, "The Perfect Wife," *New Yorker*, September 30, 2013, 63.

8. Jim Justen, interview by the author, Oakland, CA, June 28, 1996.

9. Ibid.

10. Bailey T. Walker Jr., interview by the author, Washington, DC, June 14, 1995.

11. John D'Emilio, *Lost Prophet: The Life and Times of Bayard Rustin* (New York: Free Press, 2003), 193.

12. George Chauncey Jr. and Lisa Kennedy, "Time on Two Crosses: An Interview with Bayard Rustin," *Village Voice*, June 30, 1987, 27–29; Devon W. Carbado and Donald Weise, eds., *Time on Two Crosses: The Collected Writings of Bayard Rustin* (San Francisco: Cleis, 2003), 272–303; Nancy D. Kates and Bennett Singer, dirs., *Brother Outsider: The Life of Bayard Rustin*, Independent Television Service/California Newsreel, San Francisco, 2002.

13. Gary Deane, interview by the author, New York, August 9, 1994.

14. Connie Kopelov, interview by the author, New York, July 14, 1994.

15. In 1997, Kopelov received the Lifetime Achievement Award from SAGE (Senior Action in a Gay Environment, which after 2009 changed its name to Services and Advocacy for Gay, Lesbian, Bisexual and Transgender Elders).

16. Van Alan Sheets, interview by the author, Washington, DC, June 8, 1995.

17. Tom Privitere, interview by the author, New York, March 13, 1996.

18. Ibid.

19. For a financial analysis of the costs of domestic partner benefits with a further account of New York State employee unions' campaigns to secure the coverage, see Desma Holcomb, "Domestic Partner Benefits: The Corporate Model vs. The Union Model," in *Laboring for Rights: Unions and Sexual Diversity across Nations,* ed. Gerald Hunt (Philadelphia: Temple University Press, 1999), 113–115.

20. Sections of Mage's 1960 senior thesis at Antioch College about the indigent elderly were adapted by Michael Harrington for his landmark study, *The Other America: Poverty in the United States* (New York: Penguin, 1963).

21. Judy Mage, interview by the author, New York, August 15, 1994. For an overview of Local 371, the SSEU, and the caseworkers' strike of 1965, see Joshua B. Freeman, *Working Class New York: Life and Labor since World War II* (New York: New Press, 2000), 205–206.

22. Mage interview. The Department of Welfare was later known as the Department of Social Services and then as the Human Resources Administration. For two accounts of the formation of the union and Mage's role, see Jewel Bellush and Bernard Bellush, *Union Power in New York: Victor Gotbaum and District Council 37* (New York: Praeger, 1984), 115, 131–135; Richard Henry Pereira Mendes, "The Professional Union: A Study of the Social Service Employees Union of the New York City Department of Social Services," Ph.D. diss., Columbia University, New York, 1974.

23. For more on the Daughters of Bilitis, a lesbian organization of the mid-1950s through early 1970s, and their journal, *The Ladder,* see Marcia M. Gallo, *Different Daughters: A History of the Daughters of Bilitis and the Rise of the Lesbian Rights Movement* (New York: Carroll and Graf, 2006).

24. Mage interview.

25. Freeman, *Working Class New York,* 205; Bill Schleicher, "How We Built a Great Union," *Public Employee Press,* AFSCME District Council 37, fiftieth anniversary issue, 2005.

26. Mage interview.

27. Bellush and Bellush, *Union Power in New York,* 124; Mendes, "The Professional Union," 105.

28. Mage interview. For his history of the Newark Teachers Union and the strikes of 1970 and 1971, Steve Golin interviewed female union members who had served time at the Essex County Jail. Some recalled comforting one another with gestures of affection, such as handholding after lights out. One teacher, a lesbian, described dancing and socializing with other lesbian inmates (who were not teachers) during recreation time: Steve Golin, *The Newark Teacher Strikes: Hopes on the Line* (New Brunswick, NJ: Rutgers University Press, 2002), 186–187, 199–200.

29. Schleicher, "How We Built a Great Union."

30. Premilla Nadasen, *Welfare Warriors: The Welfare Rights Movement in the United States* (New York: Routledge, 2005), 36.

31. Mage interview.

32. Bill Olwell, interview by the author, Washington, DC, June 9, 1995.

33. Ibid.; Joel Connelly, "Remembering the Man Who Rescued Seattle Labor," *Seattle Post-Intelligencer,* March 16, 2001, available at http://www.seattlepi.com/connelly/joell161 .shtml (accessed July 10, 2008).

34. Olwell interview.

35. The negotiation brought about a very early example of what labor feminists later called "pay equity": Connelly, "Remembering the Man Who Rescued Seattle Labor."

36. Olwell interview.

37. Ibid.

38. Jeanne Laberge, interview by the author, New York, May 10, 1996; Ruth Jacobsen, *Rescued Images: Memories of a Childhood in Hiding* (New York: Mikaya, 2001).

39. Laberge interview.

40. Ruth Jacobsen, interview by the author, Southampton, NY, March 6, 1995. Steve D'Inzillo to Ruth Jacobsen, letter, March 10, 1982, in the possession of Ruth Jacobsen.

41. Teresa Rankin, interview by the author, Washington, DC, June 9, 1995.

42. For a retrospective account of the J. P. Stevens campaign, see Marvin Adler, "A New Day in Dixie," *Southern Exposure* 21, no. 9 (Spring 1994): 16–27. For a detailed history of the consumer boycott and the corporate campaign, see Timothy J. Minchin, *"Don't Sleep with Stevens!": The J. P. Stevens Campaign and the Struggle to Organize the South, 1963–1980* (Gainesville: University of Florida Press, 2005), 75–126.

43. Rankin interview.

44. For more on SEIU District 925 and the emergence of the working women's movement, see Karen Nussbaum, "Working Women's Insurgent Consciousness," in *The Sex of Class: Women Transforming American Labor*, ed. Dorothy Sue Cobble (Ithaca, NY: Cornell University Press, 2007), 159–168.

45. Rankin interview.

46. Martha Voland, interview by the author, Portland, ME, July 15, 2009.

47. Ibid. Lowell Turner, "Rank-and-File Participation in Organizing at Home and Abroad," in *Organizing to Win: New Research on Union Strategies*, ed. Kate Bronfenbrenner, Sheldon Friedman, Richard W. Hurd, Rudolph A. Oswald, and Ronald L. Seeber (Ithaca, NY: Cornell University Press, 1998), 124–127.

48. Alexandra Lescaze, dir., *Where Do You Stand? Stories from an American Mill*, Firebrand Productions/California Newsreel, San Francisco, 2004.

49. Voland interview.

50. "Timeline," in Lescaze. *Where Do You Stand?*

51. Ibid.

52. Voland interview. The union prevailed when Pillowtex kept its pledge not to interfere in a final election supervised by the NLRB in 1999. A contract ratified in February 2000 became the first in the industry to provide paid sick days. The victory was short-lived. Following congressional ratification of the North American Free Trade Agreement of 1994, U.S. textile firms lost their markets to global producers in Turkey, India, China, and Brazil. Some businesses survived by extending operations globally and then selling trademarked imports at Walmart and other major discounters. Pillowtex, weak with debt, could not compete. The company filed for bankruptcy in fall 2000, recovered briefly, and then liquidated entirely in 2003. In Kannapolis, 4,340 workers lost their jobs, the largest permanent layoff ever in North Carolina: Lescaze. *Where Do You Stand?*

53. Voland interview; Desma Holcomb and Nancy Wohlforth, "The Fruits of Our Labor: Pride at Work," *New Labor Forum* 8 (Spring–Summer 2001): 19.

54. For a historical and analytical review of labor racketeering and federal trusteeships, see James B. Jacobs, *Mobsters, Unions, and Feds: The Mafia and the American Labor Movement* (New York: New York University Press, 2006).

55. For practical discussions of contemporary union democracy movements, see Jane Slaughter, *A Troublemaker's Handbook 2: How to Fight Back Where You Work—and Win!* (Detroit: Labor Notes, 2005).

56. For a broad study of labor insurgencies from 1959 to 1995, see Herman Benson, *Rebels, Reformers and Racketeers: How Insurgents Transformed the Labor Movement* (Bloomington, Indiana: 1st Books, 2004).

57. Donna Cartwright, interview by the author, Cliffside Park, NJ, July 16, 2001.

58. Cartwright was following the Standards of Care for the Health of Transsexual,

Transgender, and Gender Nonconforming People (sometimes known as the Benjamin Standards). These commonly accepted preliminary protocols are used by professionals who work with gender-variant people to delineate prerequisites for hormone replacement therapy and sexual reassignment surgery. During the "real-life experience" phase, candidates for transition live publicly in their preferred gender role. They dress according to the role; they let themselves be seen in their communities; and they talk about the transition they are intending with family members, friends and colleagues.

59. Cartwright interview.

60. Ibid.

61. Ed Hunt, interview by the author, Oakland, CA, June 29, 1996. For more on unions at Boston City Hospital, see Dan La Botz, *A Troublemaker's Handbook: How to Fight Back Where You Work—and Win!* (Detroit: Labor Notes, 2001), 63–64, 169–170.

62. For a history of organizing battles at Briggs, see Charles Williams, "Reconsidering CIO Political Culture: Briggs Local 212 and the Sources of Militancy in the Early UAW," *Labor* 7, no. 4 (Winter 2010): 17–43.

63. For a general history of black resistance in the UAW and the League of Revolutionary Black Workers during the 1960s and 1970s, see Dan Georgakas and Marvin Surkin, *Detroit, I Do Mind Dying: A Study in Urban Revolution* (New York: St. Martin's Press, 1975); Heather Thompson, *Whose Detroit? Politics, Labor, and Race in a Modern American City* (Ithaca, NY: Cornell University Press, 2001), 103–127.

64. For more on George Wallace's appeal to white members of the UAW in Detroit's northeastern suburbs, see R. David Riddle, "The Rise of the 'Reagan Democrats' in Warren, Michigan, 1964–1984," Ph.D. diss., Wayne State University, Detroit, 1998.

65. Gary Kapanowski, interview by the author, Philadelphia, February 12, 2001.

66. Ibid. On the Mack wildcat, see Thompson, *Whose Detroit?* 199–203. For another version of the battle at the Mack plant gates and the closing of the Sterling Heights factory, see Georgakas and Surkin, *Detroit, I Do Mind Dying*, 193–195.

67. Kapanowski interview.

68. Kim Ramsey, interview by the author, Tacoma, WA, July 14, 1995.

CHAPTER 3

1. Dan Baum, *Citizen Coors: An American Dynasty* (New York: William Morrow, 2000), 91.

2. California Public Interest Research Group, "CalPIRG's Preliminary Report on the Coors Beer Boycott," April 4, 1979, 8–10, in Ephemera—Subjects, International Gay Information Center Collection, 1951–1994, New York Public Library. An Equal Employment Opportunity Commission lawsuit in 1975 spurred improvements to Coors's female and minority hiring policies. At the time of settlement in 1977, 13 percent of the Coors workforce were minorities, and 16 percent were women.

3. Baum, *Citizen Coors*, 90–91.

4. Important histories of queer working-class communities include Brett Beemyn, *Creating a Place for Ourselves: Lesbian, Gay, and Bisexual Communities* (New York: Routledge, 1997); Nan Amilla Boyd, *Wide-Open Town: A Queer History of San Francisco to 1965* (Berkeley: University of California Press, 2003); George Chauncey, *Gay New York: Gender, Urban Culture and the Making of the Gay Male World, 1890–1940* (New York: Basic, 1994); John D'Emilio, *Sexual Politics, Sexual Communities: The Making of a Homosexual Minority in the United States, 1940-1970* (Chicago: University of Chicago Press, 1983); Lillian Faderman and Stewart Timmons, *Gay L.A.: A History of Sexual Outlaws, Power Politics, and Lipstick Lesbians* (New York: Basic, 2006); Elizabeth Lapovsky Kennedy and Madeline D. Davis, *Boots of Leather, Slippers of Gold: The History of a Lesbian Community* (New York: Routledge, 1993);

Marc Stein, *City of Sisterly and Brotherly Loves: Lesbian and Gay Philadelphia, 1945–1972* (Chicago: University of Chicago Press, 2000); Josh Sides, *Erotic Cities: Sexual Revolutions and the Making of Modern San Francisco* (New York: Oxford University Press, 2009).

5. This was true for approximately seventy-two janitors, cashiers, and exotic dancers employed at the Lusty Lady Theater in San Francisco. In 1996, they contacted the Exotic Dancers Alliance and then signed union cards to petition for representation by SEIU Local 790. The NLRB election in August was a union win, 57–15. Management balked at negotiations and then initiated a lockout, but the union persisted, and a contract was ratified in April 1997. Many union members were lesbian or bisexual: Heidi M. Kooy, "Trollops and Tribades: Queers Organizing in the Sex Business," in *Out at Work: Building a Gay-Labor Alliance*, ed. Kitty Krupat and Patrick McCreery (Minneapolis: University of Minnesota Press, 2001), 112–133; Vicky Funari and Julia Query, dirs., *Live Nude Girls Unite!* documentary film, Icarus Films, Brooklyn, NY, 2000.

6. Frank Bardacke, *Trampling Out the Vintage: Cesar Chavez and the Two Souls of the United Farm Workers* (London: Verso, 2011), 362–385.

7. Allan Baird, interview by the author, San Francisco, April 11, 1995.

8. Randy Shilts, *The Mayor of Castro Street: The Life and Times of Harvey Milk* (New York: St. Martin's Press, 1982), 83–84. Howard Wallace was the first openly gay man to be hired in fulfillment of Baird's pledge; he worked on a Falstaff beer truck in 1975: Baird interview; Howard Wallace, interview by the author, San Francisco, January 12, 2001.

9. Baum, *Citizen Coors*, 46, 66. Coors employees asserted in sworn affidavits that they were subjected to such questions. As the boycott pressed, company officials both denied having asked some of the questions offensive to the gay market and claimed to have eliminated them from the pre-employment polygraphs. Questions about "subversive, revolutionary or communistic activity" remained on the test: California Public Interest Research Group, "CalPIRG's Preliminary Report on the Coors Beer Boycott," 1.

10. Howard Wallace, interview by the author, San Francisco, April 8, 1995.

11. The Adolph Coors Company and Coors family members have been or continue to be major supporters of right-wing organizations, among them the John Birch Society, the National Right to Work Committee, and the Free Congress Foundation (a distributor of anti-gay literature): Russ Bellant, *The Coors Connection: How Coors Family Philanthropy Undermines Democratic Pluralism* (Boston: South End Press, 1991), 63–65, 82.

12. Baum, *Citizen Coors*, 166–183.

13. Ibid., 226–227.

14. Tim Kingston, "Rocky Mountain Venom: Coors and Queers," *San Francisco Bay Times*, March 24, 1994, 6–8.

15. Baum, *Citizen Coors*, 129–157, 213–224.

16. Ibid., 178.

17. Ibid., 178–179.

18. Ibid., 201.

19. Ibid., 206.

20. Kingston, "Rocky Mountain Venom."

21. Baum, *Citizen Coors*, 278.

22. Jonathan P. Hicks, "Coor [*sic*] Mends Minority Fences," *New York Times,* July 25, 1985; Baum, *Citizen Coors*, 289–291.

23. Baum, *Citizen Coors*, 311.

24. Gary Dotterman, interview by the author, Boston, March 23, 1995.

25. Christian Arthur Bain, "A Short History of Gay and Lesbian Labor Activism in the United States," in *Laboring for Rights: Unions and Sexual Diversity across Nations*, ed. Gerald Hunt (Philadelphia: Temple University Press 1999), 70.

26. Baum, *Citizen Coors*, 319–321.

27. Sarah Wildman, "Plain Sight: The Relationship between Family and Sexual Identity," *The Advocate*, September 12, 2000, 27–30; "Brewing Controversy," *The Advocate*, March 2, 1999, 14.

28. The Teamsters' Gay, Lesbian, Bisexual, and Transgender Caucus joined the union's Human Rights Commission in 2005.

29. Baird interview.

30. Michael Rubino, interview by the author, New York City, March 15, 1989.

31. "News Briefs," *The Advocate*, August 4, 1983, 12.

32. Jim Mitchell, interview by the author, New York, August 11, 1995.

33. Bain speculates that the statement by the AFT Executive Council may have been "precipitated" by the involvement of the civil rights leader Bayard Rustin in the rough politics of a strike by the United Federation of Teachers (the AFT's largest affiliate) in the fall of 1969 in New York City: Bain, "A Short History of Gay and Lesbian Labor Activism in the United States," 62, 84n9. For more on Rustin's troubles as a gay man in the movement, see John D'Emilio, *Lost Prophet: The Life and Times of Bayard Rustin* (New York: Free Press, 2003), 99–105.

34. Bain, "A Short History of Gay and Lesbian Labor Activism in the United States," 84n12.

35. Tom Ammiano, interview by the author, San Francisco, April 7, 1995. For more on internal politics within California teachers' unions to oppose the Briggs amendment, see Sara R. Smith, "Struggling for Equality: Rank-and-File Teachers' Organizing in California after World War II," chapter 4, Ph.D. diss., University of California, Santa Cruz, forthcoming.

36. Victor Basile, interview by the author, Baltimore, July 19, 2007.

37. Bailey T. Walker Jr., interview by the author, Washington, DC, June 14, 1995.

38. Walker interview; Basile interview. For more details on pre-convention politicking, see Bain, "A Short History of Gay and Lesbian Labor Activism in the United States," 66–68.

39. Walker interview. The argument about sex with animals is often cited by religious fundamentalists who oppose LGBT rights. The biblical text that commands, "You shall not have sexual relations with any animal and defile yourself with it. . . . [I]t is perversion" (Lev. 18:23) follows directly the text that commands, "You shall not lie with a man as with a woman" (Lev. 18:22). Thus, for literal readers of scripture, bestiality does "come next" after male homosexuality: "The Hebrew Bible," in *The New Oxford Annotated Bible*, augmented 3d ed. (New York: Oxford University Press, 2007), 169.

40. Walker interview. In the spring of 1968, William Lucy was working for AFSCME and was dispatched to Local 1733 in Memphis, where sanitation workers were sustaining a long and difficult strike. Dr. Martin Luther King Jr. traveled to Memphis to support the struggle and was assassinated on April 4.

41. Bain, "A Short History of Gay and Lesbian Labor Activism in the United States," 68.

42. Howard Wallace, "AFL-CIO Takes Strong Stand for Gay Rights," *San Francisco Vector*, October 13, 1983, 1.

43. Craig A. Rimmerman, *From Identity to Politics: The Lesbian and Gay Movements in the United States* (Philadelphia: Temple University Press, 2002), 127–129; Dudley Clendinen and Adam Nagourney, *Out for Good: The Struggle to Build a Gay Rights Movement in America* (New York: Simon and Schuster, 1999), 299–311.

44. For more on Anita Bryant and Save Our Children, see Clendinen and Nagourney, *Out for Good*, 303–307.

45. Hank Wilson, interview by the author, San Francisco, April 12, 1995.

46. Clendinen and Nagourney, *Out for Good*, 328.

47. "UTD Sets the Record Straight on Human Rights" (advertisement), *Miami Herald*, May 24, 1977; Annette Katz, interview by the author, Miami, July 29, 2004.

48. Wilson interview.

49. Ibid.

50. Madelyn Elder, interview by the author, Portland, OR, July 17, 1995.

51. Ibid.

52. Ibid.

53. Barry D. Adam, *The Rise of a Gay and Lesbian Movement*, rev. ed. (Boston: Twayne, 1995), 113.

54. Amber Hollibaugh, Diane Ehrensaft and Ruth Milkman, "Sexuality and the State: The Defeat of the Briggs Initiative and Beyond, an Interview with Amber Hollibaugh," *Socialist Review* 45 (May–June 1979): 55–56.

55. The Tenth U.S. Circuit Court of Appeals struck down Oklahoma's Helm Act in 1985 as a violation of First Amendment free speech rights. An appeal to the Supreme Court resulted in a 4–4 tie (with one abstention), which allowed the lower court's ruling to stand: Clendinen and Nagourney, *Out for Good*, 533.

56. Ibid., 378–379.

57. California voters' pamphlet, general election, November 7, 1978, 28–31, 41, available at http://librarysource.uchastings.edu/ballot_pdf/1978g.pdf (accessed July 7, 2008).

58. Hollibaugh et al., "Sexuality and the State," 56.

59. Peter Tenney, interview by the author, San Francisco, April 10, 1995.

60. "Stop Briggs, No on 6, Protect Your Rights," campaign brochure, Bay Area Committee against the Briggs Initiative, 1978, in *Solidarity in Action: An Historical Scrapbook*, ed. Howard Wallace (San Francisco: SEIU Local 250, 1994), n.p.; "Labor Unions Join Anti-Briggs Fight," *Bay Area Reporter*, July 6, 1978, 30.

61. Johnson interview.

62. Tenney interview. David McDonald's speech is reprinted in *Speaking for Our Lives: Historic Speeches and Rhetoric for Lesbian and Gay Rights (1892–2000)*, ed. Robert B. Ridinger (Binghamton, NY: Harrington Park, 2000), 295–297.

63. Hollibaugh et al., "Sexuality and the State," 59, 61–63.

64. For a discussion of Reagan's decision to recommend "no" on Proposition 6, see Clendinen and Nagourney, *Out for Good*, 385–388.

65. "Two Million Union Members—No on 6," *Bay Area Reporter*, November 9, 1978, 12.

66. Virginia LaGasa, interview by the author, Seattle, July 14, 1995.

67. Sal Roselli, interview by the author, San Francisco, April 13, 1995.

68. Tenney interview.

69. Miriam Frank and Desma Holcomb, *Pride at Work: Organizing for Lesbian and Gay Rights in Unions* (New York: Lesbian and Gay Labor Network, 1990).

70. Karen Wheeler, interview by the author, Boston, March 26, 1995.

71. Ginny Cutting, interview by the author, Boston, March 24, 1995.

72. Tom Barbera, interview by the author, New York City, April 14, 2000.

73. Wheeler interview.

74. Janice Loux, interview by the author, Boston, March 23, 1995.

75. Amy Gluckman, "Laboring for Rights: An Interview with Susan Moir," in *Homo Economics: Capitalism, Community and Lesbian and Gay Life*, Amy Gluckman and Betsy Reed, eds. (New York: Routledge, 1997), 229–231. See also Harneen Chernow and Susan Moir, "Lesbian and Gay Labor for Health Care," *Forward Motion* 8 (4) December 1989, 42–45.

76. Gluckman, "Laboring for Rights," 231. GALLAN's writings on class and the unionization of gay community services and businesses attest to the group's intensive internal discussions and public presentations: letters by Harneen Chernow, Andrea Denahewsji, and Anne Herbst; Janice Loux; and Ed Hunt and Karen Wheeler in *Gay Community News* 20, no. 3 (Fall 1994): 3, 30–31.

77. Ed Hunt, interview by the author, Oakland, CA, June 29, 1996.

78. The AIDS memorial quilt was the subject of the Academy Award-winning documentary *Common Threads: Stories from the Quilt*, dir. Robert Epstein and Jeffrey Friedman, Telling Pictures, San Francisco, 1989.

79. AFL-CIO Committee on the Evolution of Work, "The Changing Situation of Workers and Their Unions," report, Washington DC, 1985, 14–16, 18–19.

80. Frank and Holcomb, *Pride at Work*, 1–2.

81. Barbera interview.

82. Shirley Clarke, interview by the author, Boston, March 27, 1995.

83. The CWA's Executive Council announced an explicit "No Discrimination" policy statement that included sexual orientation in 1999.

84. Cal Noyce, interview by the author, Detroit, April 30, 1995.

85. Ibid.

86. Ed Mayne, interview by the author, Salt Lake City, July 27, 2000.

87. Noyce interview.

88. For more on the genesis of Pride at Work, see Desma Holcomb and Nancy Wohlforth, "The Fruits of Our Labor: Pride at Work," *New Labor Forum* 8 (Spring–Summer 2001): 9–20.

89. John Nichols, *Uprising: How Wisconsin Renewed the Politics of Protest, from Madison to Wall Street* (New York: Nation, 2012).

CHAPTER 4

1. Sally Otos, interview by the author, New York City, August 10, 1998. For an extensive history of the unionization of Columbia's clerical and technical workers, see Sharon Kurtz, *Workplace Justice: Organizing Multi-identity Movements* (Minneapolis: University of Minnesota Press, 2002).

2. Otos interview.

3. Ibid.

4. Patricia Yeghissian analyzes the interaction of municipal politics and bus drivers' union activism in Ann Arbor during the 1970s in "Towards a More Perfect Union: The Making of the Transportation Employees' Union," Ann Arbor, 1979, unpublished ms. in my possession.

5. "Sexual orientation" and "domestic partners" have been standard terms since the mid-1980s. But nomenclature for sexual diversity varied wildly and widely in municipal and state laws, union contracts and similar legal documents of the 1970s and early 1980s: "sexual preference," "affectional preference," "homosexual practices," "lifestyle," or "sexual predilection" connoted sexual orientation; "mate" or "spouse equivalent" connoted domestic partner.

6. Susan Schurman, interview by the author, Silver Spring, MD, July 18, 2001 .

7. AFSCME Local 2083, the Seattle Public Library Workers, negotiated similar protections that same year: Christa Orth, "Brothers and Sisters (and Everyone in Between): Sexuality and Class in the Pacific Northwest, 1970–1995," master's thesis, University of Oregon, Eugene, 2002, 40.

8. Schurman interview.

9. Harry Kevorkian, interview by the author, Boston, June 6, 1999.

10. Schurman interview.

11. Ibid.; John Mitzel, "My Friend Kitty, Sweet Dreams," *The Guide,* March 2002, available at http://archive.guidemag.com/magcontent/invokemagcontent.cfm?ID=1B80EE56-7E67-4964-9867A2CE50CD68A6 (accessed December 19, 2011).

12. Yeghissian, "Towards a More Perfect Union," 27.

13. Ibid., 30–33.

14. Kevorkian interview.

15. Ibid.

16. Linda Romero, interview by the author, Washington, DC, June 10, 1995.

17. Kitty Krupat, "Out of Labor's Dark Age: Sexual Politics Comes to the Workplace," in *Out at Work: Building a Gay-Labor Alliance*, ed. Kitty Krupat and Pat McCreery (Minneapolis: University of Minnesota Press, 2001), 10–12.

18. The *Village Voice*'s agreement about benefits was not actually written into the contract until a few years after the original memorandum of understanding of 1982. Bert Pogrebin, a management lawyer, coined the phrase "spouse equivalent" to describe all unmarried family arrangements. For more on the *Village Voice*, see Miriam Frank and Desma Holcomb, *Pride at Work: Organizing for Lesbian and Gay Rights in Unions* (New York: Lesbian and Gay Labor Network, 1990), 40–45; Miriam Frank, "Lesbian and Gay Caucuses in the U.S. Labor Movement," in *Laboring for Rights: Unions and Sexual Diversity across Nations,* ed. Gerald Hunt (Philadelphia: Temple University Press, 1999), 91–92; Krupat, "Out of Labor's Dark Age," 9–14. For an outline of obstacles presented by the insurance industry, see Frank and Holcomb, *Pride at Work,* 53–56.

19. Krupat, "Out of Labor's Dark Age," 11; Frank and Holcomb, *Pride at Work,* 47–48.

20. These employers were liberal public interest groups whose domestic partner benefits were not negotiated through collective bargaining: the American Psychological Association (1983), the American Friends Service Committee (1987), and the National Organization for Women (1987). The first commercial companies to adopt the reform were start-up ventures, similarly liberal and nonunion: Ben and Jerry's Homemade in Vermont (1989), followed by Lotus Industries in Massachusetts (1991). Bronx Montefiore Medical Center, a private hospital, had collective bargaining, but not for doctors; the settlement of a lesbian doctor's lawsuit in 1991 made domestic partner benefits available to same-sex partners of doctors only. Levi Strauss was the first *Fortune* 500 company to adopt the benefits, first at corporate headquarters in San Francisco in 1992; two years later, the company granted the benefits to the same-sex partners of all its production workers based in the United States, including those who were represented by the Amalgamated Clothing and Textile Workers Union.

21. As ever larger employers adopted the benefits, actuarial data continued to indicate that, even with AIDS-related claims, there were few disparities in costs between domestic partners and married couples: Desma Holcomb, "Domestic Partner Health Benefits: The Corporate Model versus the Union Model," in Hunt, *Laboring for Rights,* 107, 109–110.

22. Ibid., 110.

23. Ibid., 107. For more on the New York City campaign, see also Tamara Jones, "'Top-Down' or 'Bottom-Up'? Sexual Identity and Workers' Rights in a Municipal Union," in Krupat and McCreery, *Out at Work,* 188–189; Kelly Anderson and Tami Gold, dirs., *Out at Work: A Documentary,* AndersonGold Films, New York, 1997.

24. Janice Loux, interview by the author, Boston, March 23, 1995.

25. Ibid.

26. Holcomb, "Domestic Partner Health Benefits," 112–113.

27. Trudy Rudnick, interview by the author, New York City, August 16, 2000.

28. Krupat, "Out of Labor's Dark Age," 11–12; Keith Bradsher, "Big Carmakers Extend Benefits to Gay Couples," *New York Times,* June 9, 2000.

29. Bradsher, "Big Carmakers Extend Benefits to Gay Couples."

30. Krupat, "Out of Labor's Dark Age," 14–15; Bradsher, "Big Carmakers Extend Benefits to Gay Couples"; Norihiko Shirouzo, "Gay Couples to Get Benefits at Auto Makers," *Wall Street Journal,* June 9, 2000.

31. Bradsher, "Big Carmakers Extend Benefits to Gay Couples."

32. For more about "open shop" arrangements, see Chapter 5.

33. Walter Johnson, interview by the author, San Francisco, April 11, 1995; Christian Arthur Bain, "A Short History of Gay and Lesbian Labor Activism in the United States," in Hunt, *Laboring for Rights,* 61.

34. Ron Woods, interview by the author, Detroit, April 27, 1995.

35. Quoted in Anderson and Gold, *Out at Work,* 1997.

36. Ibid.

37. Woods interview.

38. Not until the summer of 1982 did federal health agencies agree on a name for the disease: acquired immune deficiency syndrome. For a summary of the early years of the epidemic, see Dudley Clendinen and Adam Nagourney, *Out for Good: The Struggle to Build a Gay Rights Movement in America* (New York: Simon and Schuster, 1999), 450–452, 461–464.

39. Suzanne Hanen, interview by the author, New York City, July 20, 1994.

40. Netsy Firestein, interview by the author, New York, March 20, 1989.

41. "Labor Blood Drive Launched," *Public Employee Press*, August 24, 1984.

42. Vivienne Freund, interview by the author, New York City, July 13, 2005.

43. Susan Moir, "AIDS: Unions Taking Care of Our Own," panel presented at the Pride at Work conference, District Council 37, New York City, June 6, 1992.

44. Tess Ewing, interview by the author, Boston, March 25, 1995.

45. Gary Kapanowski, interview by the author, Philadelphia, February 12, 2001.

46. Ellis Boal, interview by the author, Detroit, November 3, 1992.

47. "John Ware Selected Chronology," Ellis Boal to UAW Convention Appeals Committee, February 21, 1992, in my possession.

48. Ibid.

49. UAW Conventions Appeals Committee, *John Ware v. International Executive Board*, October 7, 1992, in my possession.

50. Boal interview.

51. Frank, "Lesbian and Gay Caucuses in the U.S. Labor Movement," 92–93.

52. John Mehring, interview by the author, San Francisco, August 18, 1997.

53. Ibid.

54. Bob Lewis, interview by the author, Oakland, CA, June 28, 1996.

55. Frank, "Lesbian and Gay Caucuses in the U.S. Labor Movement," 92–93.

56. John Mehring, "California Service Employees Local Placed in Trusteeship after Strike," *Labor Notes*, March 1987, 3.

57. Mehring interview.

58. John Mehring, "New Constitution and Bylaws Provide Foundation to Rebuild Local," *Labor Notes*, March 1988, 12; Sal Roselli, interview by the author, San Francisco, April 13, 1995.

59. Frank, "Lesbian and Gay Caucuses in the U.S. Labor Movement," 93.

60. Ibid., 88–89; *Gay Teachers Association Newsletter*, March 1978, November 1979.

61. Tom Ammiano, interview by the author, San Francisco, April 7, 1995; Hank Wilson, interview by the author, San Francisco, April 12, 1995; "Behind the S.F. School Board Fight," *San Francisco Bay Guardian*, July 11, 1975, 8.

62. For a broader discussion of Briggs, see Chapter 3.

63. *New York Teacher*, October 22, 1978.

64. Sara R. Smith, "Gay and Lesbian Teachers and the Struggle against the Briggs Initiative," paper presented at the How Class Works conference, State University of New York, Stony Brook, June 4, 2010.

65. Deborah Dickson, dir., *Ruthie and Connie: Every Room in the House*, Donald Goldmacher Production, San Francisco, 2002.

66. Jones, "'Top Down' or 'Bottom Up'?" 172–195; Frank, "Lesbian and Gay Caucuses in the U.S. Labor Movement," 96–97.

67. Jones, "'Top Down' or 'Bottom Up'?" 186–187.

68. Holcomb, "Domestic Partner Health Benefits," 111–112.

69. Michael Dias, interview by the author, Detroit, April 19, 1995.

70. Frank, "Lesbian and Gay Caucuses in the U.S. Labor Movement," 95.

71. Joyce Murdoch and Deb Price, *Courting Justice: Gay Men and Lesbians versus the Supreme Court* (New York: Basic, 2001), 252.

72. Oklahoma's statute was struck down in 1984 by the Tenth Circuit Court of Appeals. The U.S. Supreme Court heard the appeal in 1985 and returned with a tied vote, which left standing the Tenth Circuit's decision: Murdoch and Price, *Courting Justice,* 254–260.

73. Jean Hardisty, "Colorado's Right-Wing Attack on Homosexuals," *Public Eye,* March 1993, available at www.publiceye.org/magazine/v07n1/conshomo.html (accessed December 11, 2013).

74. Craig Rimmerman, *From Identity to Politics: The Lesbian and Gay Movements in the United States* (Philadelphia: Temple University Press, 2002), 142–143.

75. Didi Herman, *The Antigay Agenda: Orthodox Vision and the Christian Right* (Chicago: University of Chicago Press, 1997), 112. For an extended analysis of theory and practice in the campaign for Amendment 2, see ibid., 114–148.

76. Murdoch and Price, *Courting Justice,* 454.

77. J. A. Stanford Jr., interview by the author, Palm Springs, CA, February 25, 2008; J. A. Stanford Jr., "The Death of Colorado's Amendment 2: Judicial Activism, or a Rescue from Capricious Government?" 1998, 11–12, unpublished ms. available at http://www.ask stanford.com/TeacherCenter/documents (accessed February 10, 2008).

78. The AFL-CIO withdrawal from the organizing drive in Golden included a truce in 1987 that ended its part in the boycott. Coors's anti-union influence lived on in donations by individual family members to the National Right to Work Committee. For more on Coors, see Chapter 3.

79. Colorado's Amendment 10 appealed broadly across the electorate and was an important first step in the national movement to set statewide mandates on proposed taxes and spending. The influential Taxpayer Bill of Rights limits funding of public services by pegging all state, county, municipal and school district expenditures to a percentage rate that combines population growth with inflation and then subjects taxes to a statewide referendum. Colorado's tax rebels also made their mark in the national presidential election by giving H. Ross Perot's United We Stand America campaign one of its biggest wins over the incumbent efforts of Republican George H. W. Bush. The popular vote gave neither Perot nor Bush nor the Democrat Bill Clinton a majority; the Electoral College vote went to Clinton.

80. Murdoch and Price, *Courting Justice,* 456. For an overview of the boycott see Stanford, "The Death of Colorado's Amendment 2," 19–22.

81. For thorough accounts of the path that *Romer v. Evans* took through the courts, see Murdoch and Price, *Courting Justice,* 456–482; Lisa Keen and Suzanne B. Goldberg, *Strangers to the Law: Gay People on Trial* (Ann Arbor: University of Michigan Press, 1998), 195–266. In 1996, when John Roberts was a partner in the law firm Hogan and Hartson, he contributed to the firm's pro bono work for the plaintiffs by participating in a moot court to rehearse arguments for the Supreme Court. In 2005, he was appointed chief justice by President George W. Bush.

82. Heather MacDonald, dir., *Ballot Measure 9,* Oregon Tape Project, Portland, 1995; Patricia Jean Young, "Measure 9: Oregon's 1992 Anti-Gay Initiative," master's thesis, Portland State University, Portland, OR, 1997.

83. Oregon voters' pamphlet, 1992. See also Ann Montague, "We Are Union Builders, Too: Oregon Union Tackles Discrimination Based on Sexual Orientation," *Labor Research Review* 20 (1994): 78–83; Miriam Frank, "Labor Movement," in *Lesbian Histories and Cultures: An Encyclopedia,* ed. Bonnie Zimmerman (New York: Garland, 2000), 430–431.

84. Beckie Capoferri, interview by the author, Portland, OR, July 17, 1995.

85. For perspectives on comparable worth and its implementation, see Helen Remick, ed. *Comparable Worth and Wage Discrimination: Technical Possibilities and Political Realities* (Philadelphia: Temple University Press, 1984).

86. Ann Montague, interview by the author, Portland, Oregon, July 16, 1995.

87. Capoferri interview.

88. Ibid. Measure 8 was later struck down by the Oregon Court of Appeals as an unconstitutional infringement of free speech: *Harriet P. Merrick v. Board of Higher Education and State of Oregon,* Court of Appeals of Oregon, February 12, 1992 (CA A60997 1992.OR4227; 111 Or. APP414; 823 P. 2d 1044).

89. Sara Diamond, *Not by Politics Alone: The Enduring Influence of the Christian Right* (New York: Guilford, 1998), 161–162; Richard Peddicord, *Gay and Lesbian Rights: A Question—Sexual Ethics or Social Justice?* (Kansas City, MO: Sheed and Ward, 1996), 130; Scot Nakagawa, "Introduction," in National Gay and Lesbian Task Force, *Fight the Right Action Kit* (Washington, DC: National Gay and Lesbian Task Force, 1993).

90. Beckie Capoferri, "Organizing Organized Labor," in National Gay and Lesbian Task Force, *Fight the Right Action Kit*; Capoferri interview.

91. Montague, "We Are Union Builders, Too," 81–83.

92. Capoferri interview. See also Bob Ralphs, "Bigot Busting," in National Gay and Lesbian Task Force, *Fight the Right Action Kit*.

93. Oregon voters' pamphlet.

94. Capoferri interview.

95. Ibid.

96. Montague, "We Are Union Builders, Too," 83.

CHAPTER 5

1. Martin Jay Levitt and Terry Conrow, *Confessions of a Union Buster* (New York: Crown, 1993), 150. For a general history of union-busting, see Robert Michael Smith, *From Blackjacks to Briefcases: A History of Commercialized Strikebreaking and Unionbusting in the United States* (Athens, Ohio: Ohio University Press, 2003).

2. Bill Olwell, interview by the author, Washington, DC, June 9, 1995.

3. "Let the workers organize. Let the toilers assemble. Let their crystallized voice proclaim their injustices and demand their privileges. Let all thoughtful citizens sustain them, for the future of labor is the future of America": John L. Lewis, October 15, 1936, quoted as the epigraph to the introduction in Peter L. Francia, *The Future of Organized Labor in American Politics* (New York: Columbia University Press, 2006), 1.

4. On gay male community and commerce in San Francisco, see Randy Shilts, *The Mayor of Castro Street: The Life and Times of Harvey Milk* (New York: St. Martin's Press, 1982), 81–94, 111–126; on lesbian-feminist communities and businesses in Chicago, Detroit and St. Paul-Minneapolis, see Anne Enke, *Finding the Movement: Sexuality, Space and Feminist Activism* (Durham: Duke University Press, 2007), 1–101, 217–251.

5. Criss Romero, interview by the author, San Francisco, March 16, 2010.

6. Lillian Faderman and Stuart Timmons, *Gay L.A: A History of Sexual Outlaws, Power Politics and Lipstick Lesbians* (New York: Basic, 2006), 204–205; J. G. Sappell, "Workers' Strike at Gay Center," *Lesbian Tide* 4, no. 7 (July–August 1975): 3, 36–38; Jeff Sternberg, "Problems Surround Local Gay Community Center," *LA Free Press*, May 16, 1975, 2.

7. Faderman and Timmons, *Gay L.A*, 205–207; Sternberg, "Problems Surround Local Gay Community Center." Yolanda Retter, interview by the author, Los Angeles, June 9, 2001. For more on the Gay Community Service Center strike, see also Yolanda Retter, "On the Side of the Angels: Lesbian Activism in L.A., 1970–1990," Ph.D. diss., University of New Mexico, Albuquerque, 1999.

8. The Labyris strike received wide attention in the feminist press. "Locally it is sometimes known only as 'the troubles,'" wrote Joss Eldredge and Sandra Marilyn in "Working with Women: The Labyris Experience," *Tradeswomen* 2, no. 4 (Summer 1983): 10–15. In a twice anthologized essay, Kathleen Weston and Lisa Rofel assigned pseudonyms to the business and its owners because "this strike has generated a certain amount of controversy, and we want to be able to explore the theoretical issues it raises without reducing those issues to the sum of the personalities involved": Kathleen Weston and Lisa B. Rofel, "Sexuality, Class and Conflict in a Lesbian Workplace," *Signs* 9, no. 4 (Summer 1984): 623–646. But the shop and its principals were widely identified before, during, and after the conflict: Ann Meredith, "Working Women," *Plexus*, November 1981, 10, 15; Kelly Eve, "Women's Labor Dispute,"

Plexus, April 1982, 6; "Labyris Employees Association Grieves" and "Worker's Rights: A Smokescreen?" letters, *Plexus*, May 1982, 2–3; Fran Taylor, "Labyris Breaks Down," *Union WAGE* 70 (May–June 1982): 12.

9. Weston and Rofel, "Sexuality, Class and Conflict in a Lesbian Workplace," 624–625.

10. Eldredge and Marilyn, "Working with Women," 10–11.

11. Weston and Rofel, "Sexuality, Class and Conflict in a Lesbian Workplace," 626–627; Meredith, "Working Women."

12. Eldredge and Marilyn, "Working with Women," 10–11.

13. Ibid.; Weston and Rofel, "Sexuality, Class and Conflict in a Lesbian Workplace," 625

14. Harvey Milk's circle of labor supporters included Jim Elliot, an officer of Automotive Machinists Local 1305. Shilts, *The Mayor of Castro Street*, 150–152. Elliot is interviewed in Rob Epstein, dir., *The Times of Harvey Milk*, documentary film, Telling Pictures, San Francisco, 1983.

15. Eldredge and Marilyn, "Working with Women," 13.

16. Ibid., 12–13.

17. Mary Ellen Churchill, "Local 2 and the Alliance of Rank and File," September 1999, available at http://www.foundsf.org (accessed July 1, 2011); for a critical view of the caucus and its role in the trusteeship, see Julius G. Getman, *Restoring the Power of Unions: It Takes a Movement* (New Haven, CT: Yale University Press, 2010), 53–60.

18. "S.F. Hotel Workers Ratify Three-Year Contract, Ending 26 Day Strike," *San Francisco Chronicle*, August 12, 1980.

19. Vince Quackenbush, interview by the author, San Francisco, April 7, 1995.

20. Peter Tenney, interview by the author, San Francisco, April 10, 1995.

21. David Lamble, "Workers, Owners Battle It Out at S.F. Gay Hotel," *Gay Community News*, December 12, 1980.

22. Tenney interview.

23. Lisa Lawes, "The Bakery," *Dishrag* 1, no. 1, 1980. *Dishrag*, subtitled "America's Leading Journal for Lesbian and Gay Hotel, Restaurant and Bar Employees," was a one-issue newsletter published and distributed independently by Local 2's lesbian and gay committee. "*Dishrag* is born out of the belief that gay women and men who work in hotels, restaurants and bars are in a unique position to explore the relationships between gayness and work," a front-page editorial declared. "We won't choose any longer between job security and simple respect and support around being gay—we want it all."

24. Warren Hinckle, "Workers at the Mercy of S.F. Gay Establishments," *San Francisco Chronicle*, April 9, 1981.

25. Lamble, "Workers, Owners Battle It Out at S.F. Gay Hotel." Some 125,000 "undesirable" Cubans left their country from the Port of Mariel from April to October 1980, many of them lesbians and gay men. The U.S. Coast Guard participated in the boatlift and the landings in southern Florida: Kelly Anderson, dir., *Looking for a Space: Lesbians and Gay Men in Cuba*, videorecording, Filmmakers Library, New York, 1994.

26. Gary Guthman, interview by the author, Los Angeles, August 21, 2009.

27. Quackenbush interview; Guthman interview.

28. Guthman interview.

29. Ibid.

30. Mike Hippler, "N.Y. City Deli Bucks Workers," *Bay Area Reporter*, April 21, 1983, 1.

31. Working Women, National Association of Office Workers, "Race against Time: Automation of the Office: An Analysis of the Trends in Office Automation and the Impact of the Office Workforce." Report. (Cleveland: The Association, 1980).

32. Karen Nussbaum, "Women in Labor: Always the Bridesmaid?" in *Not Your Father's Union Movement: Inside the AFL-CIO*, ed. JoAnn Mort (London: Verso, 1998), 55–56, 67–68.

33. Alfred Vogel, "Your Clerical Workers Are Ripe for Unionism," *Harvard Business Review* 49 (March–April 1971): 48–54.

34. Lucius Cabins, "Office Workers on Strike—San Francisco 1981," in *Bad Attitude: The Processed World Anthology*, ed. Chris Carlsson (London: Verso, 1990), 103–112; Ramon Castellblanch, "Lessons from the Blue Shield Strike," *Labor Center Reporter*, no. 113 (February 1984).

35. Nancy Wohlforth, interview by the author, San Francisco, April 11, 1995.

36. Ibid.

37. Larry Kramer's autobiographical play *The Normal Heart* (New York: New American Library, 1985) dramatizes the first years of the epidemic and the origins of the Gay Men's Health Crisis.

38. Joe Izzo, interview by the author, Washington, DC, July 18, 2001.

39. Scott Melvin, interview by the author, New York City, February 27, 2001.

40. The clinic was named for Edmund D. Edelman of the Los Angeles County Board of Supervisors. Edelman represented the Third District, which included West Hollywood and other queer neighborhoods. He was a longtime advocate for gay rights and a former assistant to the general counsel of the NLRB, an appointment made by President John F. Kennedy. A generation before the clinic was founded, Edelman had helped the Gay Community Services Center obtain its first government grants. The center became the scene of a raucous workers' rebellion in 1974, described earlier in this chapter: Faderman and Timmons, *Gay L.A.*, 195, 204–205, 215–216.

41. Kathy Ketchum, interview by the author, Los Angeles, June 28, 2010.

42. Celia Noriega, interview by the author, Los Angeles, June 28, 2010; Ketchum interview.

43. Christa Orth, "Brothers and Sisters (and Everyone in Between): Sexuality and Class in the Pacific Northwest, 1970–1995," master's thesis, University of Oregon, Eugene, 2002, 63.

44. Marc Earls, interview by the author, Seattle, August 2, 2001.

45. Orth, "Brothers and Sisters (and Everyone in Between)," 64–72.

46. Earls interview; Orth, "Brothers and Sisters (and Everyone in Between)," 65–69.

47. Orth, "Brothers and Sisters (and Everyone in Between)," 68–69.

48. Ibid., 74

49. Christa Orth, interview by the author, Seattle, August 3, 2001.

50. Earls interview.

51. For a review of PATCO events and their consequences, see Arthur B. Shostak and David Skocik, *The Air Controllers' Controversy: Lessons from the PATCO Strike* (New York: Human Sciences, 1986) and Joseph A. McCartin, *Collision Course: Ronald Reagan, the Air Traffic Controllers, and the Strike That Changed America* (New York: Oxford University Press, 2011).

52. Jim Hubbard, dir., *United in Anger: A History of ACT-UP*, videorecording, Film Collaborative, Los Angeles, 2012.

53. Izzo interview.

54. Kramer, *The Normal Heart*.

55. Craig A. Rimmerman, *From Identity to Politics: The Lesbian and Gay Movements in the United States* (Philadelphia: Temple University Press, 2002), 102; Mireya Navarro, "Diversity but Conflict under Wider AIDS Umbrella: At the Gay Men's Health Crisis, a Struggle to Serve Competing Groups of Clients," *New York Times*, May 28, 1993.

56. Melvin interview.

57. Ibid.

58. Ibid.

59. Donna Minkowitz, "Lavender Labor Lost?" *Village Voice*, December 7, 1993, 13.

60. GMHC campaign leaflet, 1993.

61. Melvin interview.

62. Peter Steinfels, "Cardinal O'Connor, 80, Dies: Forceful Voice for Vatican," *New York Times*, May 5, 2000; Jason DeParle, "111 Held in St. Patrick's AIDS Protest," *New York Times*, December 11, 1989.

63. Raymond L. Rigoglioso, "AIDS Goes Union," *Gay Community News* 20, nos. 1–2 (June 1994): 9–10, 27–28.

64. Melvin interview.

65. Article III-B, Constitution of Local 1199, Drug, Hospital and Health Care Employees, Division of RWDSU, 1992. It was not until March 1994, a month after the GMHC election, that the union's Executive Council approved the inclusion of sexual orientation in the union's antidiscrimination statement: Rigoglioso, "AIDS Goes Union."

66. "Gay Men's Health Crisis Unionization," National Archive of Lesbian, Gay, Bisexual, and Transgender History, New York, collection 76, folder 128.

67. Melvin interview.

68. Ibid. Duncan Osborne, "GMHC: Naming Names," *Village Voice*, March 15, 1994, 10.

69. Melvin interview. Marilynne Geiffert, New York State Department of Health, to Jeff Richardson, Executive Director, GMHC, February 24, 1994; Marilynne Geiffert, New York State Department of Health, to Scott Melvin, April 21, 1994, "Gay Men's Health Crisis Unionization," folder 79.

70. Melvin interview.

71. A different dynamic was reported by Duncan Osborne: "Knowing that defeat was assured, the organizing committee opted to divide the employee voting bloc into two units two days before the vote. [They] feared retaliation and felt that even a small unionized department might protect them": Duncan Osborne, "GMHC's Labor Blues," *Lesbian and Gay New York* (prototype issue), November 1994, 10. For another report on the division of the unit, see Raymond Rigoglioso, "AIDS Goes Union," *Gay Community News*, June 1994, 9–10.

72. Melvin interview.

73. Florence Cepeda, interview by the author, San Francisco, March 14, 2010.

74. Romero interview.

75. Ibid.

76. Terry Beswick, "SFAF's Christen Breaks through $200 K Mark," 3, and "Another Year, Another Raise," Editorial, 6, *Bay Area Reporter*, May 25, 2000.

77. Melvin interview.

78. Romero interview.

79. Greg Pullman, interview by the author, Oakland, CA, March 21, 2010.

80. Romero interview.

81. Pullman interview.

82. "Gay Men's Health Crisis Unionization," folder 120.

83. Romero interview.

84. Stephanie Batey, interview by the author, Oakland, CA, March 21, 2010.

85. Romero interview.

86. Batey interview.

87. Susan Ferris, "AIDS Foundation Accused of Bias," *San Francisco Examiner*, February 16, 1995.

88. Batey interview.

89. Cepeda interview.

90. Romero interview.

91. Cynthia Laird, "Current, Former SFAF Workers Allege Discrimination," *Bay Area Reporter*, April 16, 1999.

92. The NLRB scheduled the election to decertify for September 12, 2001; this turned out to be the day after the terrorist attacks on the World Trade Center in New York City and the Pentagon in Washington, DC, and was declared by Congress a National Day

of Unity and Mourning. (H. J. Res. 61 and S. J. Res. 22 became Public Law 107–139 on September 18, 2001).

93. Izzo interview; Paula Park, "Race for the Cure," *Washington City Paper*, June 19, 1998, available at http://www.washingtoncitypaper.com/articles/15224/race-for-the-cure (accessed December 31, 2010).

94. Shostak and Skocik, *The Air Controllers' Controversy*, 109; "Former PATCO Strikers Jailed in Texas," *Labor Notes*, May 26, 1983, 1; Bob Baker, "Ex-Air Traffic Controllers Recall Strike with Regret," *Los Angeles Times*, July 27, 1991; Michael Sangian, "PATCO Stalwart Remembered for Lifting Spirits," *Cleveland Plain Dealer*, July 21, 1994; Ron Taylor, interview by the author, Martin County, FL, August 17, 2001; Arthur B. Shostak, interview by the author, Philadelphia, October 15, 2001.

95. Izzo interview; "Joe Izzo," in Raymond C. Holtz, *Listen to the Stories: Gay and Lesbian Catholics Talk about Their Lives and the Church* (New York: Garland, 1991), 60–65.

96. At the time Division 1199-E was not affiliated with District 1199 in New York City: Izzo interview.

97. Ibid.; Whitman-Walker organizing letter, October 6, 1993, in my possession.

98. Izzo interview.

99. Ibid.; William T. Taylor and Joe Izzo to Jim Graham, correspondence, November 11, 1993, in my possession.

100. Izzo interview.

101. Ibid.; Olwell interview; "Whitman-Walker Votes Union Yes!" *Union Voice*, 1199-E DC SEIU, Winter 1994, 4; Desma Holcomb, "Washington AIDS Clinic Agrees to Quick Representation Election," *Labor Notes*, February 1994, 5.

102. Izzo interview; Olwell interview.

103. Izzo interview; Becky Reeve, interview by the author, Washington, DC, January 17, 2012; "Out and Organized," printout from www.1199seiu.org/media/magazine/jun_2006 (accessed August 18, 2011; now inoperative).

EPILOGUE

1. Jane LaTour, "Marriage Equality, Members Make It Work," *Public Employee Press*, September 2011, 13.

2. Debra E. Bernhardt and Rachel Bernstein, *Ordinary People, Extraordinary Lives: A Pictorial History of Working People in New York City* (New York: New York University Press, 2000), 184.

3. Same-sex marriage was not on the gay-labor political agenda during the 1970s and 1980s, when activists were first writing antidiscrimination safeguards into union constitutions. Later, when they negotiated domestic partner benefits, the aim was to establish economic parity rather than to obtain the sanction of the state. During the 1990s, LGBT scholars and strategists debated the centrality of marriage as a goal for the movement: Paula Ettelbrick, "Since When Is Marriage a Path to Liberation?" in *Lesbians, Gay Men and the Law*, ed. William B. Rubenstein (New York: New Press, 1993), 401–406. The controversy continues, even as reforms gain ground.

4. Carmen Acosta, interview by the author, New York, February 29, 2012.

5. Desma Holcomb, interview by the author, New York, December 27, 2011.

6. Acosta interview.

7. Ibid.

8. Joan Reutershan, interview by the author, New York, December 18, 2011.

9. Acosta interview.

10. Ibid.

11. Alana Samuels, "Advocates Help Gay Marriage Hit Home in Maine," *Los Angeles*

Times, October 18, 2012. See also Mainers United for Marriage website, available at http://www.mainersunited.org (accessed August 23, 2013).

12. James Cersonsky, "How Organized Labor Helped Win Marriage Equality in Maryland and Washington—And What We Can Learn," April 15, 2012, AlterNet website, available at http://www.alternet.org/story/154925 (accessed August 23, 2013).

13. The gay rights heritage of UFCW Local 21 goes back to 1969, when the union was Retail Clerks Local 1001 and Bill Olwell came out during his campaign for reelection for the presidency of the local.

14. "For Unions, Opposition to Marriage Amendment Swells from Grassroots," *Union Advocate* St. Paul, MN), October 29, 2012, available at http://advocate.stpaulunions.org (accessed August 23, 2013); Steve Share, "Vote 'No' on Marriage Amendment, Unions Urge," *Minneapolis Labor Review*, November 5, 2012, available at http://www.minneapolisunions.org/cluc_labor_review.php (accessed August 23, 2013); Baird Helgeson, "In Historic Vote, Minnesota House Approves Gay Marriage Bill, 75–59," *Minnesota Star Tribune*, May 10, 2013.

Bibliography

ARCHIVES

International Gay Information Center Collection, 1951–1994. New York Public Library.
Lesbian Herstory Archives. Lesbian Herstory Educational Foundation, Brooklyn, NY.
National Archive of Lesbian, Gay, Bisexual, and Transgender History, New York.
Northeastern University Archives and Special Collections, Boston.
ONE National Gay and Lesbian Archives. University of Southern California, Los Angeles.
Robert F. Wagner Labor Archives (RFWLA). Tamiment Library, New York University.
Walter P. Reuther Library of Labor and Urban Affairs. Wayne State University, Detroit.

FILM AND VIDEO RECORDINGS

Anderson, Kelly, dir. *Looking for a Space: Lesbians and Gay Men in Cuba.* Videorecording. Filmmakers Library, New York, 1994.
Anderson, Kelly, and Tami Gold, dirs. *Out at Work.* Documentary film. AndersonGold Films, New York, 1997.
Barneys Runway. Videorecording. Local 340, ACTWU/UNITE, New York, 1996.
Dickson. Deborah, dir. *Ruthie and Connie: Every Room in the House.* Documentary film. Donald Goldmacher Production, San Francisco, 2002.
Epstein, Rob, dir. *The Times of Harvey Milk.* Documentary film. Telling Pictures, San Francisco, 1983.
Epstein, Rob, and Jeffrey Friedman, dirs. *Common Threads: Stories from the Quilt.* Documentary film. Telling Pictures, San Francisco, 1989.
Funari, Vicky, and Julia Query, dirs. *Live Nude Girls Unite!* Documentary film. First Run/Icarus, Brooklyn, NY, 2000.
Hubbard, Jim, dir. *United in Anger: A History of ACT UP.* Documentary film. Film Collaborative, Los Angeles, 2012.
Kates, Nancy D., and Bennett Singer, dirs. *Brother Outsider: The Life of Bayard Rustin.* Videorecording. Independent Television Service/California Newsreel, San Francisco, 2002.
Latham, Liz, dir. *"We're Here to Stay": The History of Hands Off Washington.* Documentary film. Lizard Productions, Seattle, 1998.
Lescaze, Alexandra, dir. *Where Do You Stand? Stories from an American Mill.* Videorecording and study guide. Firebrand Productions/California Newsreel, San Francisco, 2004.
MacDonald. Heather, dir. *Ballot Measure 9.* Documentary film. Oregon Tape Project, Portland, 1995.

INTERVIEWS

Acosta, Carmen. New York, February 29, 2012. Transcript, in my possession.

Ammiano, Tom. San Francisco, April 7, 1995 Audiotape, RFWLA.

Ashbrook, Connie. Portland, OR, July 16, 1995. Audiotape, RFWLA.

Baird, Allan. San Francisco, April 11, 1995. Audiotape, RFWLA.

Barbera, Tom. New York, April 14, 2000. Audiotape, in my possession.

Basile, Victor. Baltimore, July 19, 2007. Transcript, in my possession.

Batey, Stephanie. Oakland, CA, March 21, 2010. Transcript, in my possession.

Boal, Ellis. Detroit, November 3, 1992. Transcript, in my possession.

Brown, Nancy. Detroit, May 1, 1995. Audiotape, RFWLA.

Bryner, Gary. Detroit, August 12, 2002. Transcript, in my possession.

Burrell, Bob. Detroit, July 24, 2002. Transcript, in my possession.

Capoferri, Beckie. Portland, OR, July 17, 1995. Audiotape, RFWLA.

Cartwright, Donna. Cliffside Park, NJ, July 16, 2001. Audiotape, in my possession.

Cepeda, Florence. San Francisco, March 14, 2010. Transcript, in my possession.

Christian, Joni. Ravenna, OH, July 28, 2002. Transcript, in my possession.

Clarke, Shirley. Boston, March 27, 1995 Audiotape, RFWLA.

Crites, Shelley. Seattle, July 14, 1995. Audiotape, RFWLA.

Cutting, Ginny. Boston, March 24, 1995. Audiotape, RFWLA.

Deane, Gary. New York, August 9, 1994. Audiotape, RFWLA.

de la Fuente, Ramon. Washington, DC, June 10, 1995. Audiotape, RFWLA.

De Santis, Robert. New York, June 29, 1996. Audiotape, RFWLA.

Dias, Michael. Detroit, April 19, 1995. Audiotape, RFWLA.

Dotterman, Gary. Boston, March 23, 1995. Audiotape, RFWLA.

Earls, Marc. Seattle, August 2, 2001. Transcript in my possession.

Elder, Madelyn. Portland, OR, July 17, 1995. Audiotape, RFWLA.

Ettinger, Shelley. New York, September 11, 1998. Audiotape, in my possession.

Ewing, Tess. Boston, March 25, 1995. Audiotape, RFWLA.

Feldman, Richard. Detroit, July 23, 2002. Transcript, in my possession.

Firestein, Netsy. New York, March 20, 1989. Transcript, RFWLA.

Flanders, Cliff. New York, January 12, 1998. Transcript, in my possession.

Freund, Vivienne. New York, July 13, 2005. Transcript, in my possession.

Guthman, Gary. Los Angeles, August 21, 2009. Transcript, in my possession.

Hanen, Suzanne. New York, July 20, 1994. Transcript, in my possession.

Harris, Jackie. New York, March 1, 1995. Audiotape, RFWLA.

Holcomb, Desma. New York, December 27, 2011. Transcript, in my possession.

Hunt, Ed. Oakland, CA, June 29, 1996. Audiotape, RFWLA.

Izzo, Joe. Washington, DC, July 18, 2001. Audiotape, in my possession.

Jacobsen, Ruth. Southampton, NY, March 6, 1995. Audiotape, RFWLA.

Jochems, Ann. New York, February 24, 1999. Audiotape, in my possession.

Johnsen, Marcy. Tacoma, WA, July 13, 1995. Audiotape, RFWLA.

Johnson, Walter. San Francisco, April 11, 1995. Audiotape, RFWLA.

Justen, Jim. Oakland, CA, June 28, 1996. Audiotape, RFWLA.

Kapanowski, Gary. Philadelphia, February 12, 2001. Audiotape, in my possession.

Katz, Annette. Miami, July 29, 2004. Transcript, in my possession.

Ketchum, Kathy. Los Angeles, June 28, 2010. Transcript, in my possession.

Kevorkian, Harry. Boston, June 6, 1999. Transcript, in my possession.

Kopelov, Connie. New York, July 14, 1994. Audiotape, RFWLA.

Laberge, Jean. New York, May 10, 1996. Audiotape, RFWLA.

LaGasa, Virginia. Seattle, July 14, 1995. Audiotape, RFWLA.

Lara, Sandra. New York City, March 21, 1995. Audiotape, RFWLA.

Levitt, Donna. San Francisco, February 17, 1999. Transcript, in my possession.

Lewis, Bob. Oakland, CA, June 28, 1996. Audiotape, RFWLA.

Loux, Janice. Boston, March 23, 1995. Audiotape, RFWLA.

Mage, Judy. New York City, August 15, 1994. Audiotape, RFWLA.

Mayne, Ed. Salt Lake City, July 27, 2000. Transcript, in my possession.

Mehring, John. San Francisco, August 18, 1997. Transcript, in my possession.

Melvin, Scott. New York, February 27, 2001. Audiotape, in my possession.

Mitchell, James. New York, August 11, 1995. Audiotape, RFWLA.

Moir, Susan. Boston, March 24, 1995. Audiotape, RFWLA.

Monk, Jim. Windsor, ON, April 28, 1995. Audiotape, RFWLA.

Montague, Ann. Portland, OR, July 16, 1995. Audiotape, RFWLA.

Noriega, Celia. Los Angeles, June 28, 2010. Transcript, in my possession.

Noyce, Cal. Detroit, April 30, 1995. Audiotape, RFWLA.

Olwell, Bill. Washington, DC, June 9, 1995. Audiotape, RFWLA.

O'Neil, Dennis. New York City, February 9, 1999. Transcript, in my possession.

Orth, Christa. Seattle, August 3, 2001. Transcript, in my possession.

Otos, Sally. New York, August 10, 1998. Audiotape, in my possession.

Privitere, Tom. New York, March 13, 1996. Audiotape, RFWLA.

Pullman, Greg. Oakland, CA, March 21, 2010. Transcript, in my possession.

Quackenbush, Vincent. San Francisco, April 7, 1995. Audiotape, RFWLA.

Ramsey, Kim. Tacoma, WA, July 14, 1995. Audiotape, RFWLA.

Rankin, Teresa. Washington, DC, June 9, 1995. Audiotape, RFWLA.

Reed, Scott. Seattle, July 13, 1995. Audiotape, RFWLA.

Reeve, Becky. Washington, DC, January 17, 2012. Transcript, in my possession.

Retter, Yolanda. Los Angeles, June 9, 2001. Transcript, in my possession.

Reutershan, Joan. New York, December 18, 2011. Transcript, in my possession.

Riegel, Rosalie. New York, February 14, 1995. Audiotape, RFWLA.

Roberts, Bill. Los Angeles, May 19, 1995. Audiotape, RFWLA.

Robinson, Faith. Detroit, April 30, 1995. Audiotape, RFWLA.

Romero, Criss. San Francisco, March 16, 2010. Transcript, in my possession.

Romero, Linda. Washington, DC, June 10, 1995. Audiotape, RFWLA.

Roselli, Sal. San Francisco, April 13, 1995. Audiotape, RFWLA.

Rubino, Michael. New York, March 15, 1989. Transcript, RFWLA.

Rudnick, Trudy. New York, August 16, 2000. Transcript, in my possession.

Schurman, Susan. Silver Spring, MD, July 18, 2001. Audiotape, in my possession.

Sheets, Van Alan. Washington, DC, June 8, 1995. Audiotape, RFWLA.

Shostak, Arthur B. Philadelphia, October 15, 2001. Transcript, in my possession.

Smith, Irving. New York, August 9, 1999. Audiotape, in my possession.

Soloway, Irene. New York, March 4, 1999. Audiotape, in my possession.

Stanford, J. A., Jr. Palm Springs, CA, February 25, 2008. Transcript, in my possession.

Sushman, Sidney. Boston, March 22, 1995. Audiotape, RFWLA.

Taylor, Ron. Martin County, FL, August 17, 2001. Transcript, in my possession.

Tenney, Peter. San Francisco, April 10, 1995. Audiotape, RFWLA.

Trees, Barbara. New York, October 29, 1987. Transcript, in my possession.

Truett, Keith. Detroit, April 27, 1995. Audiotape, RFWLA.

Voland, Martha. Portland, ME, July 16, 2009. Transcript, in my possession.

Walker, Bailey T., Jr. Washington, DC, June 14, 1995. Audiotape, RFWLA.

Wallace, Howard. San Francisco, April 8, 1995. Audiotape, RFWLA.

———. San Francisco, January 12, 2001. Audiotape, in my possession.

Wheeler, Karen. Boston, March 26, 1995. Audiotape, RFWLA.

Wilson, André. Ann Arbor, January 12, 2012. Transcript, in my possession.

Wilson, Hank. San Francisco, April 12, 1995. Audiotape, RFWLA.

Wohlforth, Nancy. San Francisco, April 11, 1995. Audiotape, RFWLA.
Woods, Ron. Detroit, April 27, 1995. Audiotape, RFWLA.

NEWSPAPERS, NEWSLETTERS, AND MAGAZINES

The Advocate
Bay Area Reporter
Bay Windows
Body Politic
Cleveland Plain Dealer
Detroit Free Press
Dishrag
1199 SEIU Magazine
Fag Rag
Gay Community News
Gay Teachers Association Newsletter
The Guardian (UAW Canada)
The Guide
John Herling's Labor Letter
Labor Notes
LA Free Press
Lesbian and Gay New York
Lesbian Tide
Los Angeles Times
Miami Herald
Minneapolis Labor Review
Minnesota Star Tribune

New Yorker
New York Newsday
New York Teacher
New York Times
Plexus
Public Employee Press
San Francisco Bay Guardian
San Francisco Bay Times
San Francisco Chronicle
San Francisco Examiner
San Francisco Vector
Seattle Post-Intelligencer
Southern Exposure
UAW Solidarity
Union Advocate
Union Voice
Union WAGE
UNITE!
Village Voice
Wall Street Journal
Washington City Paper

REFERENCES

Adam, Barry D. *The Rise of a Gay and Lesbian Movement*, rev. ed. Boston: Twayne, 1995.

Adler, Marvin. "A New Day in Dixie." *Southern Exposure* 12, no. 1 (Spring 1994): 17–27.

AFL-CIO Committee on the Evolution of Work. "The Changing Situation of Workers and Their Unions." Report. AFL-CIO, Washington, DC, 1985.

Aptheker, Bettina. "Keeping the Communist Party Straight, 1940s–1980s." *New Politics* 12, no. 1 (Summer 2008): 22–27.

Aronowitz, Stanley. *From the Ashes of the Old: American Labor and America's Future.* Boston: Houghton Mifflin, 1998.

Babson, Steve. *Working Detroit: The Making of a Union Town.* Detroit: Wayne State University Press, 1986.

Badgett, M. V. Lee. "The Wage Effects of Sexual Orientation." *Industrial and Labor Relations Review* 48, no. 4 (July 1995): 726–739.

Balay, Anne. *Steel Closets: Voices of Gay, Lesbian and Transgender Steelworkers.* Chapel Hill: University of North Carolina Press, 2014.

Bardacke, Frank. *Trampling Out the Vintage: Cesar Chavez and the Two Souls of the United Farm Workers.* London: Verso, 2011.

Baum, Dan. *Citizen Coors: An American Dynasty.* New York: William Morrow, 2000.

Baxandall, Rosalyn Fraad. *Words on Fire: The Life and Writing of Elizabeth Gurley Flynn.* New Brunswick, NJ: Rutgers University Press, 1987.

Baxandall, Rosalyn Fraad, Linda Gordon, and Susan Reverby. *America's Working Women: A Documentary History, 1600 to the Present.* New York: W. W. Norton, 1995.

Beemyn, Brett, ed. *Creating a Place for Ourselves: Lesbian, Gay, and Bisexual Community Histories.* New York: Routledge, 1997.

Bellant, Russ. *The Coors Connection: How Coors Family Philanthropy Undermines Democratic Pluralism.* Boston: South End, 1991.

Bellush, Jewel, and Bernard Bellush. *Union Power and New York: Victor Gotbaum and District Council 37.* New York: Praeger, 1984.

Benson, Herman. *Democratic Rights for Union Members: A Guide to Internal Union Democracy.* New York: Association for Union Democracy, 1979.

———. *Rebels, Reformers, and Racketeers: How Insurgents Transformed the Labor Movement.* Bloomington, IN: 1st Books, 2004.

Bernhardt, Debra, and Rachel Bernstein. *Ordinary People, Extraordinary Lives: A Pictorial History of Working People in New York City.* New York: New York University Press, 2001.

Bernstein, Mary, and Verta Taylor. *The Marrying Kind? Debating Same-Sex Marriage within the Lesbian and Gay Movement.* Minneapolis: University of Minnesota Press, 2013.

Bérubé, Allan. *Coming Out under Fire: The History of Gay Men and Women in World War Two.* New York: Free Press, 1990.

———. *My Desire for History: Essays in Gay, Community and Labor History.* Ed. John D'Emilio and Estelle B. Freedman. Chapel Hill: University of North Carolina Press, 2011.

Bérubé, Allan, and Charlie Shively. "My Name Is Tangerine: Sylvia Sidney." *Fag Rag,* Summer 1972.

Bielski, Monica Lynn. "Identity at Work: U.S. Labor Unions Efforts to Address Sexual Diversity through Policy and Practice." Ph.D. diss., Rutgers University, New Brunswick. NJ, 2005.

Boyd, Nan Alamilla. *Wide-Open Town: A History of Queer San Francisco to 1965.* Berkeley: University of California Press, 2003.

Brisbin, Richard. *A Strike like no Other Strike: Law Resistance during the Pittston Coal Strike of 1989–1990.* Baltimore: Johns Hopkins University Press, 2002.

Bronfenbrenner, Kate, Sheldon Friedman, Richard W. Hurd, Rudolph A. Oswald, and Ronald L. Seeber. *Organizing to Win: New Research on Union Strategies.* Ithaca, NY: Cornell University Press, 1998.

Bronski, Michael. *A Queer History of the United States.* Boston: Beacon, 2011.

Buhle, Paul. *Taking Care of Business: Samuel Gompers, George Meany, Lane Kirkland and the Tragedy of American Labor.* New York: Monthly Review, 1999.

Campbell, J. Louis. *Jack Nichols, Gay Pioneer: "Have You Heard My Message?"* New York: Harrington Park, 2007.

Canaday, Margot. *The Straight State: Sexuality and Citizenship in Twentieth-Century America.* Princeton, NJ: Princeton University Press, 2009.

Carbado, Devon W., and Donald Weise, eds. *Time on Two Crosses: The Collected Writings of Bayard Rustin.* San Francisco: Cleis, 2003.

Carlsson, Chris, ed. *Bad Attitude: The Processed World Anthology.* London: Verso, 1990.

Castellblanch, Ramon. "Lessons from the Blue Shield Strike." *Labor Center Reporter,* no. 113 (February 1984).

Chauncey, George. *Gay New York: Gender, Urban Culture and the Making of the Gay Male World, 1890–1940.* New York: Basic, 1994.

Chauncey, George, Martha Vicinus, and Martin Duberman, eds. *Hidden from History: Reclaiming the Gay and Lesbian Past.* New York: Penguin, 1990.

Cheney, Mary. *Now It's My Turn: A Daughter's Chronicle of Political Life.* New York: Threshold, 2006.

Chernow, Harneen, and Susan Moir. "Lesbian and Gay Labor for Health Care." *Forward Motion* 8, no. 4 (December 1989): 42–45.

Clendinen, Dudley, and Adam Nagourney. *Out for Good: The Struggle to Build a Gay Rights Movement in America.* New York: Simon and Schuster, 1999.

Cobble, Dorothy Sue. *The Other Women's Movement: Workplace Justice and Social Rights in Modern America.* Princeton, NJ: Princeton University Press, 2004.

———, ed. *The Sex of Class: Women Transforming American Labor.* Ithaca, NY: Cornell University Press, 2007.

———, ed. *Women and Unions: Forging a Partnership.* Ithaca, NY: Cornell University Press, 1993.

D'Emilio, John. *Lost Prophet: The Life and Times of Bayard Rustin.* New York: Free Press, 2003.

———. *Sexual Politics, Sexual Communities: The Making of a Homosexual Minority in the United States, 1940–1970.* Chicago: University of Chicago Press, 1983.

D'Emilio, John, and Estelle B. Freedman. *Intimate Matters: A History of Sexuality in America,* 2d ed. (Chicago: University of Chicago Press, 1997).

Diamond, Sara. *Not by Politics Alone: The Enduring Influence of the Christian Right.* New York: Guilford, 1998.

Duberman, Martin. *Stonewall.* New York: E. P. Dutton, 1994.

Eaklor, Vicki L. *Queer America: A People's GLBT History of the United States.* New York: New Press, 2011.

Eisenbach, David. *Gay Power: An American Revolution.* New York: Carroll Graf, 2006.

Eisenberg, Susan. *We'll Call You if We Need You: Experiences of Women Working Construction.* Ithaca, NY: Cornell University Press, 1998.

———. "Women Hard Hats Speak Out." *The Nation,* September 18, 1989, 272–276.

Eldredge, Joss, and Sandra Marilyn. "Working with Women: The Labyris Experience." *Tradeswomen* 2, no. 4 (Summer 1983): 10–15.

Enke, Anne. *Finding the Movement: Sexuality, Contested Space, and Feminist Activism.* Durham, NC: Duke University Press, 2007.

Faderman, Lillian. *Odd Girls and Twilight Lovers: A History of Lesbian Life in Twentieth-Century America.* New York: Columbia University Press, 1991.

———. *To Believe in Women: What Lesbians Have Done for America.* Boston: Houghton Mifflin, 1999.

Faderman, Lillian, and Stuart Timmons. *Gay L.A.: A History of Sexual Outlaws, Power Politics, and Lipstick Lesbians.* New York: Basic, 2006.

Feldman, Richard, and Michael Betzold. *End of the Line: Autoworkers and the American Dream.* New York: Weidenfeld and Nicholson, 1988.

Feinberg, Leslie. *Stone Butch Blues: A Novel.* Ithaca, NY: Firebrand, 1993.

Firestone, Shulamith, and Anne Koedt, eds. *Notes from the Second Year: Women's Liberation: Major Writings of the Radical Feminists.* New York: Radical Feminism, 1970.

———. *Notes from the Third Year: Women's Liberation.* New York: Notes from the Third Year, 1971.

Francia, Peter L. *The Future of Organized Labor in American Politics.* New York: Columbia University Press, 2006.

Frank, Dana. *Buy American: The Untold Story of Economic Nationalism.* Boston: Beacon, 1999.

Frank, Miriam. "Hard Hats and Homophobia: Lesbians in the Building Trades." *New Labor Forum* 8 (Spring–Summer 2001): 25–36.

Frank, Miriam, and Desma Holcomb. *Pride at Work: Organizing for Lesbian and Gay Rights in Unions.* New York: Lesbian and Gay Labor Network, 1990.

Freedman, Estelle B. *No Turning Back: The History of Feminism and the Future of Women.* New York: Ballantine, 2002.

Freeman, Joshua B. *Working Class New York: Life and Labor since World War II.* New York: New Press, 2000.

Gallo, Marcia M. *Different Daughters: A History of the Daughters of Bilitis and the Rise of the Lesbian Rights Movement.* New York: Carroll and Graf, 2006.

Garson, Barbara. *The Electronic Sweatshop: How Computers Are Transforming the Office of the Future into the Factory of the Past.* New York: Simon and Schuster, 1998.

Georgakas, Dan, and Marvin Surkin. *Detroit, I Do Mind Dying: A Study in Urban Revolution.* New York: St. Martin's Press, 1975.

Getman, Julius. *Restoring the Power of Unions: It Takes a Movement.* New Haven, CT: Yale University Press, 2010.

Gluckman, Amy, and Betsy Reed, eds. *Homo Economics: Capitalism, Community, and Lesbian and Gay Life.* New York: Routledge, 1997.

Golin, Steve. *Newark Teacher Strikes: Hopes on the Line.* New Brunswick, NJ: Rutgers University Press, 2002.

Gore, Ariel. *Portland Queer: Tales of the Rose City.* Portland, OR: Lit Star, 2009.

Green, Venus. *Race on the Line: Gender, Labor and Technology in the Bell System, 1880–1980.* Durham, NC: Duke University Press, 2001.

Guess, Andy. "Trans-ition." *Inside Higher Ed,* March 30, 2009.

Harrington, Michael. *The Other America: Poverty in the United States.* New York: Penguin, 1963.

Herman, Didi. *The Antigay Agenda: Orthodox Vision and the Christian Right.* Chicago: University of Chicago Press, 1997.

History Project. *Improper Bostonians: Lesbian and Gay History from the Puritans to Playland.* Boston: Beacon, 1998.

Holcomb, Desma, and Nancy Wohlforth. "The Fruits of Our Labor: Pride at Work." *New Labor Forum* 8 (Spring–Summer 2001): 9–20.

Hollibaugh, Amber, Diane Ehrensaft, and Ruth Milkman. "Sexuality and the State: The Defeat of the Briggs Initiative and Beyond, an Interview with Amber Hollibaugh." *Socialist Review* 45 (May–June 1979): 55–72.

Holtz, Raymond C., ed. *Listen to Their Stories: Gay and Lesbian Catholics Talk about Their Lives and the Church.* New York: Garland, 1991.

Hunt, Gerald, ed. *Laboring for Rights: Unions and Sexual Diversity across Nations.* Philadelphia: Temple University Press, 1999.

Hunt, Gerald, and David Rayside, eds. *Equity, Diversity, and Canadian Labour.* Toronto: University of Toronto Press, 2007.

———. "The Geo-politics of Sexual Diversity: Measuring Progress in the U.S., Canada and the Netherlands." *New Labor Forum* 8 (Spring–Summer 2001): 37–47.

Hutchinson, John. *The Imperfect Union: A History of Corruption in American Trade Unions.* New York: E. P. Dutton, 1970.

Jacobs, James B. *Mobsters, Unions, and Feds: The Mafia and the American Labor Movement.* New York: New York University Press, 2006.

Jacobsen, Ruth. *Rescued Images: Memories of a Childhood in Hiding.* New York: Mikaya, 2001.

Jay, Karla, and Allen Young, eds. *Out of the Closets: Voices of Gay Liberation.* New York: Pyramid, 1974.

Katz, Jonathan Ned. *Gay American History: Lesbians and Gay Men in the U.S.A.: A Documentary.* New York: Avon, 1976.

Keen, Lisa, and Suzanne B. Goldberg. *Strangers to the Law: Gay People on Trial.* Ann Arbor: University of Michigan Press, 1998.

Kennedy, Elizabeth Lapovsky, and Madeline D. Davis. *Boots of Leather, Slippers of Gold: The History of a Lesbian Community.* New York: Routledge, 1993.

Kramer, Larry. *The Normal Heart.* New York: New American Library, 1985.

Krupat, Kitty, and Patrick McCreery, eds. *Out at Work: Building a Gay-Labor Alliance.* Minneapolis: University of Minnesota Press, 2001.

Kurtz, Sharon. *Workplace Justice: Organizing Multi-identity Movements.* Minneapolis: University of Minnesota Press, 2002.

Kushner, Tony. *Angels in America: A Gay Fantasia on National Themes.* New York: Theatre Communications Group, 1992.

La Botz, Dan, ed. *A Troublemaker's Handbook: How to Fight Back Where You Work—and Win!* Detroit: Labor Notes, 1991.

LaTour, Jane. *Sisters in the Brotherhoods: Working Women Organizing for Equality in New York City.* New York: Palgrave Macmillan, 2008.

Lederman, Doug. "Deal for Michigan and Its Grad Students." *Inside Higher Ed,* April 4, 2005.

Lee, Janet. *Comrades and Partners: The Shared Lives of Grace Hutchins and Anna Rochester.* Lanham, MD: Rowman and Littlefield, 2000.

Levitt, Martin, and Terry Conrow. *Confessions of a Union Buster.* New York: Crown, 1993.

Mantsios, Gregory, ed. *A New Labor Movement for the New Century: A Collection of Essays from the Labor Resource Center, Queens College, City University of New York.* New York: Monthly Review, 1998.

Marcus, Eric. *Making Gay History: The Struggle for Gay and Lesbian Equal Rights.* New York: Perennial, 2007.

Martin, Del, and Phyllis Lyon. *Lesbian/Woman.* New York: Bantam, 1972.

Martin, Molly. *Hard-Hatted Women: Life on the Job.* Seattle: Seal, 1997.

McCartin, Joseph. *Collision Course: Ronald Reagan, the Air Traffic Controllers, and the Strike That Changed America.* Oxford: Oxford University Press, 2011.

McMillian, John, and Paul Buhle, eds. *The New Left Revisited.* Philadelphia: Temple University Press, 2003.

McNaught, Brian. *Gay Issues in the Workplace.* New York: St. Martin's Press, 1993.

Mendes, Richard Henry Pereira. "The Professional Union: A Study of the Social Service Employees Union of the New York City Department of Social Services." Ph.D. diss., Columbia University, New York, 1974.

Meyerowitz, Joanne J. *How Sex Changed: A History of Transsexuality in the United States.* Cambridge, MA: Harvard University Press, 2004.

Milkman, Ruth. *L.A. Story: Immigrant Workers and the Future of the U.S. Labor Movement.* New York: Russell Sage Foundation, 2006.

Milkman, Ruth, and Laura Braslow. "The State of the Unions: A Profile of Organized Labor in New York City, New York State, and the United States." Report. Joseph S. Murphy Institute for Worker Education and Labor Studies Center for Urban Research, and New York City Labor Market Information Service, City University of New York, 2011.

Minchin, Timothy J. *"Don't Sleep with Stevens!": The J. P. Stevens Campaign and the Struggle to Organize the South, 1963–1980.* Gainesville: University Press of Florida, 2005.

Moccio, Francine A. "Contradicting Male Power and Privilege: Class, Race and Gender Relations in the Building Trades." Ph.D. diss., New School for Social Research, New York, 1992.

———. *Live Wire: Women and Brotherhood in the Electrical Industry.* Philadelphia: Temple University Press, 2009.

Montague, Ann. "We Are Union Builders, Too: Oregon Union Tackles Discrimination Based on Sexual Orientation." *Labor Research Review* 20 (1993): 78–83.

Mort, Jo-Ann, ed. *Not Your Father's Union Movement: Inside the AFL-CIO.* London: Verso, 1998.

Murdoch, Joyce, and Deb Price. *Courting Justice: Gay Men and Lesbians versus the Supreme Court.* New York: Basic, 2001.

Murolo, Priscilla, and Benjamin Chitty. *From the Folks Who Brought You the Weekend: A Short, Illustrated History of Labor in the United States.* New York: New Press, 2001.

Nadasen, Premilla. *Welfare Warriors: The Welfare Rights Movement in the United States.* New York: Routledge, 2005.

National Gay and Lesbian Task Force. *Fight the Right Action Kit.* Washington, DC: National Gay and Lesbian Task Force, 1993.

The New Oxford Annotated Bible, augmented 3d ed. New York: Oxford University Press, 2007.

Nichols, John. *Uprising: How Wisconsin Renewed the Politics of Protest, from Madison to Wall Street.* New York: Nation, 2012.

O'Farrell, Brigid, and Joyce L. Kornbluh. *Rocking the Boat: Union Women's Voices, 1915–1975.* New Brunswick, NJ: Rutgers University Press, 1996.

Orleck, Annelise. *Common Sense and a Little Fire: Women and Working-Class Politics in the United States, 1900–1965.* Chapel Hill: University of North Carolina Press, 1995.

Orth, Christa. "Brothers and Sisters (and Everyone in Between): Sexuality and Class in the Pacific Northwest, 1970–1995." Master's thesis, University of Oregon, Eugene, 2002.

Orwell, George. *Why I Write.* New York: Penguin, 2005.

Peddicord, Richard. *Gay and Lesbian Rights: A Question—Sexual Ethics or Social Justice?* Kansas City, MO: Sheed and Ward, 1996.

Penelope, Julia. *Out of the Class Closet: Lesbians Speak.* Freedom, CA: Crossing, 1994.

Rasi, Richard, and Lourdes Rodriguez-Nogues, eds. *Out in the Workplace: The Pleasures and Perils of Coming Out on the Job.* Los Angeles: Alyson, 1995.

Remick, Helen, ed. *Comparable Worth and Wage Discrimination: Technical Possibilities and Political Realities.* Philadelphia: Temple University Press, 1984.

Retter, Yolanda. "On the Side of the Angels: Lesbian Activism in L.A., 1970–1990." Ph.D. diss., University of New Mexico, Albuquerque, 1999.

Riddle, R. David. "The Rise of the 'Reagan Democrats' in Warren Michigan, 1964–1984." Ph.D. diss., Wayne State University, Detroit, 1998.

Ridinger, Robert B., ed. *Speaking for Our Lives: Historic Speeches and Rhetoric for Gay and Lesbian Rights (1892–2000).* Binghamton, NY: Harrington Park, 2004.

Rimmerman, Craig. *From Identity to Politics: The Lesbian and Gay Movements in the United States.* Philadelphia: Temple University Press, 2002.

Rubenstein, William B., ed. *Lesbians, Gay Men and the Law.* New York: New Press, 1993.

Schroedel, Jean Reith, ed. *Alone in a Crowd: Women in the Trades Tell Their Stories.* Philadelphia: Temple University Press, 1985.

Schulman, Sarah. *People in Trouble.* New York: Plume, 1991.

Shaw, Randy. *Beyond the Fields: Cesar Chavez, the UFW, and the Struggle for Justice in the 21st Century.* Berkeley: University of California Press, 2008.

Sheflin, Neil, Leo Troy, Industrial Relations Data Information Service: *U.S. Union Sourcebook: Membership, Finances, Structure, Directory, 1947–1983.* West Orange NJ: IRDIS, 1985.

Shilts, Randy. *The Mayor of Castro Street: The Life and Times of Harvey Milk.* New York: St. Martin's Press, 1982.

Shostak, Arthur. *Robust Unionism: Innovations in the Labor Movement.* Ithaca, NY: Cornell University Press, 1991.

Shostak, Arthur, and David Skocik. *The Air Controllers' Controversy: Lessons from the PATCO Strike.* New York: Human Sciences, 1986.

Sides, Josh. *Erotic Cities: Sexual Revolutions and the Making of Modern San Francisco.* New York: Oxford University Press, 2009.

Smith, Robert. *From Blackjacks to Briefcases: A History of Commercialized Strikebreaking and Unionbusting in the United States.* Athens: Ohio University Press, 2003.

Smith, Sara R. "Struggling for Equality: Rank-and-File Teachers' Organizing in California after World War II." Ph.D. diss., University of California, Santa Cruz, forthcoming.

Sockell, Donna, and John Thomas Delaney. "Union Organizing and the Reagan NLRB." *Contemporary Policy Issues* 5, no. 4 (1987): 28–45.

Stein, Arlene. *The Stranger Next Door.* Boston: Beacon, 2001.

Stein, Marc. *City of Sisterly and Brotherly Loves: Lesbian and Gay Philadelphia, 1945–1972.* Chicago: University of Chicago Press, 2000.

———. *Rethinking the Gay and Lesbian Movement.* New York: Routledge, 2012.

Terkel, Studs. *Working: People Talk about What They Do All Day and How They Feel about What They Do*. New York: Pantheon, 1974.

Thompson, Heather. *Whose* Detroit? *Politics, Labor, and Race in a Modern American City*. Ithaca, NY: Cornell University Press, 2001.

Tiemeyer, Phil. *Plane Queer: Labor, Sexuality and AIDS in the History of Male Flight Attendants*. Berkeley: University of California Press, 2013.

Timmons, Stuart. *The Trouble with Harry Hay: Founder of the Modern Gay Movement*. Boston: Alyson, 1990.

Vogel, Alfred. "Your Clerical Workers Are Ripe for Unionism." *Harvard Business Review* 49 (March–April 1971): 48–54.

Vozenilek, Helen. "Changing Times, Changing Leadership: Interview with Janis Borchardt." *Tradeswomen* (Winter 1991): 19–21.

Wallace, Howard, ed. *Solidarity in Action: An Historical Scrapbook*. San Francisco: Local 250 SEIU, 1994.

Weston, Kathleen, and Lisa B. Rofel. "Sexuality, Class and Conflict in a Lesbian Workplace." *Signs* 9, no. 4 (1984): 623–646.

Williams, Charles. "Reconsidering CIO Political Culture: Briggs Local 212 and the Sources of Militancy in the Early UAW." *Labor* 7, no. 4 (Winter 2010): 17–43.

Working Women, National Association of Office Workers. "Race against Time: Automation of the Office: An Analysis of the Trends in Office Automation and the Impact of the Office Workforce." Report. Cleveland: The Association, 1980.

Young, Patricia Jean. "Measure 9: Oregon's 1992 Anti-Gay Initiative." Master's thesis, Portland State University, Portland, OR, 1997.

Zimmerman, Bonnie, ed. *Lesbian Histories and Cultures: An Encyclopedia*. New York: Garland, 2000.

Index

AATEU, 107, 108, 109

Abnormal Behaviors Initiative (OR), 129

Acosta, Carmen, 167, 168, 169–170

ACT-UP, 152, 155

ACTWU. *See* Amalgamated Clothing and Textile Workers Union

ACWA. *See* Amalgamated Clothing Workers of America

AFL-CIO. *See* American Federation of Labor–Congress of Industrial Organizations

AFSCME. *See* American Federation of State, County, and Municipal Employees

AFT. *See* American Federation of Teachers

Agency shop, 151, 159–160, 163

AGMA, 41, 83

AGVA, 41

"AIDS and the Health Care Worker," 119–120

AIDS clinics and centers, 139; in 1980s, 148–150; in 1990s, 151–153; Edelman Health Clinic, 149–150, 196n40; GMHC, 153–157; Northwest AIDS Foundation, 150–151; San Francisco AIDS Foundation, 140, 157–160; Whitman-Walker Clinic, 160–163

AIDS Coalition to Unleash Power (ACT-UP), 152, 155

AIDS crisis, 103, 108, 116–120

AIDS Labor Education Project, 120

AIDS memorial quilt, 96, 189n78

ALGFAS, 112

Alliance of Rank and File (ARF), 142

"Allies for the 90s: United for Health" fundraiser (Boston), 95

Amalgamated Clothing and Textile Workers Union (ACTWU), 12; and Barneys, 43; leadership, 59–62; Local 340, 43; merging of, 84; restructuring at, 136; and transgender rights, 2

Amalgamated Clothing Workers of America (ACWA): and Barneys, 43; Connie Kopelov at, 166; leadership, 51–52; Local 340, 43; merging of, 59

Amalgamated Meat Cutters, 57–58

Amalgamated Transit Union (ATU), 34; and lesbian bus drivers, 34; Local 1225 (SF), 34; Local 1564 (Detroit), 109; and sexual orientation protection, 109

American Civil Liberties Union, 92, 126

American Federation of Labor–Congress of Industrial Organizations (AFL-CIO): and antigay legislation, 130; Asia Pacific American Labor Alliance, 100; and Briggs amendment, 91, 92; Building Trades Council (Boston), 95; Building Trades Department, 86; Coalition of Black Trade Unionists, 85, 100; Coalition of Labor Union Women, 30, 70, 93, 97, 100, 166; Construction Trades Council (SF), 90; and Coors boycott, 79–80, 82; and Equal Protection Colorado, 126; of FL, 87; and gay rights, 6, 9, 86; Huron Valley Labor Council, 107, 108; Industrial Union Department, 86; King County Labor Council, 57, 89; Labor Council for Latin American Advancement, 100; leadership, 49; and marriage equality, 11; of MD, 172; of MN, 172; in National March for Lesbian and Gay Rights, 96–97; NYC Central Labor Council, 82; of OR, 130; and Pride at Work, 9, 77, 100–101; Randolph Institute, 97, 100; and Save Our Children campaign, 87; and SF clerical workers, 147; and social workers' strike (NYC), 56; Solidarity Day rally, 43, 182n94; Southern Maine Labor Council, 171; and J. P. Stevens boycott, 59; of UT, 99–100; and Vietnam War, 6

American Federation of State, County, and Municipal Employees (AFSCME): and AIDS crisis, 116, 117; and Ann Arbor bus drivers, 105, 106–107; and civil rights, 138; and clerical workers, 109; coalition politics in, 85–86, 94, 97, 100; and CO antigay law, 126; Council 31 (IL), 85; Council 51 (MI), 106–107; Council 75 (OR), 129; Council 93 (MA), 65; District Council 3 (MD), 172; District Council 26 (federal employees, DC), 85; District Council 37 (NYC), 94, 100, 116, 122–123, 165–166; District Council 47 (Phila.), 85; District Council 66 (Rochester, NY), 53; District Council 67 (MD), 172; and domestic partner benefits, 111; and Equal Protection Colorado, 126; and gay hot shops, 140; gay rights resolution, 18, 85–86; gay rights task force, 53; insurgency in, 64–65; leadership, 51, 53; Lesbian and Gay Issues Committee, 94, 122–123, 165; and lesbian bus drivers, 34; Local 101 (San Jose, CA), 128; Local 369 (Ann Arbor), 106; Local 371 (Social Service Employees Union, NYC), 17, 55, 56; Local 376 (Construction Laborers, NYC), 122; Local 693 (Ann Arbor), 106–107; Local 768 (public health employees, NYC), 122; Local 1108 (L.A.), 140; Local 1489 (Boston City Hospital), 64–65; Local 1549 (clerical workers, NYC), 122, 165, 166; Local 1723 (Temple University), 117–118; Local 1733 (Memphis), 138; Local 1930 (Public Library Guild, NYC), 122; Local 2021 (Off-Track Betting employees, NYC), 122; Local 2027 (Peace Corps, DC), 85; Local 2081 (Illinois Department of Children and Family Services), 85; Local 2083 (Seattle Public Library Workers), 190n7; Local 3339 (West Hollywood, CA), 111; and marriage equality, 165, 172; mass transit workers organized by, 34; and NYC social workers, 55, 56; and Oregon Citizens Alliance, 130; and Pride at Work pamphlet, 12; queer activism in, 97–98; queer caucuses in, 122, 124; and Save Our Children campaign, 89; on sexual orientation protection, 128–129; on wage inequity, 128
American Federation of Teachers (AFT): and AIDS crisis, 116; California Federation of Teachers, 91, 121–122; on discrimination based on sexual orientation, 18; on domestic partner benefits, 109, 112; Executive Council, 18, 84, 121, 188n33; on fair treatment for gay workers, 6–7; gay rights resolutions, 84–85, 188n33; Local 2 (UFT, NYC), 56, 84, 121, 188n33; Local 61 (SF), 85, 121; Local 280 (New Rochelle, NY), 17–18, 84; Local 1974 (United Teachers of Dade, Miami, FL), 87;

Local 3550 (GEO, University of Michigan), 2–3; Local 3882 (United Staff Association of NYU), 109, 112, 116; on transgender rights, 2
American Guild of Musical Artists (AGMA), 41, 83
American Guild of Variety Artists (AGVA), 41
American Motors, 37, 49–50
American Postal Workers Union (APWU), 90
Ammiano, Tom, 159
Ann Arbor Transit Employees Union (AATEU), 107, 108, 109
Ann Arbor Transportation Authority, 32, 33, 106
Apprenticeships: in auto plants, 36, 40; in building trades, 6, 21, 23, 25–26, 28, 29, 46; in IATSE, 58; at Labyris Auto Repair, 141, 142
APWU, 90
ARF, 142
Ashbrook, Connie, 23–24, 25, 27, 32
Association of Lesbian and Gay Faculty, Administrators, and Staff (ALGFAS), 112
AT&T, 20, 28, 31
ATU. See Amalgamated Transit Union
Auto plants: AIDS awareness at, 118–119; changing gender at, 38–39; domestic partner benefits in, 113; gay men at, 34–38; UAW politics and queer identity at, 39–41

BACABI, 91
BAGL, 78, 121
Baird, Allan, 77–79, 83
Bankruptcy filing, and successor statement, 44–45
Barbera, Tom, 95, 98
Barneys, 43–45
Basile, Victor, 85
Batey, Stephanie, 159, 160
Bay Area Committee against the Briggs Initiative (BACABI), 91
Bay Area Gay Liberation (BAGL), 78, 121
Bay Area Physicians for Human Rights, 119
BEBASHI, 117–118
Bell Wringer, 30, 31
Bender, James K., 89
Bereavement leave, spousal equivalent, 103, 108, 110
Bérubé, Allan, 4, 42
Bill the Boilermaker, 1–2, 12
Black Panther Party, 78
Blacks Educating Blacks about Sexual Health Issues (BEBASHI), 117–118
Blood drives during AIDS crisis, 116
Blue Shield, 146, 147
Body Politic, 39
Bonavita, Joe, 65
Borchardt, Janis, 34

Boston: AIDS epidemic, 111, 117; Boston
  Tradeswomen's Network, 28; Building
  Trades Council, 95; Coors boycott, 81; do-
  mestic partner benefits, 111–112; GALLAN,
  81, 94–96; queer work in, 43; school bus
  drivers in, 33, 34, 117
Boston City Hospital, 8, 64–65, 94
Boycotts: of CA grapes, 75, 95, 97, 107; Coors,
  77–82; of CO tourism, 126; counter-boycott
  of Chrysler Products, 113; of FL oranges, 87;
  of Gay Community Service Center, 140; of
  J. P. Stevens textiles, 59–60
Brewery Workers Union Local 366 (Coors
  Plant, Golden, CO), 75–76, 79–80
Briggs Beautyware, 66–69
Briggs Initiative (CA), 89–92, 121–122, 124, 170
Brotherhood of Sleeping Car Porters, 51
Brown, Clayola, 2
Brown, Nancy, 22, 23, 26–27
Bryant, Anita, 86–88
Bryner, Gary, 38–39
Buddy teams for AIDS, 148
Building trades: apprenticeships in, 23, 28;
  buddy relationships in, 26–27; dyke-baiting
  in, 24–26; gay men in, 21, 179n9; lesbians in,
  22–24
Burrell, Bob, 36, 37–38
Bus drivers: AIDS and, 117; in Ann Arbor,
  105–109; in Boston, 32–34; lesbians as,
  32–34; school, 33, 34, 117
Bush, George H. W., 151–152
Bywater, Bill, 70–71

California Federation of Teachers, 91, 121–122
California Nurses Association, 91
California Proposition 6, 89–92, 121–122, 124,
  170
California Teachers Association, 91
Canada: legalization of homosexual behavior
  in, 40, 181n79; Windsor Gay Unity, 39
Canadian Auto Workers Union (CAW), 113
Cannon Mills, 61–62, 185n52
"Can We Talk" brochure, 119
Capoferri, Becky, 128–131
Card check, 137, 144–145, 162
Cartwright, Donna, 51, 63–64
CAW, 113
CBTU, 85, 100
CDU, 119–120
Cement Masons, 89
Cepeda, Florence, 157, 160
CFV, 124–127
Chavez, Cesar, 95, 97, 138
Cheney, Mary, 82
Chicken Soup Brigade (Seattle), 151

Christen, Pat, 158–159
Christian, Joni, 38–39
Christian Coalition, 124, 131
Chrysler Corp.: AIDS awareness at, 118;
  contract enforcement at, 115–116; domestic
  partner benefits at, 113; gays on production
  line at, 35–36, 37, 39, 40–41; People of Diver-
  sity, 113; plant closing at, 66–69
Church Street Station (SF), 143
CIO, 4. See also American Federation of La-
  bor–Congress of Industrial Organizations
Cisek, Johnny, 38
Citizens for Limited Taxation (MA), 96
Civil Marriage Protection Act (MD), 171
Civil Rights Movement: LGBT identities in, 51;
  queer activists from, 97
Clarke, Shirley, 98
Clerical workers, 31, 41, 104, 122, 146–147
CLUW, 30, 70, 93, 97, 100, 166
Coalition(s), 75–101; in AFL-CIO, 96–97;
  in AFSCME and SEIU, 97–98; in Boston,
  94–96; against Briggs amendment, 89–92;
  in Coors boycott, 77–82; formation of
  Pride at Work, 100–101; in Miami-Dade
  County, 86–88; in NYC, 93–94; in OR,
  127, 130–131; against repeal of gay rights
  ordinances, 86–89; in Seattle, 88–89; in SF,
  92–93; at union conventions, 82–86; in UT,
  98–100
Coalition of Black Trade Unionists (CBTU),
  85, 100
Coalition of Labor Union Women (CLUW), 30,
  70, 93, 97, 100, 166
Co-determination, 106–107
Colorado: antigay laws (Amendment 2), 105,
  124–127; Coors boycott, 75–76, 79–80, 126,
  193n78; for Family Values (CFV), 124–127;
  Taxpayer Bill of Rights (Amendment 10),
  126, 193n79
Columbia University, 102–104, 109
Committee for a Democratic Union (CDU),
  119–120
Communication Workers of America (CWA):
  and lesbians in telephone crafts, 28–32; Local 1101 (NYC), 30, 31; Local 4100 (Detroit),
  29, 30; Local 7704 (Salt Lake City), 98; Local
  7901 (Portland, OR), 32; Local 9102 (Seattle),
  31, 88–89; National Women's Committee,
  29–30; and Seattle Proposition 13, 88–89; in
  UT, 98–99
Communists, 4, 65, 68, 175–176n9
Compensation inequities, 3; for gay and
  bisexual men, 42, 182n88; gender-based, 57,
  128–129, 184n35
Concerned Employees against Union, 154–155

Congress of Industrial Organizations (CIO), 4. *See also* American Federation of Labor–Congress of Industrial Organizations

Congress of Racial Equality, 56

Construction jobs. *See* Building trades

Construction Trades Council (SF), 90

Contract enforcement, 113–116; and arbitration, 104, 114, 118

Coors boycott, 77–82; AFL-CIO in, 79–80, 82; and blacks, 78, 81; in Boston, 81; as coalition builder, 75–76; endorsements of, 81; financial losses due to, 80; in Golden, CO, 75–76, 79–80, 126, 193n78; and Latinos, 75, 80–81; and MADD, 81; in NY and NJ, 81–82; in SF, 75, 77–79, 80

Coors Company: and Bill Coors, 81; and Joseph Coors, 79; and Scott Coors, 82; polygraph tests, 78–79, 187n9; reorganization of, 82; support of right-wing organizations, 79, 187n11

Adolph Coors Foundation, 79, 187n11

Cracker Barrel restaurant chain, 40

Crites, Shelley, 32

Cross-dressing: auto workers, 37–38; textile worker, 62; at Whitman-Walker clinic, 2. *See also* Drag

Cuomo, Andrew, 168

Cuomo, Mario, 53, 165

Cutting, Ginny, 94–95, 123

CWA. *See* Communication Workers of America

DaimlerChrysler, 113

Dale, Alice, 130, 131

Dammasch psychiatric hospital, 128, 129

Daughters of Bilitis (DOB), 5, 55–56, 176–177n15

Davis, Madeline, 177n24

Deane, Gary, 51–53

Decertification, 105, 107; attempt at San Francisco AIDS Foundation, 160, 197–198n92; by GMHC, 150, 157; of Local 366, 80; of PATCO, 152

Defense of Marriage Act (DOMA), 170–171, 173, 183n7

Democratic National Convention: Miami (1972), 6; NYC (1992), 155

Dental work, AIDS and, 117–118

De Santis, Robert, 19–20

Detroit: AIDS awareness, 118; Coors boycott, 81; gays in auto plants, 35–38; insurgents in, 66–69; lesbians in building trades, 22; lesbians in telephone crafts, 28–30

Detroit Free Press, 29

Dias, Michael, 123–124

Dignity (org.), 161

Dinkins, David, 94, 123

D'Inzillo, Steve, 58–59

Direct recognition: by AIDS clinics and centers, 139, 149, 154, 162; process of, 137; in SF hospitality industry, 144–145

Dishrag, 195n23

District 65, 102, 104, 109, 110

District 1199: Gary Deane at, 52; organizing at AIDS clinics and centers by, 149, 150, 151, 154–157, 162; SEIU affiliation, 166–167

District 1199 East, 166–167, 169, 172

District 1199-E DC, 2, 150, 161–162

District 1199 Northwest, 48–49, 151, 172

DOB, 5, 55–56, 176–177n15

DOMA, 170–171, 173, 183n7

Domestic partner benefits: in auto industry, 113; at Boston hotels, 111–112; for CA municipal workers, 110–111; at Columbia University, 102–104; cost of, 110, 191n21; early adopters, 110, 191n20; invention of, 104, 109–113; LAGIC on, 123; narrow definitions of, 112–113; same-sex, 45, 46, 182–183n103; at San Francisco AIDS Foundation, 159; and union leadership, 53–54; at *Village Voice*, 8, 104, 109–110, 137, 191n18

"Don't Ask, Don't Tell," 19

Drag: drag fashion shows and Barneys, 44; Harry (Kitty) Kevorkian, 108; Sidney (Sylvia Sidney) Sushman, 43. *See also* Cross-dressing

Dress code: Ann Arbor bus drivers, 108; gay workplaces, 140, 163

Dyke-baiting, 21, 24–26

Earls, Marc, 151

Ed D. Edelman Health Clinic, 149–150, 196n40

Elder, Madelyn, 31–32, 88–89

Ellis, Havelock, 1

Employee associations: at Chrysler (People of Diversity), 113; at Coors (LAGER), 82; at NYU (ALGFAS), 112

Episcopal Community Service (SF), 147–148

Equal Employment Opportunity Commission (EEOC), 29, 159

Equal Protection Colorado (EPOC), 125–126

"Equal rights, not special rights," 125, 131

Equi, Marie, 175–176n9

Ernst, Carol, 106–108

Ettinger, Shelley, 32, 33, 34

Ewing, Tess, 33, 34, 94, 117

Exotic Dancers Alliance, 178n26, 187n5

Far right. *See* Right-wing politics

Federal Aviation Authority, 182n94

Federal employees, 85, 151

Feldman, Richard, 36
Fenway Health Center (Boston), 95
Fenway Park Stadium, Coors boycott at, 81
Fieldcrest, 61–62, 185n52
Flanders, Cliff, 18, 19, 21
Florida, Save Our Children campaign in, 86–88
Flynn, Elizabeth Gurley, 175–176n9
Focus on the Family, 124
Food service workers, new efforts at union-
    izing, 173
Ford, 113; Michigan Truck, 36, 37–38; Plastics
    Distribution Center (Milan, MI), 36
Frank, Barney, 97
"Freedom Summer" (MS, 1964), 5
Freedom to Marry, 168, 171
Freund, Vivienne, 93–94, 117
Friedman, Barry, 85
Frontlash, 82

GALLAN, 81, 94–96, 189n76
Gay and Lesbian Alliance against Defamation
    (GLAAD), 82
Gay and Lesbian Concerns Committee (GLCC)
    of SEIU, 123
Gay and Lesbian Independent Democrats, 52
Gay and Lesbian Labor Activists Network
    (GALLAN), 81, 94–96, 189n76
Gay businesses, 138–142
Gay civil rights bill (NYC), 122
Gay Community Services Center (L.A.), 140,
    196n40
Gay Freedom Day rally (SF), 91, 145, 147
Gay hot shops, 139–142
Gay liberation movement, 6, 50
Gay Men's Counseling Collective, 161
Gay Men's Health Crisis (GMHC, NYC), 149,
    150, 152, 153–157, 163, 166
Gay Pride Parade (NYC), 94, 170
Gay-related immune deficiency (GRID), 116
Gay Rights National Lobby, 85
Gay rights ordinances: and Briggs Initiative
    (CA), 89–92, 121–122, 124, 170; of Miami-
    Dade County, 20, 86–88, 124; municipal, 10,
    45, 87; of Seattle, 88–89, 172
Gay rights resolution: of AFL-CIO, 9, 86; of
    AFSCME, 18, 85–86; of SEIU, 98
Gay rights task force (AFSCME), 53
Gay Teachers Association (GTA, NYC), 84–85,
    94, 120–123
Gay Teachers Coalition (GTC, SF), 85, 121
GE, 66, 69–71
Gender identity and expression as protected
    class, 2, 3, 8, 19
Gender reassignment treatment and surgery:
    and auto plant work, 38–39; health care

coverage for, 2–3; protocols for, 185–186n58;
    and union leadership, 63–64
General Electric (GE), 66, 69–71
General Motors, 37, 38–39, 113
GEO (University of Michigan), 2–3
Giuliani, Rudolph, 123
GLAAD, 82
GLCC (SEIU), 123
GMHC (NYC), 149, 150, 152, 153–157, 163, 166
Goldberg, Whoopi, 168
Goldschmidt, Neil, 129
Gould, Jay, 136
Graduate Employees Organization (GEO,
    University of Michigan), 2–3
Graham, Jim, 160, 161, 162
Gresham, George, 167, 169
Grevatt, Martha, 41
GRID, 116
GTA (NYC), 84–85, 94, 120–123
GTC (SF), 85, 121
The Guardian, 39–40
Guthman, Gary, 144–145

Hands Off Washington coalition, 48–49, 172,
    183n2
Hanen, Suzanne, 116
Harassment: assaults and threats, 28–30,
    61, 185–186; defenses against assaults, 36,
    37–38, 40; dildos, 36, 40, 179n21; dyke-
    baiting in building trades, 24–26; graffiti,
    25, 36, 40, 115; in telephone crafts, 28–30; of
    transgender worker, 38–39, 181n69; in union
    election, 34, 57, 65, 68–69
Hard Hatted Women (Cleveland), 23
Harrald, Mike, 115
Harris, Jackie, 17, 18, 19, 21
Harvey Milk Gay Democratic Club (SF), 119
Hay, Harry, 176–177n15
Helm Act (OK), 89, 124
Henry, Mary Kay, 49
HIV status, 116–117, 156
HIV transmission, 116
Holcomb, Desma, 12, 47
Hospitality House (SF), 148
Hotel Employees and Restaurant Employees
    Union (HERE): acceptance of queerness
    in, 43; Alliance of Rank and File, 142;
    and Briggs amendment, 90, 91; and Coors
    boycott, 81; and domestic partner benefits,
    111–112; at Fenway Park, 81; and GALLAN,
    95; insurgencies in, 65; Local 2 (SF), 90, 91,
    139, 142–146; Local 8 (Seattle), 43; Local 9
    (Portland, OR), 131; Local 26 (Boston), 43,
    65, 111–112, 151; and queer workplaces, 139,
    142–146; Susan Schurman at, 106

Hot shops, 139–142
Human Rights Campaign, 168, 172
Human Rights Commission (SF), 158
Human Rights Party, 106, 107
Hunt, Ed, 51, 64–65, 96
Huron Valley Labor Council, 107, 108
Hutchins, Grace, 175–176n9

IAM. *See* International Association of Machinists and Aerospace Workers
IATSE (NYC), 58–59
IBEW. *See* International Brotherhood of Electrical Workers
IBT. *See* International Brotherhood of Teamsters
ILGWU, 62, 83–84
ILWU Local 10, 158
Immigrants, 173–174; and Alliance of Rank and File, 142; at San Francisco AIDS Foundation, 159
Industrial Union of Marine and Shipbuilding Workers of America Local 5 (Fore River Plant, Quincy, MA), 25
Industrial Workers of the World (IWW), 175–176n9
Information Store (SF), 148
Ingemi, John, 65
Insurgents, 62–65; and plant closings, 65–71
International Alliance of Theatrical Stage Employees (IATSE) Local 306 (Motion Picture Projectionists, NYC), 58–59
International Association of Machinists and Aerospace Workers (IAM): and domestic partner benefits, 46; and Labyris Auto Repair, 141; Local 1305 (Automotive Machinists Lodge, SF), 141; Local 1781 (airline mechanics, SF), 46
International Brotherhood of Boilermakers Lodge 27, 1, 175n4
International Brotherhood of Electrical Workers (IBEW): apprenticeships in, 23; and lesbians in building trades, 22; Local 58 (Detroit), 22; Local 354 (Salt Lake City), 100
International Brotherhood of Teamsters (IBT): in Coors boycott, 75, 77–79; and Jimmy Hoffa, 82; Local 856 (Bay Area), 78; Local 888 (beer truck drivers, SF), 75, 77–79; Local 921 (newspaper truck drivers, SF), 77; mass transit workers organized by, 34; restructuring at, 136; Western Conference, 77, 79
International Ladies' Garment Workers' Union (ILGWU), 62, 83–84
International Longshore and Warehouse Union (ILWU) Local 10 (SF), 158
International Union of Electrical Workers

(IUE): Local 1002 (GE, Seattle), 70; and plant closing, 66, 69–71
International Union of Elevator Constructors Local 23 (Portland, OR), 24
International Union of Mine, Mill, and Smelter Workers, 34, 180n46
IUE: Local 1002 (GE, Seattle), 70; and plant closing, 66, 69–71
IWW, 175–176n9
Izzo, Joe, 2, 149, 152, 160–163

Jackson, Ezekiel, 172
Jacobsen, Ruth, 51, 58–59
Jaicks, Lisa, 144
Job interview, 19–20
Jobpower, 143
Jochems, Ann, 25
Johnsen, Marcy, 48–49
Johnson, Walter, 91, 114–115
Justen, Jim, 37, 41, 49–50

Kaiser-Permanente, 110, 120
Kapanowski, Gary, 51, 66–69, 70, 71, 117–118
Katz, Annette, 87
Kevorkian, Harry, 37, 108
King, Martin Luther, Jr., 56, 86, 138, 155, 188n40
King County Labor Council, 57, 89
King County Reemployment Project, 71
Kinsey, Alfred, 5, 178n27
Koblentz, Richard, 143
Kopelov, Connie, 11, 52–53, 165, 166, 170
Kremkow, Terry, 40–41
Krupat, Kitty, 110

Laberge, Jeanne, 51, 58–59
Labor Research Association, 175–176n9
Labyris Auto Repair, 141–142, 194–195n8
The Ladder, 5, 55, 176–177n15
Lafayette Restaurant (SF), 144
LaGasa, Virginia, 92
LAGER, 82
LAGIC, 94, 122–123, 165
Lara, Sandra, 31
Latinos, Coors boycott and, 75, 80–81
Lavender Caucuses (SEIU), 49, 98, 100, 120, 124, 158, 167
Lawrence v. Texas (2003), 7–8
League of Revolutionary Black Workers, 67
League of Women Voters, 168
Legislative Black Caucus of Maryland, 172
LeRoy, Julie, 100
Lesbian and Gay Community Center (NYC), 94
Lesbian and Gay Employee Resource (LAGER), 82

Lesbian and Gay Issues Committee (LAGIC), 94, 122–123, 165
Lesbian and Gay Labor Network (LGLN, NY), 12, 82, 93–94, 117
Lesbian and Gay Teachers Association (NYC), 94, 120
Lesbian/Gay Labor Alliance (LGLA, SF), 93, 143, 148
Levi Strauss, 191n20
Levitt, Donna, 46
Lewis, Bob, 119
LGBT people, number in United States, 7, 178n27
LGBTQ Caucus (SEIU), 167, 169
LGLA (SF), 93, 143, 148
LGLN (NY), 12, 82, 93–94, 117
Lifelong AIDS Association (Seattle), 151
Lingar, Don, 115
Liska, Ed, 35
Little Italy (SF), 144–145
Log Cabin Republicans, 168
Loux, Janice, 95, 111
Lucy, William, 85–86, 188n40
Luisa's (SF), 145
Lusty Lady Theater (SF), 178n26, 187n5
Lutsky, Robin, 103

Mack Avenue Revolutionary Union Movement (MARUM), 67
MacLeod, Lynn, 141–142
Macy's, 114–115
Mage, Judy, 51, 55–57
Maine, same-sex marriage in, 170, 171
Maine Education Association, 171
March on Washington: for Jobs and Freedom (1963), 5, 6, 51
Mariel boatlift, 143, 195n25
Marine Cooks and Stewards Union (MCS), 4
Marriage equality, 165–173
MARUM, 67
Maryland, same-sex marriage in, 170, 171–172
Massachusetts: Question 3 referendum, 96; same-sex marriage in, 170
Mattachine Society, 5, 176–177n15
Mayne, Ed, 99–100
McDonald, David, 91
McEntee, Gerald, 97
MCS, 4
Meany, George, 6, 79, 177n24
Mehring, John, 119–120
Melvin, Scott, 149, 153–157, 158, 159
Metro Theatre strike, 93
Mexican American Legal Defense Fund, 28
Miami-Dade County Metro Ordinance 77-4, 86–88

Michigan Bell, 28–30
Milk, Harvey, 78, 90, 92, 141
Minnesota, same-sex marriage in, 170, 171, 172–173
Mitchell, James (Jim), 17–18, 19, 21, 84, 85
Moir, Susan, 34, 94, 95, 96, 117
Mo'nique, 171
Monk, Jim, 35, 39–40
Montague, Ann, 98, 128, 129
Monti, Frank, 83
Moore, Julianne, 168
Mormon Church, 99
Morrison and Foerster, 158

National Association for the Advancement of Colored People (NAACP), 56, 81
National Council of Churches Staff Association, 18
National Education Association (NEA): California Teachers Association, 91; Coors boycott endorsed by, 81; on fair treatment for gay workers, 6–7; Maine Education Association, 171; openly gay and lesbian activists in, 84
National Gay and Lesbian Task Force, 167, 169
National Labor Relations Board (NLRB): and AIDS clinics and centers, 140, 154, 157, 158, 160, 197–198n92; certification by, 105; and Coors boycott, 80; decertification by, 105, 107, 197–198n92; and organizing drives for gay workers, 137, 143, 144; and southern textile workers, 61, 62
National March for Lesbian and Gay Rights: in 1979, 97; in 1987, 96–97; in 1993, 100
National Office for AIDS Policy, 152
National Organization for Women (NOW): Coors boycott endorsed by, 81; domestic partner benefits at, 191n20; on lesbians in labor movement, 93; and lesbians in telephone industry, 28, 29; and Teresa Rankin, 59
National Union of Hospital and Health Care Employees District 1199, 52
National Women's Committee of Communication Workers of America, 29–30
National Writers Union, 40
Navratilova, Martina, 126
NEA. See National Education Association
Newark Teachers Union, 184n28
New Jersey, Coors boycott in, 81–82
Newspaper Guild Local 3 (New York Times), 63
Newspaper Truck Drivers Local 921 (SF), 77
Newton, Huey, 78
New York City: AIDS crisis, 116–117; Columbia University, 102–104, 109; domestic partner benefits at Village Voice, 8, 104, 109–110, 137, 191n18; dyke-baiting in, 24–26; gay civil

New York City (*continued*)
rights bill, 122; gay labor movement, 93–94;
GMHC, 149, 150, 152, 153–157, 163, 166;
GTA, 84–85, 94, 120–123; queer work in, 42,
43–45; Stonewall Rebellion, 6, 100; union
leadership in, 52–54, 55–57, 58–59; United
Tradeswomen of, 23
New York City Deli (SF), 145
New York Labor History Association, 166
New York State: Coors boycott, 81–82; domes-
tic partner benefits, 123; Empire State Pride
Agenda, 167, 168–169; Marriage Equality
Act, 165–170, 171; New Yorkers United for
Marriage, 168, 169
New York Teacher, 121
New York Telephone, 30
New York Times, 63–64
New York University, 109, 112, 116
NLRB. *See* National Labor Relations Board
Nomenclature for sexual diversity, 190n5
North American Free Trade Agreement (1994),
185n52
Northwest AIDS Foundation (NWAF), 149–151
NOW. *See* National Organization for Women
Noyce, Cal, 98–100
NWAF, 149–151

Obama, Barack, on same-sex marriage,
170–172
OCA, 27, 127, 129–131, 183n2
O'Connor, John Cardinal, 155
Office and Professional Employees Interna-
tional Union (OPEIU): Local 3 (SF/Bay
Area), 139, 146–148, 158; Local 30 (Southern
CA), 41–42
Oklahoma antigay laws, 89, 124, 189n55,
192n72
Oliver, Walter, 107
Olwell, Bill, 51, 55, 57–58, 97, 135–136, 162
O'Malley, Martin, 171
One, 5
O'Neil, Dennis, 37
OPEIU: Local 3 (SF/Bay Area), 139, 146–148,
158; Local 30 (Southern CA), 41–42
Oregon: antigay laws, 105, 127–132; Bigot Bust-
ing, 130; Measure 9 (1992), 10, 27, 127–132;
Measure 13 (1995), 27; No on 9 campaign,
130–131; Citizens Alliance (OCA), 27, 127,
129–131, 183n2
Oregon Public Employees Union, 10, 98,
127–131
Oregon State Hospital, 130
Oregon State University, 128
Orth, Christa, 151
Otos, Sally, 102–103

Pacific Bell, 20
Pacific Telephone, 20
Packwood, Robert, 127
Pataki, George, 53
PATCO, 151, 160–161, 182n94
Patio/Bakery (SF), 143
Pay equity, 3; for gay and bisexual men, 42,
182n88; gender-based, 57, 128–129, 184n35
PEF, 53–54
Perot, H. Ross, 193n79
Picketing: at Barneys, 44; of Coors, 77, 79, 81,
82; at Dammasch psychiatric hospital, 128,
129; of gay hot shops, 139, 140; by homophile
activists in 1960s, 5; at Labyris Auto Repair,
141–142; by LGLN activists, 94; of Metro
Theatre, 93; by SF restaurant workers, 142,
143, 144, 145; by social workers, 56; by UAW,
67, 69; by UFW, 138
The Pillar, 99
Pillowtex, 61–62, 185n52
Plant closings and union leadership, 65–71
Pogrebin, Bert, 191n18
Pride at Work, 77, 100–101; Oakland confer-
ence (1996), 12, 46
*Pride at Work: Organizing for Lesbian and Gay
Rights in Unions* (Frank and Holcomb), 12, 94
Privitere, Tom, 53–54
Professional Air Traffic Controllers Organiza-
tion (PATCO), 151, 160–161, 182n94
Proskauer Rose, 154, 157
Public Employee Press, 116
Public Employees Federation (PEF), 53–54
Public sector: queer union caucuses in,
120–124; strikes in, 51, 56, 108, 151
Pullman, Greg, 158–159

Quackenbush, Vince, 143
Quality of work life, 107, 108
Queer work, 41–43

Radical right. *See* Right-wing politics
Ralphs, Bob, 128, 129–130
Ramsey, Kim, 51, 66, 69–71
Randolph, A. Philip, 51
Rankin, Teresa, 51, 59–60
Reagan, Ronald: and Briggs Initiative, 92; and
Gay Rights National Lobby, 85; and NLRB,
144; and PATCO, 151–152, 160, 182n94; and
Bill Taylor, 160, 162
Recruitment drives, 135–163; at AIDS centers
in 1990s, 151–153; at AIDS clinics in 1980s,
148–150; and civil rights movements, 138; of
clerical workers, 146–148; in gay businesses,
139–142; at GMHC, 153–157; in hotel and
restaurant industry, 142–146; and LGBT

workers, 136–139; at Northwest AIDS Foundation, 150–151; process of, 137; at San Francisco AIDS Foundation, 157–160; at Whitman-Walker Clinic, 160–163
Reed, Scott, 43
Religious right. *See* Right-wing politics
Retail Clerks International Association: and Briggs amendment, 91; contract enforcement by, 114–115; Local 1001 (Seattle), 57; Local 1100 (SF), 91, 114–115; merger with Amalgamated Meatcutters, 57–58; Bill Olwell at, 57
Retter, Yolanda, 140
Reutershan, Joan, 169
Riegel, Rosalie, 30–31
Right to work legislation: in 1950s, 4–5; and antisodomy laws, 7–8; in CO, 126; and plant closings, 66, 71; and Save Our Children campaign, 87; and union recruitment of LGBT workers, 136; in UT, 99
Right-wing politics: and Briggs amendment, 89–92; and Canada, 40; challenges to employment discrimination laws by, 20, 76; in CO, 105, 124–127; and Adolph Coors Foundation, 79, 187n11; and NOW, 81; in OR, 105, 127–132; Save Our Children campaigns, 20, 86–88, 124
Rivera, Dennis, 155, 156
Roberts, Bill, 41–42
Roberts, John, 193n81
Robinson, Faith, 28–30
Rochester, Anna, 175–176n9
Romer, Roy, 125; in *Romer v. Evans* (1993), 126, 193n81
Romero, Criss, 140, 157–160
Roselli, Sal, 93, 120
Rudnick, Trudy, 112
Rupprecht, Nancy, 141–142
Rustin, Bayard, 51, 188n33

Same-sex domestic partner benefits, 45, 46, 182–183n103
Same-sex marriage, 165–173, 198n3; in CA, 170; in MA, 170; in MD, 170, 171–172; in ME, 170, 171; in MN, 170, 171, 172–173; in NY, 165–170, 171; in WA, 170, 171, 172
San Francisco: Coors boycott, 75, 77–79, 80; Gay Teachers Coalition, 85; ordinance for benefit equity, 45–46; restaurant industry, 142–146; strike by theater janitors, 92–93
San Francisco AIDS Foundation (SFAF), 140, 149, 150, 157–160, 163
San Francisco AIDS office, 158
San Francisco Labor Council, 91
San Francisco Unified School District, 85

Save Our Children campaigns, 20, 86–88, 124
Scabs, 77–78, 80, 95, 143
Schurman, Susan, 33, 106–108
Scondras, David, 81
Seattle: GE plant closing, 69–71; Northwest AIDS Foundation, 149–151; Proposition 13, 88–89; Seattle Public Library Workers, 190n7; telephone workers, 31–32
Secrecy: of labor organizing, 7; of LGBT people, 1, 7; of Mattachine Society and Daughters of Bilitis, 5, 176–177n15
Service Employees International Union (SEIU): and AIDS clinics and centers, 94, 149–151, 158–160, 161, 163; and AIDS crisis, 119–120; and Briggs Initiative, 105; District 925, 60; District 1199 East, 166–167, 169, 172; District 1199-E DC, 2, 150, 161–162; and domestic partner benefits, 110; and Equal Protection Colorado, 126; gay rights resolution, 98; and Hands Off Washington coalition, 48–49; insurgencies in, 65; Lavender Caucuses, 49, 98, 100, 120, 124, 158, 167; Lesbian and Gay Committee, 167; LGBTQ Caucus, 167, 169; Local 6 (health care, Seattle), 149–151; Local 9 (building service workers, SF), 92–93; Local 250 (health care, Northern CA), 96, 119–120; Local 285 (health care, Boston), 65; Local 399 (L.A.), 149–150; Local 415 (public employees, Santa Cruz, CA), 110; Local 500 (nonprofit and public employees, MD), 172; Local 503 (Oregon Public Employees Union), 10, 98, 127–131; Local 509 (state employees, MA), 65, 94–95, 98, 123; Local 790 (public employees, Berkeley), 110, 150, 158–160, 163, 178n26, 187n5; Local 790A (nonprofit employees, SF), 158, 159; Local 1199 Northwest (Seattle), 48–49, 151, 172; and marriage equality, 172; and Oregon Citizens Alliance, 127; and *Pride at Work* pamphlet, 12; queer activism in, 97–98, 100; queer caucuses in, 10, 123, 124; Teresa Rankin in, 59
Service sector, queer work in, 42
Sex industry, 76, 178n26, 187n5
Sex reassignment surgery. *See* Gender reassignment treatment and surgery
Sexual orientation policies: ACTWU on, 2; AFL-CIO on, 126; AFT on, 18, 87; in Ann Arbor bus drivers contract, 8; in CO, 124–125; at Columbia University, 102, 103; at Coors, 80, 82; District 1199 on, 166; of federal workers, 19; and Hands Off Washington coalition, 48; ILGWU on, 83; IUEW on, 71; NEA on, 84, 87; in OR, 128–129; at Pacific Bell, 20; as protected class, 8, 10; Retail Clerks International Association on,

Sexual orientation policies (*continued*)
114–115; in San Francisco Unified School
District, 85; in UAW constitution, 36, 40–41,
113; UFT on, 121; and union leadership,
71–72; white-collar unions on, 109
SFAF, 140, 149, 150, 157–160, 163
Sheets, Van Alan, 53
Siegel, Phyllis, 11, 165, 166, 170
Smith, Irving, 44–45
Society for Individual Rights, 5
Sodomy, 7–8
Solidarity Day rally (1981), 43, 182n94
Soloway, Irene, 26, 27
South East Michigan Transportation Author-
ity, 109
Southern Maine Labor Council, 171
Spouse equivalents, 103, 104, 109, 110, 191n18
Stabnicki, Tom, 85
Standards of Care for the Health of Transsex-
ual, Transgender, and Gender Nonconform-
ing People, 185–186n58
J. P. Stevens textile company, 59–60
Stonewall Democratic Club (SF), 145
Stonewall Rebellion (NYC), 6, 100
Strike(s): by Ann Arbor bus drivers, 108–109;
at Blue Shield, 147; of Columbia University
clerical workers, 104; for comparable worth,
128; at Coors, 79–80; by GEO, 3; of hot
shops, 139, 140; by janitors at movie theaters,
92–93; at Kaiser-Permanente, 120; at Labyris
Auto Repair, 141–142; by NYC teachers,
188n33; by PATCO, 151, 160–161; of public
employees, 51, 56, 108, 128, 151; by Seattle
telephone crafts, 32; of SF hotel and restaurant workers at businesses in gay (Castro)
community, 142–145; by social workers,
55–56; by UAW, 50, 67, 69; union leadership
during, 55–57
St. Vincent de Paul Society (SF), 148
Sushman, Sidney (Sylvia Sidney), 43
Sweeney, John, 98, 100
Sweeney, Tim, 155

Taft-Hartley Act (1947), 4
Taft-Hartley trusts, 111–112
Tavern Guild (SF), 78, 80, 142–143
Taylor, Bill, 160–162
Taylor, Elizabeth, 161, 162
Elizabeth Taylor Medical Center, 161, 162
TB, multidrug resistant, 153–154
Teamsters. *See* International Brotherhood of
Teamsters
Tea Party, 168
Telephone crafts: gay men in, 21; lesbians in,
21, 28–32

Temple University, 117–118
Tenney, Peter, 42–43, 90, 91, 93–94, 143
Textile Workers Union of America (TWUA),
52, 59–60
Alice B. Toklas Lesbian/Gay Democratic Club,
93, 145
Transgender workers: in auto production lines,
38–39; as graduate employees, 2–3; at indus-
trial laundries, 2; at Macy's, 115; at *New York
Times*, 63–64; as protected class, 2; in textile
trade, 62; in union leadership, 63–64; at
Whitman-Walker clinic, 2, 162–163
Transportation Workers Union (TWU), 34;
Local 171 (Ann Arbor), 109
Trees, Barbara, 24, 25
Truett, Keith, 36
Tuberculosis (TB), multidrug resistant, 153–154
Tultex, 61
TWU, 34; Local 171 (Ann Arbor), 109
TWUA, 52, 59–60

UAW. *See* United Auto Workers
UAW Solidarity, 40
UFCW. *See* United Food and Commercial
Workers International Union
UFT. *See* United Federation of Teachers
UFW, 75, 77, 79, 95, 97, 138
UNC, 67, 118
Union busters, 135–136, 148, 151, 155
Union conventions, coalitions at, 82–86
Union of Needletrades, Industrial, and Textile
Employees (UNITE): formation of, 62; Local
340, 43–45; on rights of sexual minorities, 84
United Airlines, 46
United Artists theater chain, 93
United Auto Workers (UAW): AIDS awareness
at, 118–119; and Columbia University office
workers, 102, 104; contract enforcement by,
115–116; District 65 (NYC), 102, 104, 109,
110; and gay men on production lines, 22,
34–41; leadership, 49–50; Local 3 (Dodge
Main Plant, Hamtramck, MI), 35; Local 72
(American Motors plant, Kenosha, WI), 37,
50; Local 122 (Chrysler plant, Twinsburg,
OH), 41; Local 212 (Briggs and Chrysler,
Sterling Heights and Detroit, MI), 66–69, 118;
Local 372 (Chrysler Engine plant, Trenton,
MI), 40, 115; Local 412 (Chrysler Tech Center,
Auburn Hills, MI), 40–41; Local 444 (Chrys-
ler, Windsor, Ont., Canada), 35, 39; Local 594
(General Motors plant, Pontiac, MI), 37; Local
600 (Ford Plastics Distribution Center, Milan,
MI), 35; Local 900 (Ford Michigan Truck,
Wayne, MI), 36; Local 961 (Chrysler Eldon
Gear and Axle plant, Detroit), 37; Local 1112

(GM plant, Lordstown, OH), 38; Local 1264 (Chrysler Sterling stamping plant, Sterling Heights, MI), 119; Local 1981 (National Writers Union, NYC), 40; and March on Washington, 6; and plant closing, 66–70; restructuring at, 136; on sexual orientation, 113; and United National Caucus, 67, 118

United Brotherhood of Carpenters and Joiners: apprenticeships in, 23; Carpenters Trust Fund, 46, 147; Local 22 (SF), 45–46; Local 257 (NYC), 27; Local 608 (NYC), 25; and women in trades, 25, 27, 45–46

United Farm Workers (UFW), 75, 77, 79, 95, 97, 138

United Federation of Teachers (UFT): and gay rights, 84; and queer union caucuses, 121; and social workers' strike (NYC, 1965), 56; strike by, 188n33

United Food and Commercial Workers International Union (UFCW): formation of, 57–58; Local 21 (WA), 172; Bill Olwell at, 57–58, 97, 135–136, 162; on same-sex marriage, 172

United Healthcare Workers East, 166–167

United National Caucus (UNC), 67, 118

United Staff Association (at NYU), 109, 112, 116

United Steelworkers of America (USWA, USW): and AIDS crisis, 117; and GALLAN, 94; and lesbian bus drivers, 34; Local 485 (Magna, UT), 99; Local 8751 (Boston), 34, 94, 117; and George Meany at 1972 national convention, 6

United Teachers of Dade, 87

United Tradeswomen (NYC), 23

United Transportation Union Local 1741 (school bus drivers, SF), 93

University of Michigan Graduate Employees Organization, 2–3

U.S. military, policy of nondiscrimination, 19

USW. See United Steelworkers of America

USWA. See United Steelworkers of America

Utah: coalition politics in, 98–100; Salt Lake Area Labor Council, 99; Utah Coalition of Gay, Lesbian, and Bi Union Activists and Supporters, 99

Vietnam War: AFL-CIO endorsement of military escalation in, 6; labor's opposition to, 51; mobilization against, 5

Village Voice, 8, 104, 109–110, 137, 191n18

Voland, Martie, 51, 60–62

Wage inequality, 3; for gay and bisexual men, 42, 182n88; gender-based, 57, 128–129, 184n35

Walker, Bailey T., Jr., 51, 85–86

Walkouts. *See* Strike(s)

Wallace, George, 67

Wallace, Howard, 78–79, 187n8

Ware, John, 118

Washington State: Initiatives 608 and 610 (1994), 48; same-sex marriage in, 170, 171, 172; Washington United for Marriage, 172

Weingarten, Randi, 183n5

Weinstein, Jeff, 110

Weld, William F., 96

West Hollywood, domestic partner benefits in, 111

Wheeler, Karen, 25–26, 94–95

Whitman-Walker Clinic (DC), 2, 149, 152, 160–163

Wildcat strikes: by Seattle telephone crafts, 32; by UAW, 50, 67, 69

Wilkinson, J. Harvie, III, 62

Wilson, André, 3

Wilson, Hank, 87–88

Windsor, Edith, v. the United States of America (2013), 183n7

Witmer, "Big Bill," 40–41

Wohlforth, Nancy, 147–148

Women's liberation, 6

Women's Trade Union League (WTUL), 175–176n9

Woods, Ron, 36, 40–41, 115–116

Workers Defense League, 166

Wurf, Jerry, 97

WTUL, 175–176n9

Wynn, William, 58

York Hotel (SF), 143

Miriam Frank is a Master Teacher of Humanities at New York University.